The Unforgiving Coast

Also by the Author

Debaters and Dynamiters: The Story of the Haywood Trial
Diamondfield Jack, A Study in Frontier Justice
U. S. Army Ships and Watercraft of World War II
Captives of Shanghai: The Story of the President Harrison (with
    Gretchen G. Grover)
American Merchant Ships on the Yangtze, 1920-1941
The San Francisco Shipping Conspiracies of World War I

The Unforgiving Coast

MARITIME DISASTERS OF THE PACIFIC NORTHWEST

David H. Grover

Oregon State University Press

Corvallis

The paper in this book meets the guidelines for permanence and durability of the Committee on Production Guidelines for Book Longevity of the Council on Library Resources and the minimum requirements of the American National Standard for Permanence of Paper for Printed Library Materials Z39.48-1984.

Library of Congress Cataloging-in-Publication Data
Grover, David H. (David Hubert), 1925-
 The unforgiving coast : maritime disasters of the Pacific Northwest/ David H. Grover.-- 1st ed.
   p. cm.
Includes bibliographical references (p.   ).
 ISBN 0-87071-541-0 (alk. paper)
 1. Shipwrecks--Northwest Coast of North America--History--20th century. I. Title.
 G525 .G78 2002
 910ʹ.9164ʹ309041--dc21

                          2001008019

Oregon State University Press
500 Kerr Administration
Corvallis OR 97331-6407
541-737-3166 • fax 541-737-3170
http://oregonstate.edu/dept/press

Table of Contents

Foreword   vi

Chapter 1   Maritime Disasters: Events and Milieus   1

Chapter 2   Fire at Sea: The *Queen*   28

Chapter 3   The *Valencia*: Disaster on Many Fronts   45

Chapter 4   *Rosecrans*: Born to Lose   71

Chapter 5   The *Mimi*: Salvage Can Be Dangerous   85

Chapter 6   The Mystery of the *Francis H. Leggett*   102

Chapter 7   *Santa Clara*: A Beach Too Crowded   122

Chapter 8   *J. A. Chanslor*: Tanker in Trouble   139

Chapter 9   The *South Coast*: Vanished Ship, Vanished Era   156

Chapter 10 The *Iowa*: Crossing the Bar   171

Notes   188

Bibliography   201

Index   205

Foreword

A double-edged commitment drives this book, first to the beauty and grandeur of the Pacific Northwest coastline, and second to the venturous nature of the human spirit that sends people out to sea as mariners or passengers. In melding these two ideals, the true tales contained in this collection focus on the unique, the curious, the inexplicable, the poignant, the ironic—all those dimensions of life that take it out of the routine and into the realm of adventure.

For most of us, the simple act of stepping aboard any kind of boat, watercraft, or ship is an adventure in itself, regardless of whether anything of interest subsequently takes place on board. When further events do occur, the result can be high adventure for those on board, either in person or in spirit. In this sense, when a shipboard adventure with an interesting cast and an exciting scenario is played out against the backdrop of, say, rounding Cape Blanco on a moonless night in a southwesterly gale, what does it matter that most of us have to participate vicariously rather than in person?

In addition to the geographical boundaries of the California border to the south and Cape Flattery to the north, I have chosen to limit the narrative to the first half of the twentieth century. I have also focused on those disasters that seem to have generated excessive numbers of casualties under the prevailing circumstances. One other restriction will also apply: the book will not investigate any disasters that reflect hostile military or naval actions. It will be enough to contend with the forces of the sea without bringing outside interlopers into the analysis of why ships have sunk with great loss of life.

In the initial chapters which provide an orientation to maritime mishaps and to the geographical setting for the book, the reader will encounter occasional comparisons to events and places on the California coast. These references are in no way an attempt to suggest that California is the standard against which other West Coast areas are measured. Instead, the inference to be drawn from the comparisons is that while the two areas have much in common in terms of coastal geography, the Northwest has been spared both the number and variety of shipwrecks which the California coast has seen. Although the Pacific Northwest was potentially a sterner coastline than that of the Golden State, unique geographical features to the north mitigated the dangers— particularly in the case of collisions.

It was highly unlikely that I could have found any eye-witnesses to the events I have described. So I have been heavily dependent on the written sources which were available, primarily newspapers and the transcripts of official investigations into the various tragedies.

With those definitions and limitations established, we can now turn to the all-important responsibility of acknowledgments. The libraries holding the vital materials which have served as sources and documentation include those of the University of California at Davis, the University of California at Berkeley, the Northern Regional Library Facility of the University of California System at Richmond, the University of Oregon, the California Maritime Academy at Vallejo, the Dudley Knox Library of the Naval Postgraduate School at Monterey, Oregon State University through the Valley Library in Corvallis and the Guin Library at the Oregon Marine Sciences Center at Newport, and the library of the U.S. Court of Appeals in Portland. Archival material from the following sources was also useful: the San Francisco Maritime National Historical Park, the Columbia River Maritime Museum at Astoria, the Oregon Maritime Center and Museum in Portland, the Oregon Historical Society in Portland, the Maritime Museum of British Columbia at Victoria, the Coos County Historical Society Museum at North Bend, the Coquille River Museum at Bandon, the Curry County Historical Society at Gold Beach, the Museum of History and Industry at Seattle, the Tillamook County Pioneer Museum, the Oregon Coast History Center of the Lincoln County Historical Society at Newport, the Maritime Museum of Monterey, and the Visitors Center at Cape Disappointment, Washington. The lone public library that was utilized was the ever-helpful Napa Public Library. The regional branches of the National Archives at Seattle and at San Bruno, California, as well as the central NARA facility in Washington, DC, were also useful sources of information.

Other agencies and corporations which supplied information include the Office of the Coast Guard Historian, the library of Chevron Corporation, and the German Consulate in San Francisco.

Individuals who have been helpful in supplying material include a unique group of West Coast mariners with interests in the history of their profession: Captain Harold D. Huycke of Seattle, former purser William Kooiman of the library of the San Francisco Maritime National Historical Park, Captain Gene Harrower of Portland, Captain Niels Nielsen of Portland, former Coast Guard Chief Petty Officer and prolific historian Dr. Dennis L. Noble of Sequim, Washington, and former Coast Guard officer James A. Mossman of Seattle, who had already helped me on an earlier book. From the East Coast, Charles Dana Gibson drew on his expertise in Army ships to provide information on two of the ill-fated ships that had once carried troops. From the Canadian province of Alberta the family of the late George Poelman, one of two survivors from the *Francis H. Leggett* disaster, supplied information on his recollections of the event.

Among other helpful westerners were three descendants of pioneer Tillamook County families who had heard stories about the wreck of the *Mimi* passed down from their parents. One was the author Jack L. Graves, who has written about the *Mimi* and also has the credentials of a former harbor commissioner in Garibaldi. Another was William Klein from Wheeler, whose keen eyes have apparently discovered from the air the long-buried hulk of the *Mimi*. The third is Don Best from Rockaway Beach, a photographer of Oregon coastal vistas, who is waiting, along with Graves and Klein, to capture the *Mimi* when winter storms have again uncovered her.

Two other people deserve recognition for their role in this book. One is Howard Allred of Sacramento, whom I first met more than a decade ago when researching my book on the passenger liner *President Harrison*, on which he served as an able seaman; I turned to him again on this book for information about steam schooners, another type of vessel on which he had served. A final word of appreciation goes to Kenneth L. Munford, the doyen of the Oregon State University Press, whose sage advice to me years ago, distilled from his experience in writing about John Ledyard's service with Captain James Cook, was, in essence, "never put words in a character's mouth unless you know that he said them." I have followed that advice assiduously.

Speaking of the OSU Press, almost forty years after that press published my first book, a word of thanks should go to those who facilitated the creation of this most recent book: Acquisitions Editor Mary E. Braun who first found merit in the manuscript, Managing Editor Jo Alexander who steered it through the production process, and text editor Paul Merchant whose sensitive touch produced the final draft.

This was the first time I have used the internet in writing a book. No one site became a gold mine of information, but I did turn up leads to sites that contained useful data. In the few cases where that information was worthy of a citation, I have tried to attribute it to the most primary source of the information, rather than to a website.

Writing this book has been an unusual experience. With death on a massive scale as the theme of every chapter, it would be cruel and inaccurate to say that I enjoyed doing it. By the same token, it would be equally inaccurate to say that it was a grisly chore that I am thankful has now ended. It has been a project of enormous personal interest and involvement, sometimes exhausting and sometimes exhilarating.

In writing the book I found myself grateful for having had the opportunity to sail once in an older ship that depended upon the magnetic compass, the winch-type sounding machine, and the taffrail log—the navigational equipment that characterized many of the ships in this book—because I can now relate to such gear and to the men who used it in an earlier era. I once utilized some of these older devices myself in helping to keep our ship from grounding in the fog in stormy seas.

In completing the book, I found much to make me proud to have been a professional mariner, and to have sailed in the waters of the Pacific Northwest. I have also found much to make me humble, as well as thankful for the personal safety I have enjoyed. The successful completion of an ocean voyage is always accompanied by such emotions.

That great old hymn, which the Navy has adopted as its own, speaks of "those in peril on the sea." My hope is that this book will provide vicariously for its readers, as it has for me, some of that same feeling of relief and thankfulness that the ocean travelers of that era experienced upon reaching safe harbors.

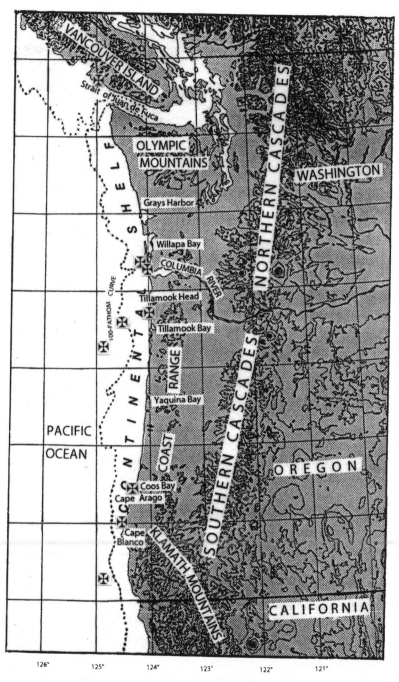

The sites of the nine maritime disasters described in this book are indicated with crosses on this map of the coastline of the Pacific Northwest, along with significant geographical features

Chapter One

Maritime Disasters: Events and Milieus

As the twenty-first century dawns, the undiminished public fascination with the sinking of the *Titanic*, an event that took place only a dozen years into the twentieth century, is a clear indication of the inherent interest that disasters at sea hold for most people. This is particularly true for younger generations who are unlikely to make ocean voyages, except on cruise ships, in their lifetime, nor to encounter the potential perils of the sea. For these people the vicarious, or in today's terminology the virtual, voyages they make aboard the *Titanic* may be their only taste of the sea.

Adding to the sustained interest in maritime disasters today is the existence of technology capable of examining ships on the ocean floor, a potential which has been provided by advances in deep diving and in self-contained and robotic submersibles. The possibility of even raising sunken wrecks not only exists, but, fortunately, has already spawned its own concern for ethical guidelines.

Shipwrecks have always fascinated people, and the histories of ancient civilizations, stories in the Bible, and accounts of the great era of exploration are replete with examples of mariners being tossed violently onto uncharted shores, with their ships destroyed behind them in the surf. Modern marine archeologists, using all the technical tools of the diving profession, have made remarkable discoveries during the last several decades in looking at ancient shipwrecks, and it is certainly conceivable that in coming years any wreck anywhere in the world at any depth can be found and explored, if not raised.

Adding further to the vast accumulated lore on shipwrecks are dozens of books in recent years that serve as guidebooks for recreational divers who wish to visit wrecks. While this desire to inspect the last resting place of ships and people who have died a violent death may be understandable as a form of the basic human instinct to explore, it is somewhat alien to the approach of this book, which seeks to honor the people who were on board those vessels, and to leave their world undisturbed while trying to understand the events that led up to their tragic deaths.

Today the term "maritime disaster" probably evokes images of a tanker lying broken apart, spilling millions of gallons of oil onto a fragile coast. Indeed that does represent disaster in the true sense of the word, but the maritime disasters to be reviewed in the pages that follow are disasters in the human sense—when loss of life was significant, at a time when no one thought to tally the gallons of fuel that had entered the sea. Unfortunately, no figures are available to indicate what the toll of human life has been in marine disasters through the ages, but it must represent a staggering total.

Even within the twentieth century no grand totals exist, although for smaller sectors of time and geography data can be found. For example, according to the U.S. Coast Guard and its predecessor agencies, during the period 1901 through 1929 there were 9,037 American ships totally destroyed in maritime accidents, an average of 312 a year, and 11,813 lives lost, an average of 407 per year.[1] Given time and a research budget, it might also be possible to extrapolate numbers for a small geographic area such as the Pacific Northwest. Indeed, just the nine disasters described in this book destroyed eight ships and took at least 360 lives.

In all fairness to the maritime industry, however, it should be noted that in the absence of any standard of comparison it is impossible to determine what kind of a safety record steamships compiled during the zenith of passenger travel. Furthermore, since the mishaps covered in this book occurred from 1904 to 1936 it is difficult to establish a base year for such comparisons. In the early 1920s the figures kept by the Department of Commerce showed one passenger lost per six million carried, but this figure included inland waterways and ferries.[2] By way of comparison, during aviation's growth years the loss of several hundred lives a year certainly was common, and yet that total may have been amassed in flying many million passenger miles. The same would be true for passenger ships.

Perhaps it is the nature of death at sea that renders it so disquieting to most people. Survivor accounts describe the hours of terror and agony for those who survive or die aboard a sinking ship, whereas most major aircraft accidents kill quickly and totally, albeit after moments of unimaginable terror for the victims.

It is not easy to know how the ocean passenger early in the century viewed the risks of his or her journey. It seems fair to conclude, however, that since shipwrecks were common enough to be featured with some regularity as front page newspaper stories, often somewhat sensationalized, the timid souls or those with queasy stomachs could easily be deterred from ocean travel that was not absolutely necessary.

The start of the twentieth century represents an appropriate point at which to begin a study of modern maritime disasters. Prior to that time wooden sailing ships predominated, and only elementary navigational equipment prevailed. Thus, ships could not always be made to go where their masters wanted. With the coming of powered steel ships, together with reliable navigational instruments such as chronometers, sextants, and proper charts and tables, it was much easier for a ship's captain to stay out of trouble. With the advent of a higher order of technology using electrical and sonic devices which appeared during the first quarter of the twentieth century, the ship captain now had no easy excuse for losing his way. Yet hundreds of them did so, endangering their cargo, crew, and passengers. It is the intent of this book to look at some of those disasters, and to try to determine why they occurred.

A broader goal of the book is to describe the world of the steamship off the Northwest coast during this era—why the ships were there, what they carried, where they went, who ventured onto them as crewmen and passengers, and what happened on board during their moment of peril. Just as a well-written obituary can be a fascinating glimpse of life in another era, a sensitive account of the demise of a ship can provide insights into earlier times and places, as well as into the character of the victims.

Apart from hostile military action, which is outside the scope of this study, there are several different mishaps that can occur to a ship and lead to disastrous loss of life. Collisions are the most obvious preventable cause of disasters, occurring generally in crowded coastal waters, but occasionally far from land, as in the case of the *Andrea Doria* and the *Stockholm* in the North Atlantic in 1956. Generally in a collision at least one of the ships remains afloat, serving as an immediate source of assistance to the other.

Perhaps the most common cause of extensive loss of life aboard American ships in bygone years has been groundings or strandings, again associated with coastal travel. Unless the ship has clearly suffered a steering casualty, such events immediately suggest navigational errors which, like collisions, are human errors. Strandings can be relatively benign if they occur on sandy beaches from which ships can readily be salvaged, but more deadly in rocky surf-swept locations where ships can quickly be battered apart. The West Coast of the United States contains many such rocky locations.

One of the deadliest forms of accident giving rise to a disaster is the sinking or foundering of a ship, an event that can sometime occur in conjunction with other types of mishap. In its most frightening form when ships capsize, foundering can result in appalling loss of life, since it is very difficult to launch lifeboats as a ship heels over. Of all the sinister things that can happen to a ship, foundering is perhaps the most insidious.

The concept of foundering often conjures up images of ships sinking swiftly with little opportunity for distress messages or the launching of lifeboats, leaving behind great mysteries of the sea, such as that of the USS *Cyclops* which vanished in 1917. Alternatively, a foundering can sometimes be a long losing battle against the sea; such was the sinking of the *Flying Enterprise* in 1952, a struggle with the sea that caught the fancy of a worldwide public.

Another disturbing element of the image of foundering is the nagging awareness that since ships are designed to stay afloat in an upright position, the responsibility for the sinking of the ship—absent any human error such as from improper loading—sometimes cannot clearly be assigned to a person or even to a set of circumstances. In the lore of the sea, and even in maritime law, such unattributable blame is sometimes identified as an "Act of God," a notion than can make us feel uncomfortable.

Perhaps the most frightening marine catastrophe of all is a fire at sea, which often leads to a sinking or grounding. The most famous American disaster of this type occurring aboard an ocean steamer was the *Morro Castle* which burned off the New Jersey coast in 1934, but the most deadly was the excursion steamer *General Slocum* in the East River of New York harbor in 1904, aboard which 1,030 lives were lost.

Ships occasionally vanish completely. The British lost a new naval vessel, the steel sloop *Condor*, which disappeared off Cape Flattery, Washington, in 1901 en route to Honolulu with 140 men aboard.[3] The presumption is that overdue ships have sunk, but in the past it has been entirely possible for derelicts to drift around the oceans of the world for years. Today, however, with satellites scanning every square foot of the surface of the earth the romantic notion of the *Flying Dutchman* or the other legendary ghost ships is a thing of the past.

There are perhaps four key elements common to each shipwreck story: the sea and its related weather, the ship, the people aboard, and the locale. These elements may become personified to some degree in the telling of the story. For the purposes of this study, those personifications can be reduced initially to obvious generalizations such as "moody but unforgiving" in the case of the sea, "old but sturdy" for the ship, "courageous but fallible" for the people aboard, and "beautiful but treacherous" for the coastal locale.

The readers and viewers of the *Titanic* epic might be surprised to realize that maritime disasters as dramatic and tragic as that which befell the great White Star liner have occurred with some regularity much closer to land, indeed in sight of land in many cases. All types of marine disaster have occurred along coasts and in harbors, rivers, and bays. With a coastline of 12,383 miles, and a total of 88,633 miles of saltwater shoreline including those around bays, islands, and estuaries, the United States is unique among the major maritime nations of the world in the opportunities that exist for coastal marine disasters. Indeed, one would be hard pressed to find many American maritime disasters that took place in mid-ocean, while there would be no difficulty in identifying dozens of major disasters in coastal waters.

⌐

In putting this book together it has been difficult to know how to strike a balance between the serious and dark side of the sea—that treated so allegorically and somberly by such writers as Melville and Conrad—and the workaday world of the sea as most seafarers have known it, sometimes hazardous but often quite routine. For centuries the sea has been regarded as a relentless disciplinarian, always ready to extract punishment from those who have transgressed against the rules of prudent seamanship. A coastline is the ultimate tribunal of this nautical justice, a place in which mariners can be held accountable for a broader array of misjudgments than they might encounter while sailing in mid-ocean waters. In this high-risk environment some offenders pay the price of death and destruction for their carelessness; others get off remarkably free.

Still others, however, may never come to trial, in that they work as mariners for many years without ever encountering the kind of crisis that calls for decisive action entailing risk. These mariners may represent a large majority of the profession, but their ordinary and uneventful careers, while countering the dark search for meaning in Melville and Conrad, are not the raw material of books, at least not of books such as this one.

The mariners are perhaps the most intriguing element in these sea stories, but collectively we know relatively little about them. While we have enough records on the ships to know the materials and techniques used in their construction and the reputation of their builders, we encounter difficulty in establishing so many years later just what the common denominators of training and experience were for the men who sailed the ships. We are probably justified in hypothesizing, however, that for the most part the officers and men aboard the early steamships were inadequately trained, in that the increasing professional demands made upon them during their careers often outstripped their narrow preparation.

Fortunately for these men, for the first two decades of the twentieth century the technology of marine transportation had changed little from the time when they had first learned their trade. Of course, radar and electronic navigation did not exist during this period; in fact, for some of the vessels whose moments of crisis are described in this book the navigation equipment was essentially no different from that found in a ship in the mid-nineteenth century. However, when the gyro compass, radio as well as radio direction finders, echo fathometers, and pit logs were coming into general use in the second and third decade of the new century, there was little formal re-training to accommodate this new technology, just as there was no re-training for the newer short-cut methods in navigation.

Prior to that time the magnetic compass, the taffrail log, and the lead line were the standard means of determining direction, speed, and water depth, while the simple expedient of blowing the ship's whistle and timing its echo was used to find one's way in the fog. These early mariners did not feel deprived in not having the equipment which we have come to look upon today as essential, simply because they knew nothing else. Furthermore, they did a respectable job of navigating their ships with the imperfect tools available to them.

Virtually all merchant marine officers of that era had "come up through the hawsepipe," meaning that they had started as seamen and worked their way up, acquiring their original and higher officer's licenses by self-study or by attending proprietary schools which taught the answers to typical examination questions. A few others were graduates of the early "schoolships," non-collegiate institutions run by local or state entities. After World War One another small group of officers had been trained as company cadets by a few steamship companies.

Of the "hawsepipe" deck officers of this era, many had started their careers in sail, and had learned much of the formal lore of the sea through rote, e. g., "boxing" the magnetic compass or using the tables in *Bowditch*, the venerable bible of marine navigation, to do a longitude time sight. Moments of force, stability, the trigonometric basis of navigational solutions—these things were alien to them, but they knew deck seamanship, the compass and leadline, and the rules of the road. Similarly, ship's engineers knew little thermodynamics, but they knew a great deal about boilers, reciprocating steam engines, and how to pack a leaky valve.

In spite of being called upon to operate in a changing technological environment in which they often did not fully understand the principles behind their actions, the mariners of that era were reasonably successful in sailing the ships entrusted to them. The mistakes that put ships aground or into other serious jeopardy were generally quantitative mistakes in judgment, not errors in failing to recognize the danger or in taking the wrong action. Misjudging the set and drift of the current or the speed made good over the ground resulted in the loss of many a ship, and yet these faulty judgments were made by captains of considerable experience who had correctly made such judgments hundreds of times before.

In the disasters reviewed in this book, freighters, tankers, and passenger ships will receive equal attention, but the latter category may merit special consideration at times. This focus not only reflects the fact that the presence of passengers has led to greater casualties in disasters, but also is justified because the lives of passengers present such a variety of great human dramas. We know from the next-of-kin declarations, which seamen of that era had to make when they signed on vessels, that many were loners with limited or no family ties. Passengers made no such declarations, but it seems reasonable to conclude that they would have had much more extensive family relationships to report than did the typical seamen.

Passengers traveling in ships are a distinctive study in dependence. Men who choose the sea as a calling have always willingly accepted the risks of their profession. The few women of that era who went to sea, largely as stewardesses on passenger ships (including one who died in one of the disasters reviewed in this book), were equally willing to accept the dangers of seafaring. Passengers, however, especially in the era when ships were the only means of crossing oceans or traveling coastwise, have been forced to entrust their lives to ships and seamen, and indeed to the sea itself—a set of variables over which they had no control. Sometimes that trust has been breached as ships have been imperiled by human error, with resultant loss of innocent passenger lives.

The popularity of the *Titanic*'s ethos is due in part to the wide appeal of the traditional image of the ocean voyage as romantic. That term suggests two human impulses. In one, romance is heroic faraway adventure; in the other, romance is love and affection. For centuries the reality and the literature of the sea have satisfied both of these aspirations. There is heroism and high adventure in every ship mishap, just as there is the potential for the moonlit tryst on the boat deck on every passenger ship.

More important than the latter, however, is the filial and spousal love that is displayed in a shipboard crisis. That love often rises above itself, being transfigured into sacrifice and heroism. No better example of that love can be imagined than that shown by the mother aboard the steamer *San Juan* who passed her small child to the waiting arms of men on the tanker which was still in contact with the passenger ship after the two had collided off the California coast in 1929; the *San Juan* sank in three minutes with the loss of many lives, including that of the young mother, while the tanker and the woman's son survived.[4]

Human behavior under stress is difficult to observe dispassionately, but the accounts of survivors of maritime disasters are often successful in representing both the best of that behavior and the worst. With good reason, newspaper interviews with survivors often focus on these aspects of a tragedy more so than on its causes, which are often beyond the ability of the passenger, or the interviewer, to understand. Because crewmen are more apt to be concerned about investigations that are held afterwards to determine causes and to fix responsibility, their comments to the press tend to be more guarded than those of the passengers who are so grateful to be alive.

⌒

When ships burn, go aground, or sink, there ought to be a reason why, and explanations ought to be forthcoming as to why the accident resulted in fatalities. Maritime disasters have generally been followed by extensive formal inquiries by the appropriate federal agency. The licensure of personnel, the certification of the seaworthiness of ships, and other matters pertaining to safety at sea have always been functions of federal agencies. Today, the United States Coast Guard combines all the duties of maritime safety in one agency, but in the early part of the twentieth century these responsibilities were in separate bureaus which had been created to meet specific and narrow needs.

The Steamboat Inspection Service initially was the agency responsible for all aspects of marine safety. Later it reviewed engineering aspects of ships and their personnel, while the Bureau of Marine Inspection and Navigation was responsible for licensure and performance of deck officers. The Lighthouse Service maintained aids to navigation, and the Lifesaving Service was responsible for rescues in coastal waters. The last-named agency merged with the Revenue Marine Service in 1915 to form the U.S. Coast Guard, but that new agency was not involved in regulatory matters concerning marine safety until all four of the agencies were united in 1942.

Post-incident hearings were held not only to determine the facts of maritime disasters, but responsibility as well. The examiners could also assess penalties against ships' officers in the form of license suspension or revocation. Monetary damages were generally determined through litigation in the courts. Legal recourse could be a frustrating process for the families of victims, since maritime law, which treated the ship as a person capable of being sued, had a number of narrow constraints which often reduced the liability of shipowners. Sometimes, for example, the only funds available to pay claims were those from the insurance on the ship, and shipowners at times carried little or no insurance on their vessels.

Steamship companies, particular in coastal service, were an interesting type of commercial enterprise because their ships, or sometimes their one ship, represented the entire assets of the company. Anyone could start a shipping line in those days by the acquisition of an older vessel which could be had for as little as twenty thousand dollars or, if one

IMPORTANT - READ THIS INFORMATION

DECALS

Apply to clean, smooth, wax-free surface at moderate temperature.

1. Peel decal from paper backing by bending backward at center and lifting edge.
2. Position decal and rub firmly to surface.

PLACEMENT OF DECAL ON BOAT

Decals must be placed on both sides of the bow, aft of and directly on line with the registration number as shown below.

PROPER DISPLAY

The number shown below is a sample and not your boat number

STARBOARD

⊠ WN -1234-ZZ

PORT

WN -1234-ZZ ⊠

Numbers painted or attached to each side of the bow. Always reading left to right.

REGISTRATION NUMBER

The registration number must be firmly placed on both sides of the bow in block letters not less than three inches in height in a color distinctively contrasting with the background. The number must read from left to right and included spaces of hyphens the width of the letters (other than "I") between the three parts of the registration number. The decals must be placed on both sides of the bow, at of and directly on line with the registration number as shown at left.

DOCUMENTED VESSELS

Affix decals to the forward half of the vessel on each side of the bow. Do not display WN registration numbers on documented vessels.

CHARACTERS
Block letters not less then three inches high.

COLOR
Must be a color contrasting to the background.

SPACING / DECAL
Hyphen or equivalent space between the 3 parts of your number. The validation decal must be within 6 inches of the number.

lacked cash, chartered from someone else. Pier space could be leased and crews hired with the expectation of revenues covering those expenses. If the company failed to meet its revenue expectations, it was as easy to stop operating as it had been to begin. Obviously, such companies did not make good "deep pockets" prospects for attorneys representing clients with claims against them.

Furthermore, hearing examiners often had difficulty in sorting out who had a legitimate claim for loss of life. Passengers and crewmen alike sometimes lost their identity on coastal vessels. One of the serious problems encountered in disasters affecting such vessels was the absence of complete rosters of who was on board. Unlike vessels making foreign voyages, coastal passenger ships could keep their personnel records as well as their passenger lists on board, which meant that these documents were often lost with the ship. In addition, last-minute crew changes and the names of walk-on passengers were often not sent ashore before sailing. When disasters occurred, determining who was aboard, who survived, and who did not became a difficult task.

Another aspect of life aboard ship that complicated the identification of accident victims was the reality that seafaring men often did not learn the names of others in the crew, even those with whom they worked closely. Some of this lack of normal sociability was a result of regulations that required that engine room personnel and deck personnel be housed and fed in separate facilities. Even within these separate worlds, however, names were rarely used. Crewmen were identified by their job, e. g. Bos'n, Chips, Sparks, the Mate, the Old Man, or, if no standard nickname existed for the position, by specific designators such as "First" [assistant engineer], "the 12 to 4 oiler," "the night cook," etc. Obviously, when survivors were asked to identify victims the results could be less than precise.

Traditions of the sea also often complicated hearings into disasters. In addition to maritime law which spells out in great detail the duties and responsibilities of masters and crewmen, there is a great body of tradition that influences accountability. One example is the expectation that the captain should go down with his ship, or, lacking that Spartan requirement, that he should be the last to leave his vessel. The former is only a tradition of long standing among seafaring men. Realistically, captains are often deeply involved in last-ditch efforts to save their vessels and cannot escape; furthermore, captains who might have had the means to escape have also been known to stay aboard voluntarily as an acknowledgment of personal failure.

Being the last to leave the ship, however, is interpreted in a variety of ways. According to the *Merchant Marine Officers Handbook* which does not cite its source,[5] such behavior is mandatory for captains. In 1991, after the captain of a sinking Greek cruise ship abandoned his passengers in escaping by lifeboat, *Time* Magazine ran a short piece examining the ethical issues of such conduct. Noting that "there is no law of the sea that requires the captain to remain to the end," the magazine reflected that captains who disregarded the traditions of the sea in such a matter risked public censure.[6]

Other traditions are incorporated into legal requirements, for example, that ships in collision shall stand by and render assistance to each other as required by federal law. Tradition, reinforced by strong pressure from the marine insurance industry, has always called upon ships to depart from their route and schedule to render assistance to nearby ships in distress. One of the great issues of the *Titanic* disaster was the role of the nearby steamer *Californian*. Her captain, Stanley Lord, spent the rest of his life trying to vindicate himself for not responding to the radio messages and visual distress signals from the sinking liner. In one instance in this book a ship may have sailed close to another ship that had just capsized in daylight, and did nothing to assist the victims in the water.

Marine disasters rarely wiped out the entire crew and passengers of a vessel. Rescue procedures, or sheer luck, often permitted some people to survive the initial accident. Ships, of course, carried minimal lifesaving equipment in the form of life jackets, life boats, and rafts. Although required life boat drills included the donning of life jackets by all hands, the jackets themselves were rarely tested, with the result that, more than once, defective life jackets have been responsible for loss of life. In the case of the sinking of the *Valencia* which grounded in 1906 trying to find her way in fog into the Strait of Juan de Fuca, life jackets filled with tule, a fiber which had only a limited ability to float, contributed to the death toll of more than one hundred lives.[7] When the *Santa Rosa* broke up on Point Arguello in California in 1911, passengers were told by the ship's officers not to use the tule life jackets since they would not float.[8]

To save expense, steamship companies of that era had been known to rotate their best lifesaving equipment from ship to ship to meet the requirements of annual inspections. It was this kind of practice that characterized the low standards of the American merchant fleet, at which the reforms of the comprehensive Merchant Marine Act of 1936 were eventually directed.

Lifeboats, too, were often more symbolic than useful. Boat drills required only that the boats be swung out of their chocks regularly, and only occasionally put into the water. Both wooden lifeboats and metal lifeboats with flotation tanks are virtually unsinkable once in the water, but launching them in high seas is fraught with difficulty and even danger, particularly if the ship is listing. Many lives have been lost at the critical moment when a boat lands in the water, and the falls, the ropes or wires supporting the boat, are released.

Lifeboats are not easy to handle in heavy seas. A well trained boat crew manned only by ship's personnel may have a reasonable chance of getting away from a sinking ship, distancing itself from the scene of the accident, and even landing through the surf onto a beach, but a big bulky lifeboat with passengers aboard and with crewmen drawn largely from the steward's department would be lucky to simply stay upright and not capsize.

Ships also carried line-throwing guns, squat little cannons called Lyle guns that shot a lightweight line attached to a 1,500-foot coil of heavier manila line. The guns were test-fired periodically as required by law, but the lines were rarely attached so that ships' crews had very little experience in how to use this system to reach shore or another vessel.

In coastal mishaps there was a strong possibility that the most immediate help could come from the shore rather than from other ships. The Lifesaving Service, which became one of the original components of the U.S. Coast Guard in 1915, operated a series of lifesaving stations and beach patrols early in the twentieth century. Using double-ended surfboats, sometimes hauled from place to place by horse drawn wagons, rescuers could go out through the surf to reach stranded or sinking vessels. By the early 1920s motorized lifeboats were in wide use from stations that launched them from boathouses on tracked ramps, and these small craft were instrumental in a number of rescues.

The most dramatic shore-based rescue system, however, was the breeches buoy. This gear consisted of a heavy trouser-like sling which traveled out and back on a line that had been shot to a stranded ship and made fast aboard her. One by one, people could be evacuated from the ship, sitting in this device as it was hauled to safety. Hundreds of seamen and passengers owe their lives to this technique, including the crew of the Japanese freighter *Tenpaisan Maru* which went aground on Copalis Beach, Washington in December of 1927,[9] and the crew of the *Oliver J. Olson* which grounded on the south jetty of the Coquille River in Oregon in November, 1953.[10]

From this discussion it should be evident that while there were strong forces at work to put ships in jeopardy, there were equally strong forces at work aboard ships in terms of their original design and construction, as well as their safety features and the competence of their crews, all acting to keep ships out of trouble. In addition, a shore-based rescue establishment and other vessels bound by a strong nautical tradition of assistance stood by to help.

This rescue and lifesaving capability evolved in the Pacific Northwest to meet the unique needs mandated by the geography of the area.

It would be unwise to try to describe in capsule form the geographical uniqueness of Oregon and Washington as coastal states, or even the coastlines themselves. Looking at the Northwest coast as a maritime milieu involves more than looking at the beautiful beaches, headlands, and lighthouses of the area, and even more than identifying the physical dangers of that coast. Rather, it encompasses recognizing the influence of those geographic and climatic factors upon the ships that served a largely agrarian and lumber economy, and upon the owners, mariners, and passengers who used the sea and those ships as a livelihood and/or as a means of transportation.

The coastline of these two northwestern states represented a somewhat different setting for ships, both physically and socioeconomically, from that of its most immediate counterpart in California. That difference played a role in the maritime mishaps of the past by reducing the risks of some types of accidents in the Pacific Northwest, and increasing the risks of others. Certain comparisons may be initially useful in understanding these influences.

Much of the California coast is high and rugged from the Oregon border down through the Big Sur, flattening out into bluffs before reaching the Mexican border. The Northwest coast presents a high profile only in selected areas. Where the Siskiyou or Klamath Mountains come to the sea on the south coast of Oregon, the mid-coast headlands such as Cape Perpetua and Cape Foulweather, an occasional high spot on the northern Oregon coast such as Neahkahnie Mountain, and the stretch of northern Washington coast where the Olympics meet the sea—these represent the higher parts of the North Pacific coast. There are, of course, many rocky and rugged spots on the less lofty stretches of the coast, so the absence of coastal heights does not assure a benign and danger-free coast for ships traveling its reaches.

There are also many miles of sandy beaches in the Pacific Northwest. In Oregon, particularly, these beaches are often interrupted by headlands and by bays, and only in a few locations are there long and continuous stretches of beach. In southwest Washington, however, the beaches are flat and straight, and the lighthouses, like their East Coast counterparts, are built as towers on the beach in the absence of the high ground on which most West Coast lighthouses are built. In this area the long spits on both sides of the entrances to Willapa Bay and Grays Harbor present an appearance not found elsewhere on the West Coast, resembling instead the sandy barrier islands common to the East Coast and the Gulf Coast of the United States.

Ships grounding on sand beaches generally have a reasonably good chance of maintaining the integrity of their hulls, and are good candidates for salvage. This salvage is carried out through the standard technique of laying out beach gear which is made up of heavy purchases of wire rope on the rescue vessel heaving on cables connected to anchors that have been placed beyond the surf line. The Calmar Line freighter

Yorkmar, a Liberty ship, was successfully hauled off the beach just north of the Grays Harbor jetty by the *Salvage Chief* using beach gear in December, 1952.[11]

Perhaps the most significant difference between the California coastline and the Northwest coast is in the number of headlands which serve as turning points. Whereas California has numerous turning points for coastal vessels—Cape Fermin, Point Dume, the Channel Islands, Point Conception and Point Arguello, Point Sur, Pigeon Point, Point Reyes, Point Arena, Punta Gorda, and Cape Mendocino—the Oregon/Washington coast has a single such point: Cape Blanco. Ships making either for the Columbia River or for Puget Sound from the south need make only this one course change, a factor which reduces the chances of both collisions and groundings. In fact, by being well offshore at Cape Mendocino in California it is possible to reach Cape Flattery at the entrance to the Strait of Juan de Fuca on a single heading. Partially as a result of this lack of turns, no significant ship collisions seem to have occurred off the Northwest coast, while the California coast has had several deadly ones, both at turning points and elsewhere.

Furthermore, the Northwest coast is much freer from offshore islands and obstructions than is the California coast. In the latter area a pair of buoyed reefs 100 miles west of San Diego known as Tanner Bank and Cortes Bank, the Channel Islands, the Farallons, Blunts Reef off Cape Mendocino, and St. George Reef off Crescent City all present hazards to navigation. Oregon and Washington have no such hazardous offshore islands or reefs, unless one counts Tillamook Rock in Oregon or Destruction Island in Washington, both of which are well inshore of the major traffic lanes. Similarly, Tatoosh Island at the entrance to the Strait of Juan de Fuca is really a part of the Cape Flattery entrance approach, as is Umatilla Reef to the south. Otherwise, only a few reefs south of Cape Blanco offer any potential for danger, and these are well inshore of the regular north-south trackline. Thus, the absence of any significant offshore geographical features strengthens the hypothesis that the Northwest coast should be somewhat safer than the California coast on several counts.

The smaller number of ports in the Northwest should also contribute to fewer accidents, inasmuch as ships frequently get into trouble trying to enter or leave port in bad weather. There are only a half dozen such ocean ports in the Northwest that have handled ships of more than 200 feet in length. These include Bandon, Coos Bay, Reedsport, and Newport on the Oregon coast, and Grays Harbor and, until recently, Willapa Bay on the Washington coast. Other small ports, such as Brookings, Gold Beach, Port Orford, Florence, Tillamook, and Bay City, could once accommodate steam schooners and smaller vessels, but generally only tugs and barges visit such ports today. Another interesting feature of the northwestern coast is the general absence of the "dogholes," those tiny little coves containing wharves or cable landings and chutes which existed on California's redwood coast farther south. Absent, too, are offshore tanker terminals and coastal piers, which have been widely used in California to create ports where nature did not intend them. Without such minimal ports, the Pacific Northwest achieved an additional margin of safety.

Offsetting that margin, however, was the fact that all the ports of the Northwest coast were, and remain, bar ports. A bar port is a harbor which can be reached only by crossing a relatively shallow bar of sand or silt which has been deposited by alluvial action outside the entrance to a port. Generally, inside a bar there is a bay into which a river has widened before entering the sea, and this slowing of the current causes sediments to drop both within the bay and outside of it.

This condition generally necessitates the establishment of jetties to stabilize the entrance channel, and dredging to maintain a prescribed depth for it. The Portland District of the Army Corps of Engineers has been charged with this responsibility, which it has carried out for a number of years in the smaller ports with such hopper dredges as the *Pacific* and *Yaquina,* augmented by commercial dredges. The Corps' larger hopper dredges have been utilized in Coos Bay, the Columbia bar, and Grays Harbor. Dredging has its own perils. The Corps lost one hopper dredge, the *William T. Rossell*, and the lives of four crewmen in a collision at the Coos Bay bar in 1957,[12] and the *Biddle* was damaged in a collision in fog at the mouth of the Columbia in August 1977.[13]

Bar ports exist to a much smaller degree in California. Eureka and Crescent City in the far north are bar ports, and San Francisco has a bar as well, but the channel into the bay through the Golden Gate is quite deep. Farther south the ports tend to be carved out of the open coastline, with or without a breakwater, or man-made in the case of Long Beach/San Pedro. Consequently, except for California's redwood coast, "crossing the bar" is a challenge to seafarers more characteristic of the Northwest than of the Golden State.

Bar ports provide little haven for ships caught at sea during storms. A perverse "damned if you do and damned if you don't" decision faces a captain who feels his ship cannot ride out a storm. If he tries to enter port he may go aground, and if he stays outside he may face an equally unpleasant alternative even farther from potential rescuers. Oregonians may remember two cases in recent years that illustrate the point. The Japanese freighter *Blue Magpie* tried to enter Yaquina Bay in 1983 after the authorities ashore had told the captain to stay out during a storm. The captain insisted on bringing his ship in without a pilot, but hit the jetty, destroying the ship and requiring a Coast Guard helicopter to rescue the nineteen crewmen.[14] In 1999 the *New Carissa,* a Philippine ship, was told by the authorities at Coos Bay to stay out during a storm because the pilot could not board her until the weather abated. The captain complied with the instructions and anchored outside, only to encounter such wind and seas that the ship dragged her anchor and went hard aground a few miles north of the entrance, again requiring an airlift evacuation.[15]

Early in the twentieth century pilotage was not compulsory at the bar ports of the Pacific Northwest, although ships often did take pilots. Entering port requires special knowledge which is normally credentialed through pilotage endorsements on the licenses of deck officers. These endorsements are earned through making a minimum number of trips into and out of the port, plus passing an examination covering courses to be steered, aids to navigation, etc. Pilotage is provided by licensed pilots from a local association whose services are provided for a fee to ships entering or leaving port. In coastal shipping, vessels are using the same ports repeatedly, so it becomes cheaper and more convenient for the steamship or tanker companies to expect their masters to acquire pilotage for the ports they visit rather than taking on a professional pilot for each visit.

The absence of compulsory pilotage requirements and the presence of many ship captains with pilotage sometimes resulted in either unskilled or overly-aggressive navigation of ships across bars in bad weather. While the local pilots may shut down during bad weather, primarily because boarding or leaving a ship from a pilot vessel is so dangerous to the pilots at such times, ship masters with pilotage may feel inclined to cross the bar at a time when the professional pilots choose not to try. For any captain who encountered trouble trying to cross the bar without either a pilot or his own pilotage endorsement, a presumption of bad judgment would probably exist at subsequent hearings.

In terms of climate, the Pacific Northwest coast represents a frontier between the massive and sometimes hostile ocean weather systems and the more benign weather ashore that has produced the verdant beauty of western Oregon and Washington. That no-man's-land of weather can be downright inhospitable at times, particularly in the winter, the season when all but two of the disasters described in this book occurred. The two exceptions occurred in September, a transitional and unpredictable month in weather.

Perhaps the most persistent and dangerous feature of that climate zone is sea water temperature, an important determinant of survival in a maritime disaster. With such temperatures generally no warmer than the fifties, victims of maritime accidents who find themselves in the water in the Pacific Northwest can quickly be numbed to the point of losing all ability to function. In those rare instances when survivors were picked up after many hours in the water it was incredible that they were still alive.

The wind, with its resultant high seas, is another demon of the North Coast. The entire West Coast personifies the infamous "lee shore" which mariners have been conditioned to dread, a shore lying downwind to a ship at sea. The winds and swells of the Pacific Ocean have been fortified by crossing thousands of miles of ocean before they come ashore, and on the Northwest coast they have often picked up the chill of the Gulf of Alaska as well. Winds have been measured at 120 knots and estimated at 160 knots at North Head Lighthouse, just north of the

Columbia River.[16] At Tillamook Rock Lighthouse seas have broken over the top of the structure, 150 feet above the sea.[17]

Even when winds are moderate, the mixing of ocean and land air generates fog on the coast during all months of the year. To be set inshore by wind and current during periods of low visibility was, and remains, an invitation to disaster on this coast. A captain or a ship that was not sturdy enough to meet the challenges of navigating this foggy coastline rarely got a second chance.

Fog not only reduces the ability of lookouts to search ahead for other ships or hazards, but it impacts negatively on the captain's ability to navigate the vessel. In coastal waters, navigators commonly plan on obtaining their position from established locations on shore which are identified on charts. Lighthouses represent the best of such locations ashore since they are normally visible at night as well as in the daytime— unless fog interferes. Mariners can determine their distance off the lighthouse by simple computations of bow and beam bearings which are rudimentary exercises in trigonometry. These exercises are so elementary that captains of coastal ships have been known to install peg boards on the wing of the bridge, by which various combinations of angles can be quickly set up, permitting the navigator simply to look over the top of the two pegs to determine when they line up with the lighthouse or other charted objects ashore.

Even more exact positions can be determined by fixes or cross bearings if two lighthouses are in sight at the same time. The Lighthouse Service in originally establishing the lights took into account, not only the need to mark potential dangers ashore, but the desirability of providing two lighthouses within the mariner's range of vision whenever possible for purposes of uninterrupted visual navigation. In addition, lighthouses provided lookouts ashore who could keep their eyes open for signs of trouble on passing ships.

On the Oregon coast lighthouses were established at Cape Blanco, Coquille River, Cape Arago, Umpqua River, Siuslaw Inlet, Heceta Head, Yaquina Head, Cape Meares, and Tillamook Rock. Although the mistakes have apparently not contributed to shipwrecks, at least two of these lighthouses were accidently built at the wrong locations. The Yaquina Head Light was supposed to have been built at Otter Crest, some three miles north, but the building materials were delivered to the wrong location in 1873, and it was too much of a task to move them. A similar mistake involving the confusion of names led to the lighthouse that was intended for Cape Lookout being built instead in 1889 at Cape Meares, ten miles north.[18]

Continuing north across the mouth of the Columbia, lighthouses were located at Cape Disappointment, North Head, Willapa Bay, Grays Harbor, Destruction Island, and Cape Flattery. Three lightships completed the system: one at the Columbia River, and two at the mouth of the Strait of Juan de Fuca, Umatilla Reef and Swiftsure Bank. For a ship bound north, the greatest distance between lights was the sixty miles between St. George Reef in California and Cape Blanco in Oregon, a particularly critical area in which to have no visual fix preliminary to approaching the turning point at Cape Blanco. Another stretch of forty-seven miles without a lighthouse lay between Grays Harbor and Destruction Island on the Washington coast.

The more important lights could be seen as far away as twenty miles. While most ships were not that far off shore, the extra distance meant that the lights could be picked up well before they came abeam, allowing the navigator to begin his computation of how far off the light he would be when it was abeam. While this network of lighthouses provided a basic system of visual coastwise navigation, it was, of course, unusable when fog shrouded the coast, although fog signals from the lighthouses could provide a rough measure of where a ship was with respect to the sound.

Although fog was common, it was generally not an overriding concern of the mariners who served aboard ships in the Pacific Northwest in the same way that it was on the northern California coast. According to the *Coast Pilot*, during a nine-year span early in the twentieth century no lighthouse on the Oregon or Washington coast reported operating its fog signals as many as 1,000 hours a year, a total exceeded by a number of California stations. Grays Harbor led all northwestern stations with 800 hours annually, followed by Umatilla Reef lightship with 746 hours, Coquille River with 723 hours, and Cape Flattery with 722 hours.[19] However, James A. Gibbs, perhaps the leading authority both on west coast shipwrecks and lighthouses, says that the Swiftsure Bank lightship off the entrance to the Strait of Juan de Fuca experienced fog for 1203 hours a year.[20]

Using 750 hours a year as an average for Pacific Northwest lighthouses, that amount represents about 8.5 percent of the time or one hour in twelve, a ratio that seems like a tolerable amount of time. Statistics, however, were no solace to the individual ship captain trying to make a landfall with his vessel enveloped in fog at a time of year and in a place where it was neither prevalent nor expected. Fog could occur at odd and inconvenient times, and when combined with other phenomena could produce strange results. The *Admiral Benson* of Pacific Steamship Company went aground in the fog on Peacock Spit at the mouth of the Columbia in February 1930, when an unusually low tide left too little water under the ship. Motor lifeboats from Point Adams and Cape Disappointment removed the passengers and most of the crew, with the rest being brought ashore by breeches buoy.[21]

If there is one truly troubling aspect of the operation of ships through many decades, it has been speed in fog. The Rules of the Road, the international guide to how ships should be handled with respect to other ships, have always specified that a ship in fog should reduce her speed, and, until recently, have required that upon hearing the whistle of a ship forward of the beam, the ship should actually stop her engines. In practice, however, most ships rarely made appreciable reductions in speed, and some did not blow the required long blast of the whistle every two minutes while in fog or skirting fog banks. Companies were often quick to criticize captains who were too cautious in such matters, particularly if it delayed their arrival, but equally quick to abandon them if their speed in fog resulted in accidents. As a result, the officers on the bridge sometimes found it necessary to play a game of speed, or what a punster might call "rushin' roulette," against the very long odds that two ships would be in the same exact location in the ocean at the same moment.

Those odds favored the mariner more on the Pacific Northwest coast than on the California coast. This comparative advantage accrued because there were somewhat fewer ships along the North Coast, and because these vessels were often passing through the area on a trackline that was well offshore, rather than going from point to point along the coast. This reality reduced the risk of broadside encounters with ships that had turned landward to enter harbors, and benefitted particularly the heavy volume of non-stop traffic going from the San Francisco Bay Area or southern California to Portland and Puget Sound. It was beneficial as well to the substantial traffic in lumber that left Grays Harbor and Coos Bay bound directly for San Francisco or southern California. While such through traffic generally stayed well offshore, avoiding the rocks and other inshore hazards, it was, of course, not immune from founderings or fires.

As the coastal shipping industry developed in the Pacific Northwest, so did a capability in search and rescue. The United States Lifesaving Service maintained lifeboat stations in the Pacific Northwest at a number of key locations, including Bandon, Coos Bay, Winchester Bay, Florence, Newport, Tillamook Bay, and Fort Stevens on the Oregon coast, and at Fort Canby, Klipsan Beach, Willapa Bay, Grays Harbor, and Neah Bay on the Washington coast.[22] Yet these stations were far enough apart that they could not respond promptly to every call for their services.

However, other assistance was sometimes available from the private sector. Coastal ships often stood by to assist, sometimes motivated by altruism and sometimes by an opportunity to share in a bit of salvage money. Furthermore, as in other coastal areas the small local ports of the Pacific Northwest contained tugs and fishing boats whose owners were generally willing to put to sea to assist disabled vessels, even though it was sometimes more dangerous to approach a grounded wreck from seaward than from the beach, rendering such proffered assistance unusable. But some areas, such as the north coast of Washington, had no communities for miles, and the captain unlucky enough to go aground there would have a long wait for any assistance, particularly if he had no radio.

The sheer number of ships sailing along the Oregon–Washington coast insured that the area had more potential for accidents to ships eighty or ninety years ago than it has at the present time. Today, after coastal shipping has declined to the point of near extinction, it is hard to remember that such shipping was once a vibrant industry, with millions of tons of cargo and tens of thousands of passengers moving up and down the West Coast each year. Uniform data to attest to the volume of this commerce are hard to find, but isolated evidence is available. Puget Sound and the Columbia River generated most of this commerce, but even the smaller ports had significant lumber shipments. In one typical week at Willapa Bay in 1909 six steam schooners brought out 3,360,000 board feet,[23] at a rate which annualized would reach 175 million board feet or 245,000 long tons. Similarly, in Oregon in 1912, eighteen oceangoing schooners and steamers visited the small port of Bandon in a week;[24] the annualized total of lumber at that rate was sixty-five million board feet or 91,000 long tons. Somewhat later in 1921 a total of 1,250,000,000 board feet of lumber or 1,750,700 long tons came out of Grays Harbor alone,[25] equivalent to 625 ships carrying two million board feet each. Most of this lumber tonnage was carried in coastwise ships.

The actual number of ships in service along the Pacific Northwest coast is hard to determine from the existing fragmentary data. However, in mid-1914, a median point which coincided with one of the disasters in this book, followed the first four incidents, and preceded the final four, there appeared to be about three hundred ships that were at work on that coast or en route to or from the area on a given day. A surprisingly large number of these vessels, perhaps as many as 25 percent, were sailing vessels.[26] Thus, the shipping lanes of the Northwest, although not as crowded as their California counterparts, could be congested at times.

It is interesting to speculate as to why passengers still elected to travel by ship after north-south railroad service existed on the West Coast. As late as 1914 eleven companies were in competition with each other for the passenger and freight business along this coast, with the Pacific Coast Steamship Company leading the pack because of the diversity of its routes.[27] Well beyond that point in time Californians continued to take passage in small ships to visit San Francisco or Los Angeles from such ports as Eureka, Monterey, Port San Luis, or Santa Barbara.

One reason for this continued steamer traffic was convenience, but another was the high intrastate railroad fares that prevailed under the monopoly of the Southern Pacific Railroad. Traveling by sea was definitely cheaper than by rail. Giles T. Brown in *Ships That Sail No More* indicates that fares on the ships of the San Francisco and Portland Steamship Company were four dollars cheaper than rail fares from Portland to San Francisco.[28] While that may seem like an insignificant saving, that amount represented more than a day's—even a week's—pay for many Americans at the time. Moreover, there was a certain glamour in coastwise passenger ship voyages, especially in the case of the famous night boats which ran between San Francisco, Los Angeles, and San Diego. However, it is difficult to imagine many Oregonians traveling from Coos Bay to Portland by steamer for either convenience or glamour, and even more difficult to visualize Washingtonians taking ships from Grays Harbor to Seattle.

Steamship companies operating in the Pacific Northwest were an interesting mixture of California-based companies and those domiciled in Puget Sound or in Portland. The leading California company was the Pacific Coast Steamship Company. Other California steamship companies included North Pacific Steamship and Independent Steamship. In addition, several large cargo lines, such as Dollar, McCormick, and Nelson, had developed from their roots as lumber firms.

Three major shipping lines were based in the Paciic Northwest. Two were owned by railroads: the San Francisco and Portland Steamship Company, belonging to E. H. Harriman of the Union Pacific, and the Great Northern Pacific Steamship Company, the property of James J. Hill of the Great Northern and Northern Pacific Railways. The third northwestern firm was the Admiral Line, owned by H. F. Alexander.

Competing against these larger companies were smaller firms, some of which were "niche" companies serving smaller ports. Other companies, often called "opposition lines," competed head-to-head with major steamship companies on important routes. Among this latter group were the New Electra Line and an outfit that briefly exploited the concept, calling itself the Opposition Line. The competitive edge for the small companies was achieved through reduced passenger fares, and by cutting costs wherever possible. Sometimes that might mean the use of marginal ships, or the cutting of other key corners in safety and comfort.

One of the interesting features of the smaller shipping companies was their tendency to acquire ships from other lines, rather than to have them built for their own needs. The net effect was a fleet of somewhat greater age than one might desire. Historians have sometimes raised questions about the safety record of these ships, an issue that was raised periodically in the popular press of the day. In about 1910 a Seattle newspaper observed:

> The passenger ships of the Pacific coast are with few exceptions so rotten that the least accident crushes them like egg shells and sends them to the bottom. The vessels used on this coast are the cast-offs from the East Coast, where they have been practically worn out and are sold for a song to the Pacific shipping companies. . . . Most of the passenger ships on this coast are so old that one can throw a rivet hammer through them.[29]

Perhaps more important than the rusty sides of these older ships were the safety features they lacked. Some had been built without double bottoms, watertight doors, or adequate compartmentation, all of which could help insure that the ship would stay afloat. Clearly, traveling by sea in the Pacific Northwest in those days could be a risky proposition, and *caveat vector* was an admonition that should have been heeded by those traveling in smaller ships. At least two of the passenger ships included in this study presented dual risks of small size and out-dated hulls.

It seems safe to conclude that the longer a ship operates, the more chances it is afforded to get into trouble. If the lifespan of an iron or steel ship is twenty-five years, which is what the naval architects and shipyards have conditioned us to believe, then the ship that operates beyond that age is, in a sense, on borrowed time. A number of the ships mentioned in this book were near or even beyond that age; only one survived disaster to go on to a long career, but the others met their violent ends in North Coast shipwrecks.

Ships are like people in having personalities or character. Two of the ships that appear in this book were "losers," star-crossed vessels that had escaped death at least once but were destined for disaster. One was just the opposite, a survivor who managed to go on for decades cheating the evil jinns of coastal waters out of their right to claim her.

Some of the smaller passenger ships on the West Coast had been built originally for East Coast service as night boats, aboard which passengers would normally spend only one night at sea. These vessels had remarkably large passenger capacities, both in first-class staterooms and in second- or third-class space—which was sometimes frankly designated as steerage. These alternative spaces sometimes did not have official capacities but could be filled as snugly as the circumstances allowed—with resourceful crewmen sometimes pocketing a bit of spare cash for accommodating stowaways.

The people who traveled in these smaller ships, both as passengers and crewmen, were ordinary people of modest means, whether they came from cities such as Seattle, Portland, or San Francisco, or from the small ports of Coos Bay or Hoquiam. When on occasion some of them died in tragic marine accidents, the papers of the West Coast generally reported their names and unique stories as best they could, often showing considerable sympathy for the plight of families affected by such accidents. However, there was little recognition nationally of the passing of these victims. Unlike the rich and famous who died in the great North Atlantic disasters of the era, these ordinary people died on relatively unknown ships in incidents whose circumstances have never become widely known. It is distressing today to encounter books that profess to enumerate all the deadly shipwrecks of the twentieth century, but make no mention of these disasters in the Pacific Northwest. Yet in their final terror and in their death throes in the frigid water these people died as brutally as had any of the first-class passengers of the *Titanic,* and they deserve as much recognition and respect.

Now, with the assurance that the name of that great liner will be invoked no further in the pages that follow, we can turn to the stories of ships and people in crisis on the coast of the Pacific Northwest.

Chapter Two

Fire at Sea: The *Queen*

If ever a ship was aptly named it was the *Queen*. Built in 1882 as the *Queen of the Pacific*, she was destined to go on to a long and resilient career, flirting with disaster time and time again, until she was finally retired and scrapped in Japan in 1935 at the unbelievable age of fifty-three. Although she was never in the same league as the great and regal ladies of the Pacific, the romantic *Lurline* and *Mariposa* of the Matson Line, the impressive *President* liners of Dollar and American President Lines, or the awesome Canadian Pacific and P. & O. liners such as the *Empress of Australia* and the *Canberra*, she was nevertheless unmatched in her ability to go anywhere and to survive any challenge.

This remarkable vessel was built at the Cramp Shipyard in Philadelphia in 1882. She was long and sleek for a coastal liner of that era, 331 feet in length at the waterline, 39 feet in beam, and 21 feet in hull depth. Her gross tonnage was 2,727 and her net tonnage 1,672. Unlike some of her counterparts built on the East Coast for service on the Pacific Coast, she was built primarily as a passenger ship for her owners, the Pacific Coast Steamship Company division of the Pacific Coast Company. Her 3,000 horsepower and speed of nearly fourteen knots were evidence of her designed ability to meet schedules.

The *Queen* was utilized in virtually all the services in which the ships of Pacific Coast Steamship Company participated, including coastal routes between San Francisco and Los Angeles, San Francisco and the

Pacific Northwest, and on to Alaska. She even made an occasional voyage to the Hawaiian Islands to prove that she was indeed a ship for all trades. The company was intensely proud of this ship. An advertisement in the late 1890s proclaimed:

> The Alaska excursions having become the excursion of the Continent, the Pacific Coast Steamship Company, in order to meet popular demand, run during the excursion seasons an excursion steamer on the route that for speed, elegance and comfort is unexcelled by scarcely any vessel afloat. This steamer (the *Queen*, 3,000 tons) is 340 feet long, and has accommodations for 250 first-class passengers. She is supplied with all modern improvements and appliances including the electric light in every stateroom, etc. The staterooms of the *Queen* are unusually large and handsome.[1]

Her most sterling endorsement came after an early voyage from Seattle to San Francisco when a passenger, Sir Charles Russell, later to be Lord Chief Justice of Great Britain, wrote:

> The *Queen* is a very fine and a very fast ship; and it is no exaggeration to say that expense and ingenuity have not been spared in making her the most luxurious boat I ever saw. My apartment is splendid. I should be content to go in the *Queen* round even by Cape Horn and so home to England.[2]

In spite of her stellar qualities, early in her career the *Queen of the Pacific* demonstrated a tendency to be accident-prone, albeit with an equally strong talent for quick recovery. In September, 1883, with her captain blinded by the smoke of a nearby forest fire, she ran aground on Clatsop Spit at the Columbia River bar, but was successfully refloated after a monumental salvage effort was undertaken by no less than five tugboats hauling on her simultaneously.[3] In 1888 she sank off the end of the long wharf at what was then called Port Harford, now known as Port San Luis, a tanker port on the central California coast. The reasons for that sinking are rarely cited, but according to one account she simply took too much water aboard through an open porthole.[4] Pictures of that era show her listing to starboard, her decks almost awash, something of an embarrassment to both the ship and the port.

The *Queen* was one of the most versatile and resilient ships on the West Coast, but she had a knack of finding trouble which other ships avoided. Here she is shown in Alaska in the 1890s. (Photo courtesy of San Francisco Maritime National Historical Park)

She was subsequently refloated, taken to a shipyard, and rehabilitated for further service. In 1888 she was somehow reported overdue and missing between Port Townsend and Honolulu, but eventually turned up safe.[5] In 1890 her owners shortened her name to *Queen*. In 1896 in San Francisco Bay she collided with the British ship *Strathdon*, whose steel bowsprit raked her sides and injured several passengers. In 1899 she touched on the Farallons, and in 1901 she scraped a reef in Alaska, but again came through each time unscathed. She then collided with the coal-laden British steamer *Adamson* in Puget Sound in 1903.[6] Her next moment of infamy, the fire which is the subject of this chapter, occurred in 1904 when she was running to the Pacific Northwest from San Francisco. This would not be the last fire aboard the *Queen*, nor the last for Captain Cousins.

Fire at sea is a singularly dreaded event aboard ship. It presents to its victims the distinct possibility of death by either of two horrible fates, burning or drowning. Furthermore, it can lead to other dangerous crises such as stranding or foundering. Unlike other accidents at sea, a fire must normally be faced alone by the ship, crew, and passengers, with no assistance from other ships or the rescue establishment. Until the modern age of helicopter rescues even the evacuation of personnel from the ship on fire has had to be achieved by the ship itself, and often the launching of lifeboats for this purpose added additional dangers to an already perilous situation.

⟝

On 25 February 1904, the *Queen* left San Francisco bound for Seattle on the 505th voyage of a career spanning twenty-two years. She was under the command of Captain N. E. Cousins, who had been the ship's master for a year. As was usually the case with wintertime voyages, the ship was not filled to capacity. A total of 218 people were on board, 88 of them as crewmen, and 130 of them as passengers. Among these passengers, 71 were traveling first class and 59 occupied second class or steerage space. The ship also had 1,300 tons of general cargo in her holds.[7]

On the morning of the second day out she was thirty miles off Tillamook Light on the northern Oregon coast. A heavy sea was running, a brisk southwesterly wind was blowing, and the sky was cloudy and dark with occasional rain squalls. At 4:05 A.M. Fourth Officer Meyer, who was going off watch, stopped in the dining saloon for a few minutes, and noticed nothing out of order. By 4:20, however, a fire had broken out in a cabin opening off the dining saloon. The night watchman on duty in that area first detected smoke, after which he notified the second steward. This man then opened the door to the unoccupied stateroom room from which the smoke was emanating, and was immediately driven back by flames and dense smoke. Slamming the door shut, he dispatched the night watchman to the bridge to report to the mate on watch.

Fanned by the fifteen-knot wind and the momentum of the ship, the fire quickly blazed up into conspicuous flames that now could easily be seen from the bridge. Second Officer Reece immediately called the captain. When Captain Cousins arrived on the bridge a few moments later clad in his pajamas, flames were whipping thirty feet into the air through the skylight of the dining saloon. The captain ordered the engines stopped, and the sounding of the fire alarm bell to wake and warn the passengers. As Cousins recalled later, "No time was lost by the crew in getting water on the fire which seemed to gather headway, until the entire after part of the ship was a seething mass of flames."

The captain knew instinctively that he was facing a major crisis. The upper deckhouses of the ship were constructed largely of wood. Years of painting and varnishing these surfaces had made them highly combustible. In addition, any possible assistance from other vessels or the shore was a long way off. Furthermore, the Oregon coast, thirty miles away, did not provide, particularly in winter time, any calm shallow water where the vessel might safely be beached.

The prudent, and perhaps the only, course of action seemed to be evacuating the ship as promptly as possible while the after wooden lifeboats were still intact. If this were done, at least the women and children could be taken off the ship first, while some of the male passengers could remain behind to help the crew fight the fire.

Captain Cousins later explained his decision to prepare the lifeboats: "When it seemed as if it would be impossible to keep the fire under control, I gave orders to clear away the boats, to swing them out, and lower them to the rails. The boats on the weather, or port, side had been lowered to the water."[8] In launching the boats Captain Cousins was fortunate to have the assistance of Captain Isaac N. Hibbard, a passenger, who was an official of another steamship company. He took over most of the responsibility for the boats, leaving the captain to direct the overall firefighting effort. Several other former seafarers among the passengers were also available to help with the boats and firefighting.

In moments of crisis there is often a person who seems to have a sense of what is needed. Aboard the *Queen* that person was a young woman who initially did not want to give her name to reporters, but was ultimately identified only as Miss L. Peckinbaugh of Seattle. When some of the women began singing hymns that reflected their despair, Miss Peckinbaugh launched into a bouncy tune called "Bedella."[9] Her indomitable spirit helped others to avoid the panic that was latent while everyone was still on board. When she was put into a lifeboat she continued in a cheerful vein, bailing seawater that slopped in from the choppy seas.[10]

Four boats were subsequently launched on the windward side of the ship, each containing three crewmen. While this side presented a more difficult launch than that which could have been made on the lee side, it had the advantage that no fire would be blowing onto the boats and their manila falls as they were launched. For loading, the lifeboats were then rowed around to the starboard or lee side of the ship. One of the problems in putting the lifeboats into the water was that the most experienced men in the deck department were remaining on board to fight the fire, leaving the boats to be commanded largely by personnel from the steward's department and the engine room. Altogether, about sixty people left the ship in the boats.

The passengers who were directed into the boats went willingly without any protest. Unfortunately, the first boat to be launched, with the second steward in charge, capsized as it drifted under the stern of the vessel, although the screw was not turning. Other boats were quickly able to rescue most of those who had been dumped into the sea, but four crewmen in that boat and one young female passenger were drowned. Another boat had been able to get well away from the burning ship, but it, too, overturned in the rough sea. Again the other boats rescued most of those who had been in this boat, but another five men were lost. Already the evacuation attempt had cost ten lives, and the issue was still in doubt with respect to the fire. Only a few of the bodies were recovered.

Back aboard the ship Captain Cousins was determined not to lose the battle against the roaring inferno. The engineers remained on station, providing enough steam to insure that the fire pumps had the proper pressure for those on deck who were fighting the fire. The fire had to be attacked largely from above, with water being sprayed from the hoses under 150 pounds of pressure and directed from the top deck through the skylight into the dining saloon.

At one point the captain rang up an ahead bell on the engine-order telegraph, and swung the bow of the ship around into the wind. This maneuver had the effect of putting the blazing stern of the ship downwind, so that the flames were moving aft onto previously burned material and out over the stern.

With the deck officers supervising the crew, and with the help of a large number of the male passengers who dragged hoses around and backed up the nozzlemen, the captain soon had reason for hope. With the ship dead in the water the effect of the wind on the fire was reduced. The dedication, resourcefulness, and sheer numbers of the men who were fighting the fire did much to turn the tide. In one of the strangest dramas in the annals of the sea, passengers now played a pivotal role in saving themselves and the ship in which they traveled. Miraculously, after several hours this unusual collection of professional seamen and untrained amateurs won their battle; the flames ran out of dry fuel, and the fire was brought under control.

Although the ship was in the main coastal shipping lane where in those days one might expect to see as many as several ships an hour, no other vessels came along to assist. Flames on a vessel have always been considered a distress signal, and any ship within ten miles of the *Queen* could easily have seen this fire.

The burnt-out deckhouse on the stern of the *Queen* provided grim testimony of her battle with flames off the Oregon coast. (Photo courtesy of San Francisco Maritime National Historical Park)

By 8:30 A.M., with the fire almost out, it was now possible to recall the boats. As soon as they heard the three-blast signal from the ship's whistle, those in charge of the remaining lifeboats ordered them rowed through the gray dawn back to the smouldering hulk of the *Queen*. Rafts were rigged as landing stages alongside, so those leaving the boats would have an interim platform on which to stand before climbing up the ladders. Soon the passengers and boat crews were scrambling back aboard the burnt-out liner, anxious to rejoin their friends and families, and to see what was left of their quarters and belongings.

The after portion of the upper decks of the ship had been consumed by the fire, with damage extending forward almost to the topside extension of the engine room spaces. The deck structures aft of the mainmast were gone. The bodies of three men from the steward's department had been found, horribly burned, in a passageway leading up from their quarters, called the "Glory Hole," deep in the ship. These deaths brought the toll of fatalities to thirteen. One elderly female passenger subsequently died of exposure from her experience in the boats, making the total of fourteen dead, eleven of whom had died in the boats and three aboard the burning ship. Four had been passengers; ten were crewmen: three from the deck department, two from the engine department, and five from the steward's department.

The fate of the three waiters who lost their way in the smoke was particularly tragic. Among the passengers the greatest sense of loss seemed to come from the drowning of the young woman, Anna Steiner, who disappeared after bobbing about for ten minutes in her life jacket while her brother who had been thrown out of the same boat tried to save her. "A big wave separated us, and I did not see her after that," he explained. "That was about five minutes before I was picked up."[11]

By 9:30 A.M., with the fire out, Captain Cousins cautiously ordered his crew to get the ship underway. All the essential systems seemed to be operational, so the now-hellish-looking vessel was able to begin moving again. When the *Santa Monica*, a 500-ton steam schooner, came into

sight, Cousins asked her to stand by the *Queen* as the liner moved slowly toward the mouth of the Columbia, some thirty miles away.

When the *Queen* reached this emergency destination, Cousins found the bar too rough to cross safely with his overextended ship and overwrought passengers. Consequently, he pressed on toward Puget Sound, two hundred miles farther north, confident that the ship's well-known reputation for sturdiness would see him through. The steward's department, with the help of other passengers, improvised arrangements to house and clothe those who had been displaced by the fire. En route north, an unusual electrical storm briefly pounded the ship near Cape Flattery, but such an anticlimax meant little at this point to Captain Cousins.

At Port Townsend at the entrance to Puget Sound the captain stopped his ship briefly to report the disaster to authorities, and to let the injured, and those passengers who chose to do so, leave the ship. While at this port a group of passengers decided that they wanted to honor the heroic work of the captain and crew during the fire. They drew up a statement which was signed by every passenger, and presented it to the captain. It read:

> We, the undersigned, passengers of the steamer *Queen*, desire to express to Capt. Cousins and the crew of the steamer our heartfelt appreciation of, and gratitude for, the splendid courage shown and perfect discipline maintained during the perilous experience we have just passed through, and it is our unanimous opinion that but for the coolness and bravery shown by the captain, officers and crew, most of us would undoubtedly have been lost and the ship destroyed.
>
> And we want to further testify to the chivalry shown in placing all the women and children in the boats first, and we believe we all owe our safety to this fact, as the crew were thus enabled to subdue the fire and thus allow us to be brought safely to port.
>
> We deplore the loss of those drowned in their efforts to save the ship and passengers, and we are deeply thankful to Almighty God the loss was not greater.[12]

With this reassuring support, Captain Cousins now directed his ship south through Puget Sound toward her original destination of Seattle, knowing he would eventually have to face the question of why eleven people died in the boats and only three in the fire. Even during this passage the tragedy continued to take its toll; another female passenger, who had been hospitalized at Port Townsend suffering from exposure, died, raising the death toll to fifteen.

One newspaper reported the arrival of the ship at Seattle as follows:

> Thousands lined the wharves when the *Queen* steamed into the harbor of her home port. Only once before had so many watched for her coming—the day when she brought home the men of Washington who had fought in the Philippines. Slowly she steamed up the bay, slackened until she seemed to come to a dead stop, then finally circled about the revenue cutter which lay at one of the city buoys, and made her way into the slip.
> When her passengers filed down the gangplank to meet those whose anxious faces were turned to theirs, each stopped to grasp the hand of the Captain who had brought them safe in port, and to thank him.[13]

The assistant general manager and the port captain for Pacific Coast Steamship Company met the ship from a tug before she docked at her Smith Cove pier around 5:30 in the afternoon. For reasons that are hard to understand, as soon as the passengers disembarked the curious crowd on the pier was allowed on board to see the results of the fire.

When time permitted, Captain Cousins issued a statement to the press, reflecting on what he had just been through:

> I have no ideas as to the origin of the fire. . . . It seemed to have burst into a full fledged fire with great suddenness. It was a vicious fire, and but for the heroic work of the crew and passengers in fighting it, the ship and all on board would have been lost. My crew behaved admirably. They could not have done better, and too much cannot be said in praise of the splendid service of the male passengers. I feel more than grateful to them for the assistance they rendered. There was no disorder, and very little excitement. It was a hard fight, and I am well nigh worn out.[14]

Several questions now remained to be answered. On 3 May 1904, just five days after the *Queen* burned, a fact-finding hearing was convened by the local inspectors of the Steamboat Inspection Service in Seattle, Captain B. B. Whitney who was concerned with navigation and seamanship, and R. A. Turner whose purview was the engineering aspects of the fire. Such hearings are normally held as soon after accidents as possible so that crew members, who have a way of wandering off into the hinterland, will still be available. The hearing lasted only one day, and twelve witnesses testified.[15]

The hearing was routine and produced no bombshells in the form of any surprise testimony. It was brief enough that the essence of it can be reviewed in a few paragraphs which may provide insights into the kind of inquiries that the inspectors conducted. For the most part the inspectors were interested in the wisdom of the decision to launch the boats, and any possible explanation for the cause of the fire. Captain Cousins was the first witness to be called. He was asked to describe the circumstances of the discovery of the fire, and the decision to launch the boats. There was considerable confusion in both the questions and answers at this point with respect to the naming of the various decks, and the location of the embarkation stations for the boats. Curiously, the captain was not asked to defend his decision to put the boats in the water.

The next witness, the passenger Captain Isaac N. Hibbard, was asked specifically about the wisdom of launching boats with the resultant loss of life. He replied that he concurred with the captain's decision, and that in spite of the loss of life he would recommend the same procedure again, even though it might result in jeopardizing lives including his own. Hibbard was an articulate witness, and spoke at length about how well things had been handled during the fire and the launching of the boats.

Another mariner who had been a passenger, Captain Stephen B. Shaw, was the next witness. He corroborated closely what Captain Hibbard had said about the smoothness and efficiency with which everything had been carried out, and he agreed that launching the boats was the only course of action available. The chief engineer of the *Queen*, W. J. McCredy, was called next. He explained the smooth, almost casual, engine room handling of the request for "water on deck," the term used for starting the fire pumps, aboard the *Queen*, and proudly reported how ample the pressure was at various deck fire stations. He described how the engine room made sure the bilge pumps could handle the water that was cascading down from the decks above (firefighting water has been known to capsize and/or sink more than one vessel), and he indicated that things went so well in the engine room that he and other engineers actually spent time on deck fighting the fire.

The chief mate, George Zeh, had little to add to what had been testified to by earlier witnesses, and was followed by Walter E. Anderson, the first assistant engineer, who was questioned only briefly. However, he offered the first possible explanation of the cause of the fire, suggesting that seawater that had come on board earlier had soaked some wiring that had to be repaired, and that shorts in this wiring may have started the fire. The inspectors did not pursue this line of questioning any further.

The second assistant engineer, a fireman, and the second mate then followed, each confirming earlier testimony except for minor details, about which witnesses might be expected to disagree. For example, the second mate insisted it was the fourth mate, not the night watchman, who notified the bridge of the fire. The next witness was Ernest Savage, the second steward. He described how the night watchman had discovered the fire, and that after opening the door and encountering flames, he—Savage—had sent the night watchman to the bridge.

The inspectors then took a new tack in trying to determine the cause of the fire, asking about the possibility of any oil-burning lamps that might have been in use. Savage denied that any such lamps would be available since they were kept in a locked cabinet. Inspector Turner asked, "Did you ever notice lady passengers having these alcohol lamps to curl their hair with?" Savage replied that he was aware of such lamps, but had not observed any on board. He concluded that the only passengers on the deck in which the fire started were two families, "and they had both been sick from the start."

The night watchman, John Poulsen, was the next to testify. He explained that he had been away from the pantry calling some of the early shift in the steward's department, and while crossing the dining saloon he noticed the smoke. He confirmed Savage's testimony about the discovery of the flames, and explained how after returning from the bridge he had awakened passengers and the rest of the steward's department personnel. This latter group including the ten or twelve men who slept in the "Glory Hole," the berthing compartment below the dining saloon.

A Seattle newspaper had reported that a woman had come out of her room, asked the night watchman for a glass of water, after which she returned to the door of her room. "As she opened this a gust of flame and smoke swept out. Her shriek of fright was the first alarm of fire."[16] The inspectors did not ask Poulsen about this story, apparently regarding it as impossible since the rooms in question were known to be empty, but it would be interesting to know how such a story was started. This was apparently the only instance in which a fanciful and patently untrue account of the fire on the *Queen* showed up in news reports.

The final witness was a waiter, James Greer, who had been asleep in the infamous "Glory Hole" at the time the fire broke out. He described how he had been awakened by the watchman, and had come up on deck through the smoke. He was questioned repeatedly about the rather circuitous route he would have to take to reach the open deck. He explained how turning the wrong way during that process would result in emerging on what he called the "fantail," a term that apparently denoted the steering-gear flat on that ship. It was in this area that the bodies of the three waiters were found.

The question of the alcohol lamps was raised again, and Greer replied that he was aware of such devices but that he had not seen any in the rooms for which he was responsible. He added that while women might carry them along, "but [on] short trips like this they are nearly all sick and they don't care to curl their hair." It was an interesting commentary on the economics of ocean travel in that era, and a reminder that in saving money one could expect to be miserable much of the time.

Another short set of questions followed, dealing with the possibility of oily rags or kerosene being left about. Greer indicated that any lamps and kerosene were kept by the porter. When asked what kind of oil the porter kept, the waiter answered "I don't know," and that answer became the final bit of testimony in the hearing. At that point the inspectors ruled that the hearing was officially concluded.

Two days later a terse report of the hearing was issued by the inspectors. It said in full: "In the matter of the investigation into the causes of fire on board the steamer *Queen*, February 27, 1904, the master and officers of the said steamer are hereby exonerated from any blame in connection herewith." It was a fully justified finding. The only disappointment came in there being no finding with respect to the cause of the fire, and no comment about the combustibility of the materials used in the deckhouses. Today, society has come to expect that fire experts can ascertain where and how any fire has started, what fueled it, and how it might have been prevented, but in 1904 no such capability existed.

It does seem strange, however, that at 4:10 A.M. the fourth officer of the ship—who was never called to testify—had been in the dining saloon and had seen no hint of fire, but by 4:20, by the night watchman's estimate, the smoke was noticeable and was quickly followed by flames. The stateroom in which the fire apparently started was on the port side of the ship near where the first assistant engineer had reported the repairs to the faulty wiring, but the rapid flare-up of the fire did not seem consistent with a wiring fire.

Thus the fire must remain for all time a mystery. How it started, however, is far less important than how it was put out, which was, in a word, magnificently.

Voyage number 505 ended for the *Queen* when she arrived back in San Francisco in late March under her own power, with cargo but no passengers aboard, to be rebuilt at the Union Iron Works.[17] This reconstruction, at a cost exceeding fifty thousand dollars, an amount of money which could buy a ship in those days, resulted in a new profile for the vessel. What must have been her original profile was shown in a photograph dating from 1895, In this picture, on top of her long deckhouse which covered about three quarters of her length can be seen two upper-level deckhouses, one from her bridge aft almost to the funnel, and another extending from her mainmast to the stern. This photograph shows both masts equipped with gaffs and booms from which, at least theoretically, fore-and-aft sails could be rigged. An even earlier picture shows yard-arms on the foremast from which square sails could be rigged.

In what must be a later picture, since the gaffs on the mast are gone, the fore deckhouse on the hurricane deck extends past the funnel, and the after deckhouse—the one destroyed by the fire—is shorter, beginning well aft of the mainmast. The lengthening of one deckhouse and the shortening of the other seems inconsistent, but there may have been fire safety considerations in the redesign.

With her new look the *Queen* soon went back into service for Pacific Coast Steamship Company, and managed to stay out of major trouble for several more years. In 1911 she burned at sea again, this time off Point Reyes on the northern California coast. Her captain was now George Zeh, who had been chief mate at the time of the 1904 fire. This time it was a fire in her forward hold, and while other ships stood by the ship's crew managed to put out the fire, allowing the ship to return to San Francisco.[18] In January of 1918, reflecting the hysteria created by World War I, the ship was a subject of a bomb scare while at a pier in San Francisco; this threat was seemingly related to sabotage charges being filed against one of the ship's oilers who had ties to the IWW, the Wobblies.[19]

As the dominance of the Pacific Coast Steamship Company waned, it was inevitable that the next giant of West Coast shipping would seek to acquire some of the better ships of the other lines. That new power, the Admiral Line, acquired the thirty-four year old *Queen* in 1916, and bought the rest of the company in 1918. Between 1916 and 1932 the *Queen* was operated by the Admiral Line in the Alaskan trade, with occasional coastal trips between Seattle and California. By this time, however, her age was catching up with her; even queens get tired.

The year 1921 was particularly difficult for the *Queen*. In January of that year the *Queen* broke a crankshaft and drifted helplessly off Point Arena on the northern California coast. After an unsuccessful effort by the crew to rig sails, she was towed back to San Francisco by the *Admiral*

Dewey and the tug *Hercules*. At San Francisco the *Admiral Watson* had been held up to carry her passengers north. However, only seventeen of the 130 passengers on board the *Queen* took advantage of the opportunity, with the rest preferring to travel by land.[20] In June of that same year the *Queen* sent an SOS when her main feed line broke and efforts to repair the break proved futile. At the time she was off the Oregon coast with 140 passengers on board. Five hours later she was taken in tow by the steam schooner *Johanna Smith*, but was subsequently able to get underway and return to San Francisco on her own.[21]

A month later, during labor troubles in 1921 the *Queen* broke down off Point Sur on the California coast. When the ship arrived in San Francisco the entire engine room force was fired because company officials felt that they were involved in sabotage. The passengers who had made the trip were not sure that the breakdown was indeed related to the labor troubles; one hundred of the 160 passengers on board signed a petition to the U.S. Shipping Board asking that the *Queen* be declared unseaworthy.[22] She was towed part of the way home by the *Admiral Farragut* with the tug *Monarch* bringing her the rest of the way to San Francisco.

Finally, the end came for the *Queen*. From her laid-up status in Lake Union in Seattle where many a good ship has spent her final days, she was sold to Japanese ship-breakers late in 1934. In September of 1935 under her own power a Japanese crew sailed the venerable ship to Yokohama on a passage that lasted fifty-three days, thanks to constant mechanical problems. It seems like a sad ending for such a resilient ship, but perhaps that bloodless demise was preferable to passing from this world in yet another disaster.

The *Queen* story, however, refused to end at that point. The former master of the *Queen*, N. E. Cousins, in 1916 was master of the finest ship in the Pacific Coast Steamship Company fleet, the 424-foot-long 7,793-ton liner *Congress*. In an incredible instance of déjà vu, on a coastal run going north from San Francisco this three-year-old ship caught fire off Crescent City and by the time she reached Coos Bay was fully ablaze. The captain stopped the vessel, and aided by the calm seas of a fine September day evacuated 253 passengers and 175 crewmen into the boats, later to be picked up by the seagoing hopper dredge

Michie of the Army Corps of Engineers. Not a life was lost. At last, Captain Cousins found himself completely vindicated for losing the fifteen lives in 1904 aboard the *Queen* and for some questionable behavior two years later under circumstances described in the next chapter.

The *Congress* was completely gutted by the fire, and unlike the *Queen* could not proceed under her own power. She was towed to Seattle, where she underwent a complete rebuilding effort, emerging as the *Nanking* of the China Mail Line in trans-Pacific service, a ship which quickly acquired a very shadowy reputation as a smuggler. After being seized by U.S. Customs, she was subsequently acquired at auction by the Admiral Line in 1923 as the *Emma Alexander*. After thirteen years of operation and a five-year lay-up she was sold to British interests in 1941 as the *Empire Woodlark*. She survived World War II under that flag and name, and was deliberately sunk in 1946 in deep water with a cargo of gas bombs. There the long shadow of the *Queen's* fire in 1904, and its aftermath throughout the fleet of Pacific Coast Steamship Company, finally ended.

Chapter Three

The *Valencia:* Disaster on Many Fronts

The loss of the SS *Valencia*, characterized as it was by struggles for survival aboard the ship, in the surf, and even ashore, was something out of a wild adventure novel that could not have taken place in real life. Yet it did occur, amidst chaos, rancor, and a high degree of confusion which still persists in trying to examine this devastating tragedy nearly one hundred years later. The story has been told and preserved in the Pacific Northwest, but nationally and internationally the *Valencia* remains virtually unknown.

The passenger ship *Valencia* had reasonably good credentials for her time. Like the *Queen of the Pacific*, she had been built at the William Cramp shipyard in Philadelphia, a yard with a fine reputation for solid construction. In 1906 when she faced her greatest crisis she was twenty-four years old, and having survived that long in the dangerous coastal waters in which she sailed seemed to be a tribute to her apparent indestructibility.

She was small, however, only 253 feet in length, and 34 feet in beam, and she was underpowered for an ocean passenger steamer, with only 950 horsepower. Her greatest problem, though, was her obsolescence. She had been built in 1882 when Chester A. Arthur was president, and, like the other iron steamers of that era, she lacked the double bottoms and compartmentation to make her as resistant to hull damage as were later generations of steamers. Although she had been modified and brought into the electric light era, structurally she was still the product of the gaslight age.

She was not a particularly handsome vessel. Like a number of other small steamers of that type, she had a relatively small deckhouse, with masts and booms for two hatches on a long forward deck. The same rigging existed aft for another hatch which was squeezed in between the principal midships deckhouse and another deckhouse on the stern. The long open foredeck was a concession to her cargo capabilities, while a string of portholes along her hull was a clue that most of her passenger space was below that main deck. Again showing a common design feature for such ships, her pilothouse was mounted only half a deck higher than the deckhouse. While this feature contributed to a sleeker look for the ship, it also limited the visibility for the mates and lookouts over what could be attained from a higher deck.

Journalistic accounts of this ship were unusually sloppy with respect to dates and other basic information, and historical accounts since that time have not done much better. Even her resumé is a bit confusing. One source indicates that she had originally been built for Atlantic and Caribbean Navigation Company and then acquired by Pacific Steam Whaling Company in 1888, after which she was acquired by Oregon

The *Valencia* had provided service on demanding routes for many years before she was asked to fill in on the Puget Sound route for another ship undergoing repairs. (Courtesy of the Puget Sound Maritime Historical Society)

Improvement Company in 1889 and by Pacific Coast Company in 1897.[1] Another source indicates that she was originally operated by the Red Star Line from New York to the Caribbean (although there was no American-flag Red Star Line), and came to the West Coast in 1898 for the whaling firm.[2]

Contemporary editions of the *Record* of the American Bureau of Shipping indicate that her original owner and operator was actually Boulton, Bliss, and Dallett, and that the ship was homeported in Wilmington, Delaware. Another reliable source adds the pertinent information that she was used in Alaskan service by the Pacific Packing and Navigation Company, but went off to war as an Army transport in the Spanish American War.[3] In 1902, according to this source, she had then been acquired by Pacific Coast Company, the diverse holding company that owned railroads and coal mines, as well as shipping lines which covered the entire West Coast.

The *Valencia* had remained on the Alaskan run for her new owners, but in 1906 she had temporarily replaced the *City of Puebla* on the company's coastal route between San Francisco and Puget Sound after that ship had lost a propeller shaft at sea. That minor crisis for the *City of Puebla* had provided an opportunity for the maritime industry and the general public to see how the Pacific Coast Steamship Company treated people. The ship had been towed all the way from the north coast of California to the entrance of the Golden Gate by two hard-working steam schooners, the *Chehalis* and *Norwood*, whose captains hoped to realize a bit of salvage money for their efforts, only to have the ship's captain cast off their lines and employ a commercial tug to tow the vessel into port.[4]

The *Valencia* was now making only her second voyage as a substitute for the *City of Puebla*, a voyage that would prove to be her last. She left the Golden Gate in late morning on Saturday, 20 January 1906, under the command of Captain Oscar M. Johnson, bound for Victoria, British Columbia, and Seattle, Washington. Aboard by one account were 164 persons,[5] while another count said 144 people,[6] and still others said there were 94 as passengers and 60 as crew for a total of 154.[7] This latter number seems to be the most widely accepted of the various totals. The list of names of those aboard which was published later in the San Francisco *Chronicle* identified 42 first class passengers, 54 second class passengers, and 65 in the crew, a total of 161. The Seattle *Times* in one edition put the total on board as 170,[8] and in another as 154; it also listed the names of a total of 181 people thought to be on board, including one stowaway.[9]

The Commission which later investigated the accident acknowledged that a firm count was impossible, but it believed that 173 were on board, 108 as passengers and 65 as crewmen.[10] It is clear that even longer coastal voyages were beset with the problem of knowing who was on board, a problem generally associated with smaller ships on shorter voyages.

Even though she was considered a second-rate passenger ship, the *Valencia* was certainly staffed adequately for passenger comfort. In the steward's department she carried a stewardess, a bartender, ten waiters, three cooks and a baker, in addition to those who served the needs of the crew. Her purser's department had three members, and the deck department carried a boatswain and carpenter, four quartermasters responsible for steering the ship, a watchman, eight seaman, and a deck boy. The engine room was crewed by five firemen, three oilers, and three coal passers. However, many of her crew had come to her from the *City of Puebla* and had not yet settled in to their new ship. This situation would present problems later in the voyage, when many crewmen did not seem to understand their duties.

Early in her final voyage the *Valencia* encountered fog, and that peril to navigation persisted all the way up the coast. Her last reliable navigational fix was obtained when passing Cape Mendocino on the California coast. After that, unable to carry out either celestial observations or piloting by using bearings on lighthouses ashore, Captain Johnson was forced to rely on dead reckoning, the use of assumed speeds and courses made good, to determine the position of the ship. Apparently on Monday 22 January[11] the second mate was able to get an azimuth of the sun, an observation used to check the accuracy of compasses, but such an observation can be achieved with a fuzzy sun and no horizon, conditions which would prevent accurate position-fixing sights from being obtained.

Although there is an off-shore southbound current on the West Coast of North America,[12] there are also strong counter currents closer inshore moving north. This latter current set the *Valencia* to the north at a faster rate than Captain Johnson had anticipated, and on the evening of 22 January, when he calculated that he was off the mouth of the Strait of Juan de Fuca, he had actually been carried some nineteen miles beyond his intended turning point north of the Umatilla Lightship.[13] The foghorn of this lightship was apparently not heard aboard the *Valencia*, suggesting that it may have been inoperative, or, more likely, that it was not foggy at that location. The second lightship, Swiftsure Bank, farther to the north and west, had not yet been established in 1906. Furthermore, shipboard radio and radio direction finders had not yet come on the scene, so the captain had little to utilize, beyond his own intuition, in feeling his way through the fog.

Several accounts of the *Valencia*'s last moments use alternate dates, indicating that the ship left San Francisco on 21 January and arrived off the Strait of Juan de Fuca on the night of 22 January,[14] which would have made her speed up the coast eighteen knots, impossible for a ship of that vintage and horsepower. Distance tables show that the distance between San Francisco and Cape Flattery is 683 miles,[15] which would mean that the ship would have been making about 11.4 knots if she departed on the 20th, a much more likely scenario. This confusion about dates and times would persist throughout the newspaper coverage of the events of the next few days.

According to various accounts, the *Valencia*'s patent log or taffrail log, the means of measuring ship's mileage in that era, was in use as the ship arrived off Juan de Fuca, but may have been producing faulty readings. Captain Johnson was convinced that in normal operation the taffrail log on the ship read 6 percent high, and that belief would become an issue in the final determination of what took place aboard the ship.

The taffrail log consists of a rotor which is streamed behind the ship on a fairly stiff line connected to a odometer-type device mounted on the ship's rail. The rotor turns the line which in turn moves the gears in the indicator, producing a measure of the ship's mileage based on how fast the rotor is turning. These so-called patent logs were not very reliable because the rotor could become clogged with drifting kelp, and also because with a current behind the ship the motion of the rotor through the water was not a measure of the ship's speed over the ground. Nevertheless, they were the only measures of speed and distance available to the mariner until pit logs, making use of Pitotstatic or pressure effects, came into use somewhat later.

According to one account, the ship's Thompson deep-sea sounding machine was out of order.[16] Later investigations made no such findings, although the infrequency of soundings was criticized. The sounding machine of that era dropped a lead weight on a long wire onto the ocean floor, accompanied by a cylinder containing a scaled glass tube which was sensitive to pressure. There was also a bit of tallow inserted into a recess in the lead; this soft material picked up a sample of the bottom which could be compared to the bottom as indicated on the chart. When the lead hit the bottom it was reeled in with a hand winch, and the depth was read on the scale of the glass tube. It was a laborious and time-consuming process, but in the hands of a good operator it was a reasonably accurate way of determining the depth of the water at the time the lead was dropped.

A distinct pattern in a line of soundings is identifiable near the Umatilla Reef Lightship. Somewhat farther north a steep drop-off in depth occurs, indicating the mouth of the Strait of Juan de Fuca, the canyon of which swings off to the southwest. However, Captain Johnson did not begin his soundings until six P.M. on Monday, and immediately found no bottom. The absence of the shallower depths characteristic of the approach should have made him suspicious. Late in the evening on 23 January, measurable depths began to be recorded, which should have given the captain some idea of where he was. The final sounding indicated a depth of thirty fathoms, not characteristic of the mouth of the Strait.

Ironically, when he was abeam of Cape Flattery Captain Johnson heard no fog signal, because that lighthouse and its counterpart Carmanah Light on the Canadian side were in clear weather all night during the fatal accident to the *Valencia*. However, the ship was well to the west of where the captain thought she was, so the signal may not have been heard even if it had been operating.

Johnson was an established captain, but there is some question as to how much experience he had accumulated. His age does not appear in any account. One source said he had worked for the company for a dozen years,[17] while another said twenty years.[18] Still another source, the Seattle *Times* mistakenly identified his background with that of a cook aboard the *Valencia* named Johnson, and reported that he had been at sea for only four years.[19]

Eight months earlier the real Captain Johnson had put the *Valencia* aground in the Inland Passage to Alaska, and considerable freight had to be jettisoned before the vessel could be refloated.[20] In spite of that accident, Captain Johnson was apparently quite confident of his own ability. However, he now faced the dilemma of all captains in fog; if he waited outside for the fog to clear, he missed his schedule, but the alternative to going in—steaming back and forth outside after two days of dead reckoning—was not necessarily safer than trying to go in. When he subsequently ordered a course change, he put into motion a series of events that would soon change forever the lives of all on board the *Valencia*.

Curiously, the collier SS *Edith*, a few hours behind the *Valencia* on the same route, had a similar experience in underestimating the effect of the current, and very nearly ran aground in the fog within a short distance of where the *Valencia* would eventually strike the shore. However, her captain wisely hauled out toward the open ocean and cruised slowly about until he was able to establish a reasonably accurate position.[21]

The first indication of trouble for the *Valencia* came when the ship hit an unseen obstruction which caused her to shudder throughout her length. According to the second mate, the captain exclaimed, "My God, where are we?"[22] After listing to one side, the ship momentarily broke free from the grasp of the underwater object. The alarm was sounded from the bridge, and the unmistakable jingle of bells being rung on the engine order telegraph, together with the ship's whistle, alerted passengers to the presence of danger. The ship swung about, and appeared to be heading away from further danger when she hit another pinnacle which penetrated the ship's tired old hull. The engine room, now under the direct supervision of the chief engineer E. W. Downing, responded to the captain's order for more steam. Again, the *Valencia* freed herself from the rocks that had impaled her, and backed away from the danger.

However, it was quickly apparent that deep water was not a refuge for the ship at this point. Water was coursing into the engine room and boiler rooms, and the pumps were unable to handle the volume. As Downing scrambled topside through an escape ladder, the surging swells from a developing southeast gale cast the ship onto the rocks, permanently.

The ship had grounded on the coast of British Columbia somewhere east of Cape Beale, a headland with a lighthouse guarding the long Alberni Inlet, which led to lumber mills and canneries in the interior of Vancouver Island. Another nearby headland was called Pachena Point. The site of the grounding was later identified as being on a fringe of Walla Walla Reef, named for a sistership of the *Valencia* which had grounded there earlier, before her ultimate demise on the California coast in 1902. The location was at the base of a high steep cliff which made both escape and rescue difficult.

The exact location of the *Valencia*'s grounding was given in one newspaper account as "Shelter bight, eleven and a half miles west of Carmanah, exactly on the 120th meridian."[23] This location was provided by Captain Cousins of the steamer *Queen* which now, only two years after her own offshore fire, was about to be cast in the role of a potential rescue vessel. If Captain Cousins meant the 125th meridian, he would have indeed been accurate, but the 120th meridian is in eastern British Columbia, and farther south corresponds to the California-Nevada border. Another specific location for the wreck was given as "Point Klanaway, five miles from Cape Beale."[24] This location also seems reasonably accurate. The name Klanaway occurs in several of the accounts, but on maps it is spelled Klanawa and a local resident in an account to be cited shortly spelled it Clanawah.

There was no life-saving station, either Canadian or American, in that area. One had once existed at Neah Bay, inside Cape Flattery on the Washington side, but it had never been properly funded or manned. The Seattle *Times* spoke cynically of the announced concept for this station, saying, "The scheme was beautiful in its inception, the argument being put forward that the Indians in their canoes could ride the biggest swells and waves the Pacific ever tossed up, but when the red men were really wanted they either couldn't be found or were incapacitated through drink."[25] Shortly after the *Valencia*'s grounding, this station would be reestablished and become an important part of a safety net for mariners at the entrance to the Strait of Juan de Fuca.

A reliable first-person account of what happened when the *Valencia* hit the rocks appears in the testimony of the ship's boatswain, T. J. McCarthy, before a coroner's jury in Victoria, British Columbia:

> I was in my bunk asleep. I got up at once and went on deck. It was thick dark, sleeting and blowing a stiff breeze. I could not see any light. I went back and got my clothes. By that time the passengers were getting out of their rooms and most of them had life preservers on. At the time the engines were working, but I don't know which way. The chief officer told me to clear away the boats, which I did. The deck was crowded and it was so dark I could not tell the crew from passengers. We only carried eight sailors and four quartermasters. We had seven boats and three rafts. The davits were drop davits.
>
> The captain shouted from the bridge to lower all boats to the saloon rail and keep them there, but the four forward boats were lowered all the way; most of them were full of passengers and there was a strain on the tackles. Of those four boats, only one, No. 2, got away from the ship's side. There was a heavy sea running, breaking almost to the bridge, and I am doubtful if those boats could have got away even in daylight. The captain turned the searchlight all around. I saw No. 2 boat off at some little distance; then someone pulled the whistle and the electric lights went out.
>
> I saw No. 1 boat smash alongside. There would be 15 or 20 people in her. I had a ladder thrown over, also some ropes, and I saw one man climb aboard. At that time the *Valencia* took a heavy list to port and No. 7 boat was lowered. I saw the firemen's mess boy in No. 6 boat. She got away from the ship's

side. One raft was also put overboard. There were at that time several people in the rigging and the rest on the hurricane deck. Some rockets were then assuring the passengers that they would be all right. At the same time the social hall and the weather side of the saloon were the only dry places on the ship.[26]

By this time the ship, her iron hull pierced at several points by the ragged rocks along the shore, was beginning to break up. The captain had ordered the boats to be lowered to the rail for subsequent launching in daylight, but the restless passengers found no seaman stationed by the boats to prevent their launching. As a result, several boats were put into the water without any authorization to do so and without proper supervision, resulting in the boats upsetting and casting occupants into the water where they quickly drowned. This night-time effort to launch lifeboats became a disaster in itself, although finally one boat, amply filled with families including women and children, was able to get free of the ship. Soon, however, it became apparent that the old life jackets were full of tule rather than cork, and had only limited buoyancy.

Distress flares were fired at regular intervals, but in the prevailing weather there seemed to be little chance of their being seen along this lonely coastline. The ship was without any power, and the only light came from a few kerosene lamps. All accounts indicate that the terrified passengers bolstered their spirits by singing, "Nearer My God to Thee," a hymn that would soon emerge as the anthem of shipwrecked passengers.[27]

Another of the crew, the chief freight clerk Frank Lehn, recalled the hideous scene:

> Screams of women and children mingled in an awful chorus with the shrieking of the wind, the dash of rain, and the roar of the breakers. As the passengers rushed on deck they were carried away in bunches by the huge waves that seemed as high as the ship's mastheads. The ship began to break up almost at once and the women and children were lashed to the rigging above the reach of the sea. It was a pitiful sight to see frail women, wearing only night dresses, with bare feet on the freezing ratlines, trying to shield children in their arms from the icy wind and rain.[28]

Boatswain McCarthy recalled what happened when dawn finally came for the stricken ship on Tuesday, 23 January:

> . . . at daylight we could see the people on the beach right under the cliff at almost low water. They would be a hundred yards or more away. Captain Johnson ordered me to get a five-inch line to shore.[29] I sent a man aloft and rigged the blocks and got the Lyle gun aft on the hurricane deck.

These people on the beach early in the morning are something of a mystery, and are not mentioned in most other accounts. Apparently, a small number of survivors had somehow reached the beach, perhaps from the boat or the rafts which had been launched during the night, and these must have been the men seen by McCarthy. As they tried to climb the cliff the exhausted men all fell to their deaths on the rocks below.[30] One account identified a seaman named Lawrence Olson as having washed ashore; this man then tried to climb the cliff along with another man who was described as limping. These two were then caught in the surf and vanished from sight.[31]

The Lyle gun made one successful shot at this time, with a line eventually reaching the beach, but there was now no one to secure it, and it was swept back into the sea. After this futile effort a fireman named Joe Segalos volunteered to take a line ashore. Making one end fast to the ship and the other to his body, he leaped into the frigid water and set out for the beach. For twenty minutes he fought his way toward the beach and had almost made it when his strength gave out. Those on board the *Valencia* hauled back on the line, expecting to find his lifeless body at the end of it. Somehow, one of the life-rafts had intercepted him and pulled him aboard, still alive.

Meanwhile, aboard the ship, as Boatswain McCarthy recalled, one more attempt to reach the shore was being made by boat:

> The tide was coming in and the seas were getting stronger and Captain Johnson asked me if I would go in the remaining boat and try and make a landing, in order to take a line. I finally got a crew and got away with No. 5 boat; Captain Johnson was in charge of lowering it. We got away with considerable difficulty; the bow oar broke. They cheered us from the ship but it was so thick we could not see her. We kept outside the

breakers but at times could not see shore; it was so thick that we could not find a place to land. I came to some rocks which I took to be the Duncan Rocks off Tatoosh Island [off Cape Flattery] and finally a heavy sea hit us. Two of the men lost their oars and we had only two left. We pulled a little farther and one of the men said he thought it was the Vancouver Island shore. Finally we made a landing in a place I afterwards found to be between Pachena Bay and Cape Beale.

The boatswain's reference to "finally" getting a crew together was an indication that his call for volunteers to man the boat had gone totally unheeded for some time, until a few crewmen finally agreed to go. This boat crew eventually reached the safety of the beach, after which they struggled along the rugged shoreline until they arrived at Cape Beale Lighthouse which was three miles from their landing point, according to a sign they found on the trail. At the lighthouse they learned from the keeper's wife that there had already been a message sent along the telegraph line describing the fate of the ship.[32]

The other boat which had been launched during the night also reached the beach at a point fifteen miles east of Cape Beale with five men remaining in it. None of the women and children in this boat had survived. It was from this crew that the word of the ship's fate first was sent along the telegraph. Through the efforts of these two boat crews help was summoned from Victoria, but there was no assurance that it would arrive in time.

Reaching the site of the shipwreck from either land or sea was extremely difficult. No roads existed ashore at that time, as indeed no roads exist today, so the only possible aid that could arrive at the cliff was from those people who traveled on foot along soggy ill-marked trails through a rain forest that received 120 inches of precipitation annually. Such trails still exist today as part of the Pacific Rim National Park. Once described as "the world's most difficult hiking trail," guidebooks now call the present trail "one of the world's great hikes."[33]

The communication network ashore was a governmental concession to the reality that this was a coastline which, although not unpopulated, was a lonely place with more than its share of shipwrecks. Between the lighthouse at Carmanah and the one at Cape Beale, roughly twenty-five statute miles, a telegraph line ran along the shore, following a rough trail that had been blazed through the forest to provide relief for shipwrecked mariners. The line has generally been described as a telegraph line, but there are several references to it that suggest it was also a voice telephone circuit, and one that says it was indeed both. The line was designed in such a way as to permit it to be broken by those in distress, with instructions on how to do this posted on signs along the trail. Such a break could be detected at a central point, with a lineman subsequently going out on the trail to locate the site where the stranded seafarers would be found.

Governmental personnel were stationed at each of the two lighthouses, and there were also other men who patrolled the line. Beyond Cape Beale to the north on Barkley Sound was the community of Bamfield, which was a cable station for an international telegraph line to the Far East, and additional personnel were stationed here. There were also native North Americans living along the coast, and at least one Indian policeman. In addition, a small community called Clo-oose contained a few residents. So, although the coast was rough and inhospitable, there were a few people ashore in a position to help.

One of the survivors who came ashore in the first boat that made it to the beach was a man named Frank F. Bunker, who was en route to Seattle to become assistant superintendent of schools. His wife and children had been lost from the boat. This man quickly became a hero, and would later play a leadership role in criticizing the Pacific Coast Steamship Company and the crew of the *Valencia*. Bunker left the others on the beach, and had found the lineman's shack at Darling Creek. From this point he was able to break into the telephone/telegraph circuit and report the shipwreck to Tom Daykin, the lighthouse keeper at Carmanah to the east.[34]

Shortly thereafter, Phil Daykin, son of the lighthouse keeper at Carmanah, started out at about 4 P.M. on the 23rd, about sixteen hours after the wreck. At Clo-oose he rounded up lineman Joe Logan, trapper Joe Martin, and a fourth man, Otto Rosander, who later dropped out somewhere along the way. The four men then pushed westward on foot through the heavy rain. When they reached the Clanawah River the water was too high for the little canoe that had been left there. They shouted across to an Indian on the other bank who had a large canoe, but the man wanted ten dollars each to ferry the men across.[35]

Lacking that much money they were forced to spend the night there. Phil Daykin later speculated that this delay may have cost them the opportunity to save lives. In the morning a couple of the men took a small canoe upstream, crossed over, and commandeered the Indian's large canoe to bring the rest of the party across. Then they set out on foot to try to reach the wreck. Finally in early afternoon on Wednesday, 24 January, three of them reached the top of the bluff, 175 feet above the beach, offshore of which lay the *Valencia*. Here they found the shot-line from the ship's Lyle gun, but it had chafed through at the point where it ran across the rocks at the top of the cliff and was useless.

The weather was not particularly bad at this time, and it looked as if a rescue might be effected. However, while the men watched the ship below them a great ridge of water came sweeping from seaward, breaking up the deckhouse and sweeping everyone from the rigging. Appalled at what they had seen, the men then went back to a line shack at Sakowis to spend the night, where eventually Bunker struggled in to join them.[36]

Meanwhile, ships from Victoria were moving toward the scene to offer assistance. The first ship to come close to the wreck never saw it and knew nothing of the *Valencia*'s peril; this was a small Canadian coaster, the *Queen City*, not to be confused with the American passenger liner, *Queen*, which would be on the scene shortly. The *Queen City* earlier on the first day had dropped off the mail at the Carmanah lighthouse to the two Daykin boys who had rowed out to meet the ship, an indication that the weather had not been particularly foul at that time. She had also dropped off the mail at Clo-oose, a location that had to be passed by when the weather was bad. This ship had then started up the coast on her regular run, and passed by the site of the *Valencia* disaster but, on account of the fog, had not seen the wreck.[37]

The first ship to reach the scene of the wreck was the *Queen* which upon arriving at Victoria about 4 P.M. on Tuesday had dropped off her passengers and started for the wreck site. She arrived in darkness and subsequently took refuge overnight in the lee of Cape Flattery, after which she approached the wreck in daylight on the 24th. She came no closer than a mile, but could see signs of life on the *Valencia*. Captain Cousins chose to launch no boats, justifying his action because of the roughness of the sea.

The state of the sea this close to the shore was a critical and disputed factor in the difficulty that vessels experienced in approaching from seaward. When the hulls of oil-burning ships are ruptured, the escaping bunker fuel often provides a calming effect on the sea. But the *Valencia* was a coal-burner, and consequently her ruptured hull provided no means of flattening the breaking seas. Ships also often carried a small quantity of "storm oil," generally an animal or vegetable oil, for this purpose. However, apparently no effort was made by any of the vessels standing by to float a patch of oil in around the wreck. Neither was there any attempt to float a line in on a raft or boat.

Curiously, though, the Daykin shore party on the bluff had noticed a lane of smooth water through the breakers that existed seaward from the *Valencia*. Perhaps storm oil or lubricating oil had leaked into the

Two days after the sinking of the *Valencia*, the seas had flattened enough to make the task of the boat crews from the *City of Topeka* much easier, as they picked up the two rafts with survivors in them. (Courtesy of the Puget Sound Maritime Historical Society)

sea. In any event, such a lane could have provided a means whereby small boats could have reached the wreck, but this phenomenon could not have been visible to ships lying further offshore.

The Canadian tug *Czar* and salvage steamer *Salvor*, responding to the distress message received at Victoria, also reached the site on Wednesday, the 24th, but were unable or unwilling to work their way close in to the perilous position of the *Valencia*. At this point some heated words were exchanged between the master of the *Queen* and his counterpart on the *Czar*, and a similar shouting match took place between the captain of the newly-arrived *City of Topeka* and the captain of the *Czar*, who told that ship to "go to hell" as he departed the scene in the tug.[38] The new arrival, the American-flag *City of Topeka*, also a sister ship of the *Valencia* under the Pacific Coast Company house flag, had diverted to the scene, coming all the way from Seattle. She relieved the *Queen* which then left to resume her regular run. Neither of these ships was able to provide any assistance. Finally on the following day, Thursday, 25 January 1906, the whaler *Orion* was able to get in close enough to the hulk of the ship to determine that there was no longer any life aboard.

Later on the 25th the *City of Topeka* came upon a life-raft with eighteen survivors in it, including the heroic fireman who had tried to take the line ashore. These half-dead people represented the largest single group of survivors to be found. The second mate, P. E. Peterson, who was on that raft, described his own experience in abandoning ship:

> I was in the main rigging on the port side. We launched the starboard raft. Captain Johnson wanted the women to go on it. We then launched the port raft with much difficulty. Six or seven men got on it, and the women refused to go. Some of the men also refused to leave the ship. There were seventeen men on it and Captain Johnson told me that I had better go on it. I jumped overboard and got on the raft. We got cleared away and later, about 12 A.M., some of the men wanted to beach it; just as we started to do this we saw some smoke, and shortly after the SS *Topeka* came and picked us up. We saw nothing of the raft that left the *Valencia* fifteen minutes before us.[39]

The other life-raft also miraculously survived, but lost several people to the deadly insanity which sometimes strikes victims of marine disasters. In this raft was the chief cook Sam Hancock. He recalled how they landed at Turret Island at the mouth of Barkley Sound:

> We struck the beach about midnight and three more went insane and died on the raft. The remaining four went into the bush until daylight, and then we walked about on the island all day Thursday. Toward evening three of us got to the beach and saw an Indian settlement about a mile away. Some Indians came and afterwards a cannery steamer took us to Toquart on Barkley Sound. In the morning the SS *Salvor* came and took us off. They went to the island and got the raft and afterwards found Connors (the man who had wandered off).[40]

By this time a small fleet of vessels was engaged in rounding up the various survivors on Vancouver Island and on the small offshore islands. In addition to the *Salvor,* the tugs *Lorne, Pioneer,* and *Bahada,* and the steamer *Shamrock,* together with the whaler *Orion* and the *Perry* and *Grant* of the U.S. Revenue Marine Service, gathered up survivors and bodies for delivery to the *City of Topeka* which remained on the scene.

From the standpoint of the maritime community, and particularly that of the families of the victims, the troubling question in the *Valencia* disaster was, could more have been done? In retrospect, it is difficult, and indeed unfair, for anyone who was not there to say that the vessels that stood by could have come in closer to launch boats or put a line on board. However, water depths appeared to be adequate within a half mile of shore, although Captain Cousins of the *Queen* would later complain that charts of the area were not reliable,[41] and a ship from that distance could have tried to float in a line to the stranded ship. Although merchant ships do not carry breeches buoy gear, any boatswain worthy of the name could rig a "bosun's chair" on such a line, and while a rescue in this fashion would have been difficult, it would not have been impossible. The point is that *nothing* was tried, and this inaction flies in the face of both the reputation for resourcefulness that seafaring men have earned, as well as the great tradition of lifesaving that has existed among them. In the words of the Presidential Commission that later investigated the disaster, ". . . there was certainly no display of the heroic daring that has often marked other such emergencies in our merchant marine."[42]

The final tally, by one account, was 117 lost, made up of 37 crewmen out of 60 and 80 passengers out of 94. Another account indicated that 126 out of 164 aboard were lost, and still another that 124 were lost from an unspecified total number aboard. The Presidential Commission concluded that 136 lives were lost. By any count, the wreck of the *Valencia* may have surpassed, or at least been a close second to, the 131 lives lost in the *Rio de Janeiro* shipwreck off the entrance to San Francisco in 1901 as the most deadly American disaster on the West Coast during the twentieth century.

When the *Valencia* went down the incident proved to be a case of survival of the fittest, and men demonstrated that they had the stamina and strength to be the only survivors. Not a single woman or child survived the disaster. Crewmen had survived in greater numbers than had passengers, not because of any disregard of their duty to passengers but because they were better small boat seamen than were the passengers who had generally been reluctant to get into the boats and rafts after the disastrous attempts to launch boats at night. It might be noted in passing that crewmen sometimes brought their own life jackets on board to use in lieu of the notoriously sinkable tule jackets furnished to the passengers.

The aftermath of the disaster produced a number of interesting themes, and much recrimination. Captain Johnson of the *Valencia* was generally praised for his constant efforts in behalf of his ship and the passengers and crew for whom he was responsible, but was blamed for the navigational mistake that had put the ship aground. Captain Thomas H. Cann of the *City of Topeka* was commended for the rescue of the eighteen survivors on the raft. The fireman Joe Segalos received a hero's welcome in Seattle, where he was awarded a medal for his bravery, after which he went on to a brief stage career answering questions about the disaster in a theater owned by a fellow Greek-American citizen. He was subsequently nominated to receive a Carnegie Medal for lifesaving.

The remains of the *Valencia* lasted only briefly before they were beaten down by the heavy swells off Vancouver Island. (Courtesy of the Puget Sound Maritime Historical Society)

In a more negative vein, Captain Cousins of the *Queen* was criticized for his timidity in not getting close to the wrecked ship, and he in turn castigated the captains of the *Salvor* and the *Czar* for the same reason. The survivors who struggled ashore and reached help were blamed for not returning to the scene of the wreck and providing assistance from the beach. The all-male group of survivors was criticized for not insuring that any women and children survived. Even the marine inspectors who conducted the follow-up investigations were faulted for certifying the tule lifejackets as safe, and one of them was accused of not having the required time at sea in command of a large vessel to qualify him for the position.

Moreover, the Revenue Cutter Service was censured for the state of disrepair of its two cutters in the area, which prevented them from providing any rescue capability. Survivor Frank Bunker condemned the steamship company, asking "why the Pacific Coast Steamship Company is willing to permit the possibility of such conditions on their boats and why the United States government does nothing to prevent such wholesale murder of her citizens." The master of the whaler *Orion* denounced the captains of the ships standing by the *Valencia,* saying that he was utterly humiliated to think that anyone following the sea would have been guilty of such cowardice in relief of the unfortunate souls facing death in the rigging of a ship about to go to pieces.

Strong language characterized all these charges; there was certainly no suggestion made by survivors, the press, the general public, or the maritime community, that under the circumstances things turned out reasonably well. There were, however, a few constructive proposals offered for needed reforms. The general manager of the Pacific Coast Company rather defensively called for a government rescue tug to be stationed at the approaches to the Strait of Juan de Fuca. Richard Chilcott, a master mariner residing in Seattle, called for wireless telegraph stations to be located at Tatoosh Island and Cape Disappointment, for telephone lines similar to those on Vancouver Island to be located between Cape Disappointment and Neah Bay, for a line of bell buoys to be established offshore, and for the establishment of a well-equipped life-saving station at Neah Bay.[43] Captain Chilcott's radio proposals are particularly interesting in that the first radio message leading to rescue at sea, that of Jack Binns on the *Republic* in 1909, was still three years in the future.

Newspaper reporters had a field day in dealing with the human-interest angles in the loss of the *Valencia.* There were stories about crewmen who had experienced premonitions of disaster and had missed the ship, about passengers who had accidentally missed the ship, and others who had decided at the last moment to board the ship, about unlikely heroes such as a young man who kept his finger in the bottom hole of the lifeboat when the plug was found to be the wrong size, about heroines such as the stewardess who instilled courage and inspiration in all those around her, about the beautiful San Francisco debutante who lost her life and was never found, about families separated in death, and all kinds of other human dramas.

One of the ironies of the tragedy was the presence of a capable young athlete aboard the *Valencia,* George H. Jesse, whose talents were not used. He was a noted oarsman, and could have been of great value in early attempts to take a line to shore. However, he was committed to aiding the young debutante, Laura Van Wyck, and he stayed at her side in the rigging of the ship until they were both lost.[44]

Another particularly tragic story was that of the passenger Donald Ross who died on the *Valencia*. Two years earlier he had lost his wife who perished when the passenger steamer *Clallam* of the Black Ball Line foundered off Point Wilson in the Strait of Juan de Fuca, en route to British Columbia ports.[45]

The first legal action resulting from the *Valencia* accident was filed by Charles Allison, an elderly white-haired man who had been in the life-raft with the seventeen other survivors. Allison had been a vocal critic of Frank Bunker and the other survivors who had reached the shore, charging them with not returning to the beach near the *Valencia* to help others, a charge that had little merit considering that, for the most part, those men were exhausted, injured, and without adequate clothing including shoes. Allison was now suing the steamship company for five thousand dollars for bodily pain and mental anguish.[46]

Soon it was time for the inevitable investigation. Within a few days after the tragedy the local inspector for the Steamboat Inspection Service, Robert Turner, and his counterpart for deck department matters, Bion B. Whitney, convened a hearing to determine the facts of the case. These were the same two men who had conducted the hearing into the disastrous fire on the *Queen* two years earlier. Although federal law specified that the hearings be conducted by the local inspectors, considerable pressure existed during the hearings to utilize a national investigative panel instead. This was particularly true after the inspectors became defensive about their role in approving the hated tule lifejackets.

As the local investigation got underway the Seattle Chamber of Commerce petitioned President Theodore Roosevelt to initiate a federal investigation, free from any influences that might be brought to bear on the local inspectors. Also critical of any local inquiry were the Seattle Commercial Club and the Elks Club, who contacted the President and the Secretary of Commerce and Labor respectively.[47]

Captain Chilkott added his voice to the petition, asking Inspector-General Uhler of the Inspection Service to establish a board free of political influence that could recommend laws prescribing such things for passenger ships as "cellular bottoms, which would have saved the *Valencia*, that they shall carry so many experienced men to handle boats, and that they shall carry life boats that are life boats, and that each shall be fitted with a sea anchor and oil bags, and a great many other details. . . ."[48] The Seattle *Times* joined in by claiming bias on the part of the local inspectors in a sub-headline that read, "*Valencia* Investigation Practically Conducted by the Pacific Coast Steamship Company and Its Employees."

Before President Roosevelt had time to respond to the petition for an investigation at the national level, the Secretary of the U.S. Department of Commerce and Labor, Victor H. Metcalf, telegraphed the local inspectors in Seattle, indicating what he wanted in the local hearings:

> Make thorough and searching investigation of *Valencia*; also full investigation of conduct of officers of steamers *Topeka* and *Queen*, pursuant to Section 4450 Revised Statutes. Also investigate all causes of wreck, the loss of life and any misconduct or neglect of duty on the part of any connected therewith. Give public hearings and take testimony of all available survivors of *Valencia* and of any witness who may desire to be heard. Your investigation must be thorough and complete and your report with all evidence forwarded to the department. Also forward me immediately full preliminary reports of facts as now understood.[49]

The Secretary also told the inspectors to cooperate with the U.S. Attorney for the area, Jesse Frye, who had been ordered by U.S. Attorney General William H. Moody to assist the inspectors. Frye felt that he had been put in an untenable position of appearing to prop up the increasingly discredited inspectors.[50] Eventually, the hearing conducted by the local inspectors generated 1,132 pages of transcript, but added little to an understanding of the tragedy.[51]

The various service clubs, fraternal organizations, and labor groups of Seattle did an unusual thing which epitomized the total response of the community to the *Valencia* disaster. These groups spearheaded a campaign to provide decent burials for the victims of the wreck, particularly those who had never been identified. There are graves of such children in Lakeview Cemetery, and a *Valencia* monument in Mt. Pleasant Cemetery.[52] Inscribed on the latter are the words: "Dedicated to the Unknown Dead of the Valencia Disaster, Jan. 22, 1906, Off Vancouver Island. Memorial Services Sept. 23, 1906. Remains Brought and Interred by Organized Labor of Seattle W[ashingto]n."[53]

On February 6, 1906, Congressman William E. Humphrey of Washington called on President Theodore Roosevelt to appoint a special commission to investigate the wreck, stating that he believed the Seattle inspectors were not competent to handle the investigation and that the Pacific Coast Steamship Company exerted too much influence over the inquiry. The following day Roosevelt ordered the Secretary of Commerce and Labor to create a "Federal Commission of Investigation" to hold independent hearings in Seattle, and to make a complete investigation of all the circumstances surrounding the wreck of the *Valencia*.[54]

The commissioners named by Roosevelt included two men who had served on the panel investigating the *General Slocum* incident, the excursion boat fire in New York Harbor in June of 1904 that had cost over one thousand lives. These men were Lawrence O. Murray, Assistant Secretary of Commerce and Labor, who chaired the new commission, and Herbert Knox Smith, Deputy Commissioner of Corporations.[55] Also serving as a member of the *Valencia* commission was Captain William T. Burwell, USN, Commandant of the Puget Sound Naval Shipyard. The commission met from 14 February to 1 March 1906. On 14 April 1906 it issued a fifty-three page report which included six pages of recommendations and ten pages of conclusions.

Perhaps the most fundamental findings of the Commission were these covered in conclusion number one, relative to the navigation of the vessel:

> 1. The *Valencia* went ashore through the faulty navigation of Captain Johnson, her Master. He appears to have been a man of good character, sober, and with a good reputation as a seaman, but his management of the vessel on this trip was unsatisfactory on several points. . . .

a) He acted upon the singular belief that his log was "overrunning 6 percent," a belief that would have been justified only on the ground that both the current and the wind were against him, whereas the wind was certainly nearly aft, and it is common knowledge among all masters along this coast that at this time of year the normal current flows toward the northward and accordingly with the course of the vessel, both of which facts would make the vessel go faster over the ground than through water, and the log would therefore fail to register the entire progress of the vessel over the ground, and thus the log would underrun, if anything, rather than overrun.

b) Although he saw no land or lights with certainty after passing Cape Mendocino at 5:30 A.M. Sunday, he did not commence to take soundings until 6 P.M. Monday, thirty-six hours later, when his last definitive point of departure was at least 450 miles behind him.

c) Even after he began to take soundings, he did not take them with sufficient frequency. He did not interpret correctly the soundings taken, and, so far as can be ascertained, he spent very little time in comparing the soundings with his chart and did not carefully study them, as he should.[56]

The criticism of the captain's belief that the taffrail log was reading high suggests that this device must have been operational during the final hours of the voyage. The report suggests also that the sounding machine was in working order. Section d) of conclusion one points out that a continuous line of soundings would have indicated his position "with reasonable certainty," and such certainty was needed in entering the twelve-mile wide entrance to the Strait of Juan de Fuca after such a long period of dead reckoning.

Other findings in the report went on to criticize the *Valencia's* practice of six-hour (rather than the standard two-hour) watches for lookouts; the lack of boat drills; and "imprudent" placing of lifeboats at the rail, rendering them prematurely available to terrified passengers. The commission also criticized rescue efforts, including the *Queen's* quick departure from the scene, and the failure of any of the rescue vessels to lower boats.

With respect to the role of the *Queen*, the report noted that Captain Cousins should have been ordered to stop at Neah Bay after leaving

Victoria en route to the accident, and there to engage the services of any or all tugs that might be available. This little harbor just inside Cape Flattery was a sheltered bay where tugs often waited for employment by large sailing vessels that needed a tow for the balance of their passage through the Strait and Puget Sound. Unfortunately, the primitive telegraph wire to Neah Bay, rigged on trees, was inoperative at that moment, so no word of the wreck on Vancouver Island had reached the tugs. The bay itself had shoals of only fourteen feet at the entrance, so large ships could not enter.[57]

The report also criticized the decision to order the *Queen* back to her regular run so quickly. At the time she turned over her watchdog responsibilities to the *City of Topeka* the latter ship had not seen the wreck and subsequently never did; the *Queen* was in the best position to know where the wreckage lay. The Commission observed:

> Had the *Queen* and the *Topeka* both remained on the spot, and had the wreck been again located, a number of boats might have been held just outside the line of breakers, and some of the survivors drifting seaward would have been picked up. Furthermore, had this close approach been made to the line of breakers with the boats the men in them might have seen reason to change their opinion that a boat could not be gotten through the breakers, and a rescue might have thus been attempted directly to the wreck.[58]

The Commission chose not to comment on the role of the *Czar* and the *Salvor* since, as Canadian vessels, it would be inappropriate to make any judgment about their performance.

The Commission noted the particularly hazardous conditions along the shoreline and the wilderness conditions ashore on both sides of the approaches to the Strait of Juan de Fuca, and commented on the frequency of shipwrecks in the area. The final conclusion was that the aids to navigation, rescue facilities, and communication capabilities within this area all left much to be desired, observing that "the dangers of this entrance are out of all proportion to the present light-house and fog-signal equipment."

Recommendations in the report included specific suggestions for adding to or improving existing navigational aids. Fortunately, many of the recommendations were subsequently carried out, including the installation of the Swiftsure Lightship and the re-establishment of the life-saving station at Neah Bay with a large rescue vessel. For their part, the Canadians soon established a lighthouse at Pachena Point. The development of wireless stations and shipboard radio would come in time.

A final recommendation was signed by only one member of the commission, Navy Captain Burwell, who was not an employee of the Department of Commerce as were his fellow commissioners. In it he recommended that:

> . . . a system be established of frequent transfers of local inspectors from one port to another; and that additional life-saving stations be provided on this coast supplemental to the proposed life-saving vessel for Neah Bay, and that some provision be made for sufficient manning of vessels by seamen.[59]

The first part of this recommendation was a clear slap at the local inspectors for being too tightly entrenched in their bureaucratic positions, and the final section of the recommendation was an acknowledgment that too many ill-trained men were at sea.

The three commissioners joined in this conclusion:

> If such a terrible disaster must occur, it must be regarded primarily in the nature of a lesson for the future—a lesson not to be disregarded—and if the Government, acting upon this lesson, shall make all reasonable provisions within its power for the safeguarding of this coast, the victims of the Valencia will not have perished in vain.[60]

Some good eventually came from the Valencia disaster, but most of the improvements applied only to the geographical area surrounding the approaches to Juan de Fuca. Within a few years, radio came into general use, but as we shall see shortly, ships continued to go aground and founder even with this new means of staying in touch with the outside world. Thus, it remained to be seen what other benefits derived from the destruction of the Valencia.

Chapter Four

Rosecrans: Born to Lose

The tanker *Rosecrans* was one of those ships whose final moments can be best understood in the context of her entire lifespan. While she had managed to survive into her thirtieth year, she had bounced around from owner to owner and crisis to crisis for a number of years, and seemed destined for a violent death. As the San Francisco *Chronicle* described her, in a somewhat mixed metaphor, she was "king of all the 'hoodoos'."[1]

Although her greatest notoriety occurred while serving as a tanker, she had not come into the world as that type of ship. She was built in Glasgow, Scotland, in 1883 as the passenger/cargo ship *Methven Castle* for the Castle Mail Service. Her name was an illustrious one in history, recalling the site in Scotland where the English defeated Robert Bruce in 1306.[2]

As soon as the ship went into service the strange occurrences which were to characterize her career began to occur. An Irish nationalist, who had turned Crown's evidence against fellow conspirators in the assassination of Lord Charles Cavendish in 1882, fled to South Africa by taking passage aboard the *Methven Castle*. Upon arrival at Capetown he was met by a squad of hit men who shot him as he came down the gangplank, committing the first of two murders that took place aboard the ship.[3]

In time, after the British steamship company became somewhat dissatisfied with the ship's performance, she was sold. Her new owners,

Barclay Curle & Company, kept her under the British flag, but renamed her *Columbia*.[4] In about 1899 she was sold again, this time American, with her latest owners, the Northern Pacific Company, homeporting her in Tacoma.[5] These newest owners soon saw the opportunity to turn a quick profit on their ship when the United States became embroiled in the Spanish-American War and desperately needed hulls. The ship was sold in 1899 to the United States Army as a transport, this time being given the name *Rosecrans*, after a prominent nineteenth-century Army general, who later served as a congressman from California, where his name is commemorated in a well-known boulevard in Los Angeles.

The tenure of the U.S. Army Transport *Rosecrans* was relatively brief in this new career under her fourth set of owners, and she was taken out of service and put up for sale in 1902. A momentary glut of ships coming out of Army service depressed the market at that time, so the Army held onto her until prices for ships firmed up. During fiscal year 1903 she was sold for fifty thousand dollars to the Matson Line where she became one of the first steamers that company put into service.[6]

The *Rosecrans* was a handsome ship, reflecting history and tradition in her name and heritage, but rather prone to trouble. Here she appears in her days as an Army transport. (Courtesy of the San Francisco Maritime National Historical Park)

Matson made no change in her name and retained her for three years. During this time the steamship company used her in Hawaiian and Alaskan service where she apparently did reasonably well. When William Matson became interested in the oil business he converted the ship to a tanker at a time when built-for-the-purpose tankships were still rare.[7]

As a tanker she presented an unfamiliar profile, one still reminiscent of her days as a passenger ship and transport. She was not an ugly duckling in any sense; she simply did not look like a tanker. By the standards of the day, she was a fairly large ship when built, measuring out at 2,979 gross tons on a hull that was 326 feet long, 38 feet in beam, and 21 feet in depth. Later in her career, after new generations of tankers had been built, she would be considered only medium-sized.

Matson continued to use the ship alternately in Alaskan and Hawaiian service. In 1906 she was sold to her sixth owner, Associated Oil, one of the pioneer West Coast oil companies in the operation of tankers. In a series of mergers and acquisitions, Associated would later merge with Tidewater. In turn, Tidewater was absorbed by Getty Oil, which consolidated with Skelly before the merger trail became difficult to follow in the 1980s. While under the "Flying A" house-flag of Associated the ship was the scene of another murder, this one in Honolulu in 1909 when a drunken crewman stabbed the third assistant engineer.[8] Within a few more years a period of bad luck began for the ship along the California coast.

When these misfortunes began the *Rosecrans* was still running to Hawaii from southern California. In March of 1912 the ship was lying at the offshore marine terminal at a place called Alcatraz in Santa Barbara county. Here a refinery was located about a mile down the coast from Gaviota where today U.S. highway 101, the coast highway, swings inland through a prominent gap in the large rock formations of the Coast Range.

Commanding the vessel was Lucien F. Johnson, in his late twenties one of the youngest captains on the entire Pacific Coast. In fact, he was younger than the ship he commanded. Johnson had been in the Navy fourteen years earlier during the Spanish-American war, serving in the *Olympia* which was Admiral Dewey's flagship at the battle of Manila

Bay.[9] He could not have been more than fifteen at that time. He had been with Associated for seven years.

As the *Rosecrans* waited to load thirty thousand barrels of oil for Honolulu, a major weather system blew in over the southern California coast, and soon huge waves came crashing through the anchorage. Eventually, the ship was driven aground, and a large hole was punched in her port side. In the attempt to launch lifeboats two men were lost and no one in the crew was able to reach shore. Eventually, a Lyle gun was brought to the narrow beach, and a projectile from this cannon reached the ship with a line on which a breeches buoy could be rigged. As spray from the high surf continued to fill the air, the crew was brought to the safety of the shore in this way.[10]

Even though the ship was declared to be a total loss as a result of this accident, the captain was soon back aboard, working out the various elements of a salvage plan that would be needed to move the *Rosecrans*. In a remarkably short time through a well-executed effort the ship was hauled off the beach by the Whitelaw Salvage Company. She was then towed to a San Francisco shipyard for repairs. Within six months she was able to return to the service of Associated Oil.

In September of the same year, at the Gaviota loading terminal a mile up the coast from where the ship had grounded during the storm in March, one of the cargo tanks of the *Rosecrans* exploded. Cut loose from the pier to prevent the resultant fire from spreading, the ship burned furiously in a manner that would have meant the end for most ships. Miraculously, this time there was no loss of life, and the ship was again spared from complete disaster. Inasmuch as tankers were not yet plentiful, the oil company again elected to rebuild the *Rosecrans*, even though the total price tag for this overhaul was almost as much as her original construction cost had been. Before the year was over, she again returned to service.

∽

However, the jinns or evil spirits of the coast would not be denied a third time. During her next brush with danger the indestructibility of the *Rosecrans* proved to be a myth. In January 1913 she was en route to

The most famous photograph of the *Rosecrans* during her tanker days is this one showing her being buffeted by a storm at a southern California anchorage less than a year before her demise on the Columbia River bar. (Courtesy of the San Francisco Maritime National Historical Park)

Portland with eighteen thousand barrels of oil. Inasmuch as she had sailed from Monterey, in those days the terminus of a pipeline from the Elk Hills field in Kern County, the cargo loaded there was probably crude oil.

Captain Johnson, the veteran of her two recent brushes with disaster in southern California, was again in command. It is not clear whether he had sailed in other ships in the meantime, or whether he had stayed ashore during the repairs to the ship. As the ship approached the Columbia bar in the early morning hours of 7 January 1913, conditions were far from favorable. It was still quite dark, and the wind was blowing hard, driving showers of sleet across the heavy swells. As a result, the bar was treacherous. However, it was a navigational error, not the roughness of the bar, that first put the ship into danger.[11]

The *Rosecrans* had a radio, but radio direction finders had not yet been developed. As a result, making a landfall required that the captain or navigator use only the visual clues available to him, clues that lost their usefulness quickly in times of reduced visibility. Bearings on visible objects and soundings with the leadline were the primary means of determining the ship's position during periods of intermittent visibility.

Coastal tankers, perhaps as much so as passenger ships, were concerned about tight schedules and quick turnarounds in loading and discharging. They were also inherently sturdy and well-powered vessels that when fully loaded rode well in heavy seas. In their relatively short period of existence they had acquired a good safety record. Unlike cargo and passenger ships, where personnel changed with every trip, the crews of tankers were generally stable, and stayed aboard for fairly long periods. As a result of all these factors, Captain Johnson, like his fellow tanker skippers, felt no reluctance to cross the Columbia bar on the proverbial dark and stormy night. It is not clear whether he had pilotage for the Columbia River bar. However, it is known that during the preceding year the *Rosecrans* had not been a regular visitor to the Pacific Northwest, although she had successfully completed a round trip to Portland during the first week of 1913.

Stories persist that someone on the bridge of the tanker apparently mistook the North Head Light on the Washington shore for the Columbia River Lightship. The story was told by one of the survivors of the accident, Fred Peters, who as a quartermaster was a member of the bridge crew:

> I was on the bridge with the second officer, C. R. Palmer, when the accident occurred, and Quartermaster F. Armstrong was at the wheel. We came on watch at 4 o'clock that morning. The wind was blowing a gale and with the rain and mist it was hard to see any distance at all.
>
> When we came on duty there was a light on our bow, which must have been North Head light, but we were told by the retiring watch it was the lightship. We headed in, intending to cruise about the lightship until after daylight, but about 5 o'clock we struck hard and took a big sea clear over us. We immediately summoned Captain Johnson who hastened onto the bridge.[12]

This story bears examination, inasmuch as mistaking the one light for the other seems unlikely under the prevailing circumstances. If the ship had been traveling a normal track-line up the coast she would have been well offshore, and probably would have approached the lightship from the southwest, treating her approach as a landfall. With reduced visibility she would have used soundings to determine her location until the time when she could have seen or heard the lightship.

Using the fog signal from the lightship as an aid, she would have passed that vessel close aboard. At this point the ship would be getting lined up to enter the buoyed and dredged channel across the bar which began three miles farther northeast. That would appear to be the normal approach to the bar and the channel.

But if, instead, the ship had homed in on the North Head Light, at least ten miles away on the Washington coast, thinking it to be the lightship, it would have encountered an entirely different line of soundings and seen an entirely different light from that on the lightship.

The three major lights in the area had very different characteristics. The Columbia River Lightship had an occulting white light every ten seconds, which meant that the light was on for ten seconds and then was off briefly before going back on for another ten seconds. The Cape Disappointment Light was an alternate flashing white and red light every thirty seconds, after which it was dark for another thirty seconds. The North Head Light was a group flashing white light, with two flashes every thirty seconds, after which it was dark for another thirty seconds.[13] Not only would those aboard the ship be able to make the distinction between these lights, but the inability to close on the light and bring it close aboard would alert them to the fact that they were using the wrong light.

It is not at all clear what course the *Rosecrans* was on when she grounded or exactly where she came aground. Peters was on the bridge but his accounts do not specify what he was engaged in doing; consequently it is impossible to know the exact sequence of events as the ship attempted to cross the bar. However, most accounts have suggested that she hit the outer edges of Peacock Spit on the Washington side of the entrance to the Columbia. An observer on Cape Disappointment who had seen her wallowing in the swells reported that she had dropped both anchors when she hit the bottom at that location, and that this action prevented her from working any closer to the beach, thus negating any possibility that a high line with a breeches buoy could reach her.[14]

Peacock Spit was largely responsible for the Columbia River entrance being dubbed the "Graveyard of the Pacific." The spit on the north side of the entrance was named for the USS *Peacock*, a brigantine rigged as an eighteen-gun sloop of war which was engaged in hydrographic survey work. Misled by inaccurate charts, this ship hit the sand bar on a clear and pleasant day in July of 1841, and went hard aground. Later when the seas rose she was hammered into a jumble of timbers and planking. Fortunately, no lives were lost, but the vessel left her name permanently on the shoal.[15]

The *Peacock* had been part of the surveying expedition of the famous naval explorer Charles Wilkes which at that time was charting the mouth of the Columbia. At the time of the survey Wilkes observed that:

> Mere description can give little idea of the terrors of the bar of the Columbia; all who have seen it have spoken of the wildness of the scene, and the incessant roar of the waters, representing it as one of the most fearful sights that can possibly meet the eye of the sailor.[16]

Those aboard the *Rosecrans* on that fatal night in January of 1913 would have agreed.

Unfortunately, no photographs seem to exist of the wreck of the tanker which would resolve the question of the ship's location with respect to the spit. In illustrating the loss of the *Rosecrans* on the Columbia bar, the standard books on West Coast shipwrecks have used only a widely-circulated photograph of the ship's first accident in her trilogy of tribulation, the grounding of the ship in southern California, showing enormous seas breaking over her.

After hitting the rocks on the spit and tearing great holes in her bottom, the ship soon slid off into the water to the north of the spit where the depth was thirty-five to forty feet. There she settled, only a few hundred yards from North Head, with her masts and stack out of the water and little else showing above the breaking seas. The first word of her fate went out with a radio message. Like other tankers of Associated Oil, the *Rosecrans* had an early radio set, with a transmitter capable of 2,500 watts of power on a frequency of 710 kilocycles.[17]

Apparently her operator, L. Prudhout, sent two wireless messages from the ship. The first as she lay aground on the spit was a report of her situation, a call that set in motion the first action from the shore. It said, "Steamer *Rosecrans* on bar, send assistance, ship breaking up fast; can stay at my station no longer." The second, sometime later, was a sad farewell. It said, "We are rapidly breaking up on the bar. . . . Goodbye." That message was interrupted, indicating the inability of the operator or the equipment to continue.

The initial response from ashore was decisive but ineffective. No less than four bar tugboats, the *Oneonta, Goliath, Tatoosh,* and *Fearless,* were dispatched to the scene. However, none of these vessels was able to get close enough to the *Rosecrans* while she was still aground on the rocks, and once the tanker slid off and settled on the bottom there was no possibility of towing her to safety.

A quartermaster, identified as Joseph Slenning, had been asleep when the ship grounded on the spit. He dressed and went out onto the spray-swept deck but, along with several others, returned below where he felt it was safer. About eight o'clock the ship broke in two, forcing those who had remained below to go out on deck. As Slenning recalled later:

> After reaching the deck I made for the mizzenmast, but how I reached it I don't know. I was thrown down and the seas washed over me, but I did not go overboard. At last I got into the rigging. I had been there but a short time when [ship's carpenter Eric] Lindmark and "Dago Joe," the oiler, climbed up.
>
> I could see the crew clinging to the house, the davits, and other objects on the deck. The gale was fierce and we could not speak to each other for the roar of the seas. I did not see Captain Johnson after I came on deck. For a long time First Officer [Thomas] Mullins was hanging on one of the davits, but after one of the waves broke over the vessel he disappeared.
>
> I guess it was about nine o'clock when the pilothouse was swept off and with it went the rest of the crew except me and the other two in the rigging. The wireless operator was one of the last to go over.[18]

By this time the first of the rescue vessels had reached the vicinity of the *Rosecrans,* but had been unable to approach close enough to render assistance. Slenning continued his explanation:

> It was a long weary wait in the rigging, clinging for dear life to the masts. We were not lashed to the mast and were wet and chilled to the bone. It was the most awful experience I ever had. An hour or two after we were in the rigging we caught sight of a tug on the inside, and I knew that they were trying to save us.

> When I saw the lifeboats getting near I felt that we were
> going to be saved. As the boat came near the men yelled for us
> to jump, but I was afraid we would never reach them in the
> raging sea. Lindmark was the first to try it. We climbed down
> and stood on the rail and the next wave carried him away from
> the ship. I followed shortly after. When I struck the water it
> was like jumping into a warm current, so thick was the oil
> upon it. "Dago Joe" jumped soon after, but was injured in
> jumping to the deck. He was dead when they picked him up.[19]

By mid-morning there were a number of rescue vessels in the water, and a crowd had gathered atop Cape Disappointment to watch the rescue drama unfolding below. The Fort Stevens crew from Point Adams had started for the wreck in their powered self-righting lifeboat shortly after eight o'clock when they first saw the wreck. The crew from Fort Canby at Cape Disappointment did not start out until eleven o'clock. They were in a power boat, but eventually had to shift to oars. En route to the wreck site, the Fort Canby boat lost three men overboard, but they were all pulled back aboard safely. The Fort Stevens boat also lost and recovered several men before succeeding in reaching the ship, and became the rescuer of the two men in the rigging. The crew in this boat also recovered the body of the oiler known as "Dago Joe," which had plunged from the rigging into the sea.

This lifeboat stalled and was drifting helplessly before the tug *Fearless* took her in tow. However, the towline parted, and the lifeboat was again on her own. Eventually, the crew was able to restart the engine. Rather than trying to return across the bar, the boat, with the two survivors and the dead man aboard, headed for the relative safety of the Columbia River Lightship anchored on station farther offshore.

This lightship, like all others, had a fixed geographical identity, into which various vessels rotated. Since 1908 the hull used in this location as the Columbia River Lightship had been Number 88 of the Lighthouse Service. Built at Camden, New Jersey, she was a rugged steam-powered vessel. After coming around Cape Horn in 1908, she replaced an earlier vessel, Number 50, which had possessed no means of propulsion other than sails.[20]

An idea of the size of lightships can be gleaned from the dimensions of Number 88, which was 135 feet long and 29 feet in beam. It is difficult to imagine life aboard such vessels, and the periodic challenge of bringing supplies aboard and rotating the dozen or so crew members ashore in heavy weather. It is even more difficult to imagine the disruption and overcrowding that having survivors on board must have caused. The Blunts Reef Lightship off the northern California coast once took aboard 155 survivors of the steamer *Bear* which had run aground nearby.[21] After the *Rosecrans* disaster Number 88 at the Columbia River had only about nine extra people aboard, two survivors of the ship and the seven-man boat crew, but the Lighthouse Service crewmen probably wished that the number could have been far more.

Unknown to either the rescuers or the rescued aboard Number 88, there had been a third survivor in the person of Fred Peters, the quartermaster. He had been washed overboard when the waves first began to break heavily on the deck of the ship. He had grabbed a plank which he found in the water, and somehow managed to propel it toward the beach. Peters explained:

> The plank wasn't very big, only about four feet long, a foot wide and two inches thick, but, let me tell you, it did me a lot of good. It must have been 3 o'clock when I hit the breakers. The sea was so rough here that I lost my board and started to make it the best way I could. About this time the tide kept washing the life preserver over my head and I had to cut it loose. About the next thing I remembered was striking bottom, and I got down on my hands and knees and crawled out into some driftwood, and just about this time a young fellow with a gun came along and helped me the rest of the way out.[22]

Thus, in a dazed condition on the North Beach peninsula near Tioga, Washington, seventeen miles from the spit at Point Peacock, Fred Peters was found. His survival was the most incredible story to emerge from the disaster.

The two other survivors, now in the lifeboat alongside the lightship, were still not out of danger. With great effort they were hauled aboard the lightship, along with the boat crew. An attempt was made to bring the lifeboat aboard as well, but it broke away and drifted out of reach with the body of the oiler still lashed to the floorboards inside it. That boat and the body of "Dago Joe" would never be seen again.

Two days would pass before the seas calmed enough to permit the *Oneonta* to reach the lightship and to bring the two seamen from the *Rosecrans*, Slenning and Lindmark, to the safety of the shore, along with the boat crew from Fort Stevens. It was a sobering moment for both the tanker survivors and the men of the boat crew.

⌇

The aftermath of the wreck was stunning. The ship was gone, her wreckage added to the debris which had been strewn on the north side of Peacock Spit from the wrecks of other ships. Gone, too, were eighteen thousand barrels of oil; although flattening the seas somewhat, this oil was now fouling the beaches below Cape Disappointment and North Head on the Washington coast. More important, thirty of the thirty-three men of the crew of the *Rosecrans* were gone forever. The bodies of the captain and three seamen were found within a few hours at Klipsan Beach, halfway to the entrance to Willapa Bay. Captain Johnson had suffered a broken leg from being battered by the breakers hitting the deck of the ship before it broke up.

Newspaper coverage of the wreck of the *Rosecrans* did not seem as personal as the coverage given to other shipwrecks. Other than an attempt to identify "Dago Joe"—as Joe Cagna, since it was the only name on the crew list that appeared to be Italian—and a report of the captain's military funeral as a Navy veteran, there was little written about the crew. This may have been because she was a tanker, an alien form of ship to the general public and the maritime community in the Northwest, who were more familiar with passenger ships and freighters carrying lumber and grain. Tankers came from faraway southern California, with crews that had generally been recruited there, giving such ships the status almost of foreign vessels. Their turnaround time in port was brief, so their seaman spent little time and money ashore. In any case, it has been difficult to get to know the crew of the *Rosecrans* from the few accounts that have been written about the ship and her men.

Similarly, the personality of the ship does not emerge from the stories about the wreck. For example, reporters failed to pick up on the irony that the *Rosecrans*, now a victim of the Columbia bar, had once borne the name *Columbia* as a Pacific Northwest ship before the Army named her for the general.

Responsibility for what happened to the ship has been difficult to assess. Like the records of most other ships in this study, the transcripts of the follow-up investigation and hearings are not at the National Archives where they should be, so it is impossible to know what the official findings were in the case of the *Rosecrans*. Obviously, there was an error in navigation that put the ship farther to the left of the entrance channel than she should have been, but whether that error resulted from steering toward the North Head Light instead of the lightship is not at all apparent.

It does seem odd, however, that the captain was apparently not called by the second mate until the ship was off course and at risk. Captain Johnson may have left night orders to be called at a particular time or distance off which had not yet been achieved; such instructions may have reflected his confidence in his ship. That confidence could have been a product of the ship's past record in surviving crises, as well as an awareness that a loaded tanker with the seas astern generally rides well in rough water. However, the bridge watch was in some confusion and could easily have justified calling the captain earlier, an action not only permitted but encouraged in the night orders written by most captains.

Soundings would have been useful to the watch at this point. However, soundings were difficult to take during the course of an ordinary watch, in that two men were generally required to carry out the operation of dropping and retrieving the lead with the sounding machine. Typically, merchant ships had only two men on the bridge, the mate and the helmsman or quartermaster. At night another seaman may have been on the wing of the bridge as the lookout, but this man was often posted on the bow or in the ship's crows-nest. If the ship carried nine seaman, an additional seaman may have been available as the "stand-by" in the mess hall below, ready to take his turn at the helm or as lookout for a rotation of an hour and twenty minutes, but even if this man were called out there would still be too few men to take soundings with safety.

With a minimum of an officer and one man required on the bridge (assuming that the lookout is sent to the sounding machine for the time being, a dangerous practice in itself) and two men on the stern to drop the lead, it was still difficult for the watchstanders to take soundings unless the captain was on the bridge freeing up the mate to supervise the soundings. However, Captain Johnson was not on the bridge of the tanker during the time that soundings might have been useful in determining the ship's location. Furthermore, crew lists show that the ship carried only six seamen, so the deck watch would have had only a mate and two men to carry out all the required duties on the bridge and elsewhere.

Apparently some sort of inquiry was held after the accident. Captain J. H. Quinan, an inspector for the Lifesaving Service, came to Portland from San Francisco to investigate the circumstances in which the Cape Disappointment and Point Adams boat crews were involved, and to ascertain the fate of the missing powered boat. At the same time, there were indications that the inspectors for the Steamboat Inspection Service, Edwards and Fuller, would also be in Portland to conduct their investigation.[23] Unfortunately, despite newspaper allusions to such an inquiry, later issues of the papers contained no reports of it.

It seems fair to conclude that the sinking of the *Rosecrans* was a tragic and entirely preventable incident resulting from poor navigation and seamanship by the watch on the bridge. On the positive side, praise for the conduct of the tireless men of the Lifesaving Service was soon forthcoming. Captain Oscar S. Wicklund who commanded the boat from Point Adams received a letter from Franklin MacVeagh, Secretary of the Treasury, commending the work of his seven-man crew in bringing off the two survivors from the doomed tanker.[24]

It was gratifying for mariners of the Pacific Northwest to be reassured that the incisive motto of the Lifesaving Service, "You have to go out, but you don't have to come back in," still meant that there would always be rescuers seeking to reach stranded seafarers. However, the dark angel that watched over Peacock Spit, the "Graveyard of the Pacific," had misconstrued the slogan, and thirty men of the *Rosecrans* became the ones who did not come back in.

Chapter Five

The *Mimi*: Salvage Can Be Dangerous

The four-masted barque *Mimi* was one of those unlucky ships that survived an initial shipwreck crisis, only to be destroyed at the hands of well-meaning but incompetent salvors.

The *Mimi* was unlike any other ship in this book in a number of ways. First and foremost, she was a sailing ship, albeit both large and steel-hulled. Second, she was under German registry and had a German crew. Third, she may have gone aground largely due to the indifference of another ship, most likely an American, that did not provide the simple information the *Mimi*'s captain needed in order to know where the ship was. Fourth, she was in no great danger during two months aground. Fifth, her salvors created the dangers that ultimately destroyed the ship, along with eighteen innocent human lives.

Built by Russell & Company at Port Glasgow, Scotland, in 1893, the *Mimi* had originally been the British *Glenclova* for W. O. Taylor & Co. of Dundee, but had been acquired in 1909 by Hans H. Schmidt of Hamburg who renamed her *Mimi*. Schmidt obviously liked the name; he had owned an iron barque named *Mimi, ex-Staffordshire,* in 1900-01, and after the demise of the *Mimi, ex-Glenclova,* he would own another *Mimi, ex-Port Logan,* a steel full-rigged ship, from 1913 until 1920.[1]

The *Mimi* of this story was one of a number of steel-hulled sailing vessels that still prowled the oceans early in the twentieth century in search of bulk cargoes of grain, coal, and lumber. Her ample dimensions of 283 feet in length, 43 feet in beam, and 25 feet in depth gave her a capacity of 1,984 gross tons, and her barque rig provided good capabilities for such a tramp service.

Little is known about her early service. She had last visited the Oregon coast two years earlier when she had called at Portland for a grain cargo. Now in 1913 she was headed again for the Columbia, this time in ballast to load a lumber cargo at Astoria for Antofagasta, Chile, under a charter to Comyn, Mackall & Company of San Francisco. Some sources say that she had taken the place of the British barque *Torrisdale* which had been wrecked on the Grays Harbor jetty in late December of 1912, but the *Mimi* was at sea, without a radio, at that time and could not have been ordered in to fill the new charter.[2]

⌒

On the evening of 13 February 1913—which was a Thursday, but might as well have been Friday the 13th for the bad luck it produced—the *Mimi* was fifty-four days out of Callao, Peru, groping her way up the Oregon coast in a dense fog. Her captain, Ludwig Westphal, at thirty-three a veteran of eighteen years at sea including eight as a master, had gone three days without a decent observation to determine accurately the position of his ship. All of the problems of navigating by dead reckoning in a fog are compounded for a sailing vessel, which cannot control her speed or her course nearly as well as a steamer.

Earlier that day an opportunity had finally opened up for the *Mimi* to learn where she was, when a large steamer came along during a brief lifting of the fog. Using international flag hoists, which are multi-lingual in that the code book is printed in many languages, Captain Westphal asked the steamer for a latitude and longitude. Although this other ship was in sight for an hour, no reply whatsoever came from her. So the *Mimi*'s last chance to determine her position passed by, going north up the coast.[3]

It is difficult to assess the importance of this encounter to the fate of the *Mimi*. Realistically, the chances of assistance as a result of the flag hoist message were not great. While license examinations for mates and masters do contain questions on signaling, this aspect of bridge seamanship was not highly developed on the typical American ship of that era. Single-flag hoists used regularly, such as those in connection with the need for a pilot or in clearing quarantine, were familiar to these officers, but more complicated two and three letter hoists were not. Furthermore, some of the longer hoists were not always clear in meaning; for example, the hoist L–F–V is identified as meaning "what is my present position?" but asking this question, out of context, to an unknown ship might not result in a helpful response. Adding additional information for context could easily make the hoist too complex to be decoded readily.

In further defense of the steamer, there may also have been problems in seeing flag hoists flying amidst the spars, masts, and sails of a barque, and the visibility during the break in the dense fog may not have been enough even to notice the signals. Apparently Captain Westphal had chosen to make his flag hoist an administrative type of message rather than an emergency signal, and no rockets were fired at that time to attract attention. Thus, either from visual limitations or from a lack of a sense of urgency, no response was forthcoming.

Westphal later described the steamer as having three masts, and what appeared to be a white letter "S" on her stack. Two companies on the West Coast had stack marks resembling what Westphal described. One was the Standard Oil Company of California which operated traditional tankers that the captain could have recognized as such. The other was the Dollar Line which carried a white dollar sign on a black funnel, easily resembling an "S" at a distance. Although Dollar did not acquire the large passenger ships for which the line was famous until after World War I, that company did operate freighters in 1913. Thus, it might have been a Dollar Line ship that did not see the message or failed to provide the needed position.

An examination of the listings in the San Francisco shipping paper, *The Guide*, for 13 February 1913, shows that both a Dollar Line and a Standard Oil ship were in that area, but southbound. In addition, a Standard Oil tanker, the *Asuncion*, was northbound, two days out of San Francisco en route to Vancouver. This ship, with a standard engines-aft profile, may be what Captain Westphal saw.

⌒

Within four hours of that disappointing incident the *Mimi* went aground. The location was Nehalem Spit, about twenty-five miles north of Tillamook. Ironically, there was no compelling reason why Captain Westphal should have remained lost to the point of going aground. Presumably the steamer that he saw was on a trackline for either the Columbia Lightship or Cape Flattery. Westphal might well have simply followed in the direction that the steamer took, trusting that he could eventually get his bearings, literally and figuratively, or find another more cooperative steamer when the visibility improved.

The Cape Blanco–Columbia River trackline would normally be at least ten miles offshore at Nehalem, so if the *Mimi* reached shore in four hours after encountering the steamer she must have made good a course with a substantial easterly component. In any case, on a high tide and with only a moderately rough sea the barque grounded gently on the beach in a fog so dense that the shore could not be seen. Rockets were fired, bringing out the Garibaldi Lifesaving Station boat crew under Captain Robert Farley, but these rescuers found that the ship was stable and safe and apart from several crewmen who came ashore experimentally by breeches buoy no personnel evacuations were effected.[4]

Two tugs appeared the next day from Astoria, the *Fearless* and *Oneonta*, but neither of these vessels had a long enough line to tow the barque off the beach. Captain Westphal was understandably frustrated, for he believed that at that time a simple tow would have been enough to free the ship from the sand.[5]

Fortunately, no harm came to any of the thirty men aboard. The saga of the strange shipwreck thus began on a benign, almost casual, note. For some reason, the Tillamook area had for some time been the scene of a number of groundings of large sailing ships, and many of these groundings were visited and photographed by hundreds of people. One explanation offered for this phenomenon was that an area strangely devoid of wind existed off Neahkahnie Mountain, just north of Nehalem Bay, and the absence of wind made sailing vessels unmaneuverable.[6] In any case, the *Mimi* proved to be another highly-photogenic beached sailing ship, and would remain on the spit for the curious to observe

MI-On Neah-kah-nie beach Feb. 13 - 1913 -

The *Mimi* spent two months ashore on the spit at Nehalem Bay on the Oregon coast, attracting a number of visitors. (Courtesy of the Tillamook County Pioneer Museum)

and photograph for the next two months, sustaining no damage in her dry and stable position but working her way further into the grasp of the sand.

Nehalem Bay, on whose seacoast side the *Mimi* went aground, is the northernmost of a series of bays along the Oregon Coast, all in Tillamook County. It was, however, of no great consequence as a port. Although a few tugs and barges served the mills located on this bay, it had little of the commerce of the larger Tillamook Bay, ten miles to the south. On the latter bay a few oceangoing ships operated, including steam schooners built at Bay City, and small steamers that linked Tillamook with the trains at Astoria until the railroad reached Tillamook in 1912. On both bays, the seafaring men were generally fishermen, rather than merchant seamen.

The crew of the *Mimi* initially remained aboard the vessel, and at low tide the ship could be reached on foot. Soon several surveyors for the insurance underwriters arrived at the scene, principally Captain E. C. Generaux of Seattle, representing the German underwriters, and Captain Albert Crowe of Portland, representing the San Francisco Board of Marine

Underwriters. The latter individual had recently represented the same group in the aftermath of the *Rosecrans* disaster. After examining the site Captain Generaux reported:

> The bark is making no water. She is in good position and one anchor with 75 fathoms of chain is out. She is heading pretty well off shore and lies about 500 feet from low-water mark. There is from six to seven feet of water around her at high tide and she has a slight list to starboard. The vessel is absolutely tight and shows no sign of straining. They are filling the forepeak tank with water, so as to "keep her down by the head"and that will tend gradually to work her stern around. She is now heading about south–southwest magnetic.[7]

That amount of water alongside the ship at high tide corresponded roughly to the height of the tides at Nehalem as reported in tide tables. Thus, the ship at low tide was clearly "high and dry." Photographs taken at the time confirm that status.

The grounding was considered routine, and was not even reported in some of the West Coast newspapers which normally carried significant amounts of maritime news. The owner of the *Mimi* initially had considered selling the empty ship in a "where she lies" condition if a good price could be obtained, but was otherwise inclined to abandon her to the underwriters and to collect the sixty thousand dollars insurance on the hull. However, upon positive recommendations by the surveyors he agreed that if she could not be sold for a satisfactory price the underwriters could have her removed from the beach by salvors.[8]

It should be noted that there was considerable difference in the way various sources reported the financial transaction that led to the salvage of the vessel, particularly with respect to the actual ownership of the vessel at various times after the grounding. Additional perspectives on that subject were provided in a recent book on the *Mimi*'s demise, in the form of an historical novel, pseudo-authentic in its approach. This book was the work of Jack L. Graves of Garibaldi, Oregon, a town at the north end of Tillamook Bay, after hearing parts of the story from his parents, who knew some of the participants. Although he can privately identify what is literary invention and what is reality in his book, for the public the book serves the unintended purpose of illustrating how difficult it is to separate fact from fiction throughout the story of the *Mimi*.[9]

According to the San Francisco *Chronicle*, a request for bids was disseminated, calling for the salvaged vessel to be delivered safely over the Columbia River bar. The contract was on a "no cure, no pay"basis, which was commonly used in ship salvage. Six bids were subsequently submitted, ranging from $14,000 to $48,000. The mid-range bid of $24,850 was accepted, that of Watt and Holyfield of Brighton Beach, Oregon, a community on Nehalem Bay.[10]

The salvage plan, however, was created by Fisher Engineering and Construction Company of Portland. This firm had been the high bidder on the salvage job, but it had apparently acquired the rights to the vessel from the underwriters who had paid off on the insurance, thus putting the principals of the firm in the position of owners of the ship. The Fisher firm planned to use beach gear laid out through the surf, with wood-fired steam-driven donkey engines supplying the power to inch the ship off the beach at high tide. It was a standard salvage technique, generally effective in removing ships from sandy beaches.

As a means of lightening the *Mimi*, some of the yardarms were removed, but this was only a token amount of weight. In looking around for other weights that could be removed, the salvors found the ship's 1,300 tons of permanent ballast, and this discovery led to fatal flaws in their reasoning.

Ships are sometimes built with permanent ballast in place to insure that they do not bob too high in the water when empty, and, in the case of steamers, to insure that their screw is still largely in the water when empty. Permanent ballast is also part of the stability designed into the ship by the builders, and it is intended to be, as it name indicates, permanent. It is sometimes in the form of poured concrete, or it could be something more portable such as heavy stones or pig iron, which was apparently the case in the *Mimi*.

Charles S. Fisher, the principal salvor, was sometimes called "Captain," but he was apparently an engineer, rather than a seafaring man. He and Captain Crowe decided that it was necessary to remove some of this permanent ballast in order to lighten the ship properly. Against the advice of Captain Robert Farley of the nearby Garibaldi Life Saving Station, Fisher directed that the ballast be taken off the ship. The ship's crew then began removing the ballast, and apparently about a third of it was ultimately taken off.[11]

Shortly before the salvage attempt was made, a curious event disturbed the crew. One of the mates experienced an unsettling dream. This man was identified as Frederick Fischer by the two Tillamook newspapers, while the *Oregonian* called him William Fischer in one account and Frederick Flagg in another—the latter being the name which writer Jack Graves says he invented for the chief mate who is the central character in his novel. In this dream the *Mimi* became an underwater hotel for the dead, with bloated corpses entangled in seaweed bobbing in and out of the submerged hatches. When the mate related his story to others, a near-panic developed. All three mates deserted the ship by going hand over hand along a cable to the beach, followed by three men of the salvage crew. Superstitious grumbling broke out among the remaining crewmen, causing the captain to use a pistol to enforce his orders and to keep more men from defecting.[12]

Other crewmen also must have deserted, however, for when the final salvage effort was made on Sunday 6 April 1913, there were only about a dozen men left aboard, supplemented by the salvors. A number of the young Germans in the crew had developed friendships ashore, and some of these men remained away from the ship during the salvage effort.

The weather was not yet severe, but gale warnings had been issued and a storm was known to be working its way up the coast. It was apparent that the weather was not going to be conducive to the salvage project, but passing up a high tide would delay the effort for another month. Consequently, although the highest tide of the month was still two days away, the decision was made to proceed ahead of the storm, even though the required tugboats were not yet available.

The beach gear was operated by J. E. Holyfield from the nearby community of Brighton, who had recruited men from logging companies and mills to assist on the salvage job. The beach gear layout included two four-ton anchors placed beyond the surf line, connected to the two donkey engines on the deck of the *Mimi*, These engines powered winches whose drums pulled on the heavy block and tackle rigs that were connected to the anchors.

It was to be a difficult salvage effort, in that the ship would be pulled off broadside, rather than by the bow or stern. When the tide was full a strain was taken on the beach gear, and soon the ship began to move, literally inch by inch. Apparently the first part of the operation was conducted on Saturday afternoon, 5 April, and the concluding portion shortly after midnight on Sunday when the tide was at its highest. The wind and seas increased in intensity as the ship moved slowly across the sand. As the *Mimi* reached deeper water she became lively, and then unmanageable. As Holyfield observed from his position on the winch, "I felt sure I had a nice fortune in my hand . . . when we heard the cracking of timbers and the boat keeled over. She remained this way several minutes before the steel mast buckled and she turned entirely over."[13]

While later recuperating from the ordeal, Captain Westphal explained what happened. In what was purportedly a newspaper interview, but does not sound like the words of a German sea captain, he said:

> Shortly after three A.M. Sunday morning as I was walking forward to tell the donkey engine man not to pull the *Mimi*, but to anchor her where she was, a sudden lurch took the vessel and I was pinned to the forward deckhouse by a fallen top spar. This lurch immediately preceded the capsizing of the *Mimi*. I distinctly remember hearing Captain Crowe (of the wrecking crew) speaking, but when we reached there, no one was to be seen nor were there any signs of life on the forward part of the ship at all. The donkey engine, mounted there, had slid into the sea. After a two hour endeavor to prevent sailors from leaping overboard and telling them that their best course was to stay by the ship, my efforts proved all for naught by their plunging overboard. Had it not been for the seven-foot board that ran around the vessel we would all have been carried away. To this alone we owe our escape.[14]

This "seven-foot board" was the unusually high bulwark that surrounded the main deck of the *Mimi*. Why the ship was built this way is not entirely clear, although the bulwark appears to have been a later modification to facilitate carrying deck loads of lumber. Such a bulwark could possibly be beneficial in keeping seas from sweeping over the deck while underway, but with the ship in a normal upright position it would seem to represent, in effect, a walled-in prison for those working on the main deck, who could not see the horizon without climbing to the top of a deckhouse or into the rigging.

The ship now lay on her port side, her deck facing the shore while seas crashed against her exposed bottom. Captain Westphal described working his way aft, finding no one alive along the way. Here he found Fisher, the salvor, and a man from the salvage crew. This man died as Fisher and Westphal tried to pull him out of a submerged location. Westphal continued his explanation of what happened aboard the ship as she lay on her side:

> The other sailors died during the course of Sunday night. One man went crazy early Sunday morning after the first lurch and before she capsized. We called for three hours before an effort was made by the lifesaving crew to launch their boat. I guess they could not hear us and it was then that we undertook the dangerous efforts to attract attention by climbing up in the scupper and waving to those on shore. With the coming of darkness we gave ourselves up for goners, as we knew the tide was higher than that of the night before—and that almost covered the boat.[15]

The erstwhile salvor, Holyfield, bemoaned the fate of the ship and the loss of his fee as a contractor, saying, "Captain Crowe and others had assured us we had more than sufficient ballast and I can't understand how it happened."[16]

Captain Farley was summoned from the Lifesaving Station at Garibaldi, and brought his lifesaving crew and equipment by train to the north end of Nehalem Bay and then overland by team to the spit. In spite of thirty-foot combers breaking over a tangle of wreckage from the mast and spars surrounding the deck of the capsized barque, Farley took his surfboat out three times on Sunday in a futile rescue effort. Because of the wild surf that was now running it was impossible to get near the wreck by boat. Furthermore, because there was nothing standing upright on the wreck to which a line for a breeches buoy could be made fast, that type of rescue was also impossible.

As Captain Westphal indicated, Sunday night was critical in the survival of those on board. Charles Fisher recalled later:

> My whole life put together did not seem as long as the hours between sunset Sunday and daybreak this morning (Monday). It seemed years. All we could do was wait. Often during the long hours I thought I would give up my hold and fall into the water to join the others we knew had gone before us. Several times I lost heart but something seemed to cause me to cling. I was frozen with the cold of the water, was sickened by the cries of the people about us and was faint from hunger and thirst. I cannot see how I held on as long as I did. I shall return to my home and attempt to recover from the shock and horror of it all.[17]

Captain Westphal had similar thoughts during the two long nights following the capsizing while those remaining alive waited for dawn and the rescue they hoped was coming:

> All night long we cheered each other by telling of other wrecks and situations worse than ours, where men had been rescued. With the coming day and the sighting of the lifesaving crew standing by out toward us on the way to our rescue, our hopes rose higher. The most sickening feeling anyone could have was experienced when the last attempt at rescue failed Sunday night. It looked as though our lives were to sink out with the dying sun. But we held fast and prayed. My God, how we prayed and hoped and clung. It is too horrible to relate the horrors of that second night in our danger. We were paralyzed from the cold, sickened by the exposure and faint from hunger and thirst. The smell of the sea was horrible. Young Ludwig (the unconscious boy) stood to his waist in water almost Arctic in temperature for 28 hours. That we survived is a wonder. I want to forget it all.[18]

On the following day, Monday 7 April, the lifesaving crew from the Garibaldi station again tried to reach the wreck. This time they succeeded in bringing off four survivors: Captain Westphal, Fisher, the salvor who had conceived the ill-fated project, and two young German seamen. One was named Johan Kusher or Koschr, according to the *Oregonian*, or Hans Konchard, according to the San Francisco *Chronicle*; the other was Fritz Ludwig. Ludwig told an interesting story of the final hours aboard the ship:

> We wanted to come ashore before the attempt to pull the *Mimi*
> off, but we were held back by the captain at the point of a
> gun. He threatened to shoot the first man that left the ship.
> We boys saved the captain's life when he was pinned down by
> the fallen forward yard. We felt no ill will toward him, as it was
> his duty to prevent desertion and it was our duty to help
> him.[19]

Ludwig went on to describe how many of the crewmen, contrary to the captain's orders, tried to swim ashore from the wreck and were drowned in the pounding surf. The young man's loyalty to his captain must have been severely tested when Captain Westphal later denied using a gun, saying "It would be silly for anyone to say that I or anyone else could have held the men on deck with a threat that the first to jump would be shot."[20] Westphal also changed his story and in a later interview said that he had been hurled into the ratlines instead of being pinned down by a yardarm.

Captain Farley of the Lifesaving Service who was responsible for bringing the survivors to safety, said later: "It's a wonder anyone lived, and had it not been for the high bulwark around the *Mimi*'s deck, no one would have been left. I could not believe anyone was alive, and would not risk the lives of my men until I saw them, waving from the ship."[21]

The dead included fourteen of the ship's crew, plus four men from the salvage party. Only one or two bodies were recovered. Among the dead salvors were Captain Albert Crowe, surveyor for the San Francisco Board of Underwriters, a onetime sailing ship captain who was highly regarded in the maritime community in Portland and was the father of two teenagers, and Russell Blackman, the corporate secretary of the Fisher engineering firm, who had been married only five days before the tragedy. The crew of the *Mimi* was quite young and generally unmarried; the news of the deaths among this group would soon be sent to parents in Germany.

In a peculiar twist of events, the rescuer Captain Farley was soon blamed for the tragedy by a segment of the press and the public, as well as by the salvage company. One local paper inveighed against the lifesaving crew in these blunt words:

... the crew seemed to lack the stamina to go into the breakers and failed to heave on their oars effectively so that they never got farther than forty yards from shore at any time during the fifteen minute effort, after which they returned to land and gave up the job for the day leaving the poor fellows who were enduring untold physical agony to their fate for twelve long hours until daybreak the following morning to die of exposure or drown in the meantime. The crowd implored them to make another attempt before darkness came upon the scene and many even volunteered to take the places of the life savers in the boat, but Capt. Farley steadfastly refused to entertain such an idea.[22]

This account then goes on to describe how the mood of the crowd turned ugly and even dangerous.

It was then that the crowd was in a mood to resort to force if necessary to get possession of the boat but for some unknown reason their anger subsided sufficiently to bring them to their senses and this purpose was abandoned. It was a narrow escape for Capt. Farley, however, and he may thank his lucky stars that he escaped from the vengeance of any angry mob without sustaining serious injury in his refusal to comply with their wishes.[23]

Charges were made in other newspapers that the lifesaving crew, fatigued from its efforts to save the men of the *Mimi*, was drunk on duty. These impressions had been gained erroneously when the surfboat crewmen literally staggered ashore, their legs wobbly from fatigue.

Captain Westphal was particularly ungracious to his rescuers, saying, "The water between the wrecked ship and the lifeboat was no rougher

The lifeboat crewmen who tried to rescue survivors from the *Mimi* were vilified by local newspapermen who thought they had done too little. (Courtesy of the Tillamook County Pioneer Museum)

After capsizing during her salvage, the hull of the *Mimi* spent a week in the surf before suddenly disappearing. (Courtesy of the Tillamook County Pioneer Museum)

than the surface of the Nehalem River. I can see no reason why we were not taken off at this time. . . . The sea was not rough and I can see no reason why there should have been any trouble experienced in getting to us."[24]

Eventually, however, public opinion was defused after several respected maritime men in the community came to the defense of Captain Farley and his crew, and criticized the mobs who knew little about the problems of small-boat handling in the surf. A week after the accident the hull of the *Mimi* slipped from sight rather quickly, apparently the result of an undertow which had eroded away the beach on the seaward side of the ship.[25] It was this undertow that Captain Farley had insisted was one of the serious perils in taking the lifesaving boats to the wreck. It is curious, though, how a hull forty-three feet in breadth could drop out of sight so completely on a relatively flat beach—where 750 feet out from the high water mark the depth was only two fathoms—and never show itself again. It is surprising that winter storms in ensuing years have not uncovered this hulk, but that may now be happening, as we soon shall see.

⌒

The investigation conducted after the *Mimi* disaster was entirely different from those conducted after other shipwrecks. It was an investigation of the rescue attempts, rather than an inquiry into the accident itself. As such, it was conducted by the Lifesaving Service, one of the predecessor agencies of the Coast Guard, rather than by the

Steamboat Inspection Service. The fact that the ship flew the German flag ruled out normal investigative procedures to determine how the barque was navigated, but the rescue and the criticisms levied against the rescuers were within the jurisdiction of American governmental agencies.

The Germans held their own inquiry in Portland, presided over by the consul from Seattle, Baron Wolf Engelhard von Loehneysen. Many of the key figures of the tragedy, including the survivors as well as the three mates who saved themselves by defecting, were present at this inquiry, but there was no public report of what transpired.[27]

Captain Gay N. Quinan of San Francisco chaired the closed-door inquiry for the Lifesaving Service. The *Oregonian* identified him as representing the Revenue Marine Service, the other federal agency which in 1915 would be merged with the Lifesaving Service to form the Coast Guard, but this officer, identified then as J. H. Quinan, had appeared earlier that year in Portland in the aftermath of the *Rosecrans* disaster as an inspector for the Lifesaving Service. Initially various townspeople around Nehalem Bay testified, a number of whom aired their concerns about the ineffectiveness of the rescue and the behavior of the surfboat crew.[28]

Later, witnesses from the ship were called to testify. Fisher repeated the charge that the boat crew was intoxicated, and accused the boatmen of inefficiency and cowardice. The water toward the shore from the capsized vessel, claimed the salvor, was "quiet as a pond,"[29] and there was no reason why the boat should not have reached the capsized ship and rescued her crew on the first day.

During his testimony, which was also critical of Captain Farley and his men, Captain Westphal was allowed to question the two members of his crew who had survived the ordeal. While each man changed certain details of his testimony under this cross-examination, each man also reiterated his earlier statement that he had been given no chance to leave the ship, and having been offered such a choice would have elected to leave the ship before the salvage began.[30]

Ultimately, after a thorough investigation, Captain Quinan found no substance to the allegations against the boatmen, and vindicated the lifesaving crew. The report of the investigation observed:

> The charges of drunkenness were unfounded, and the major
> portion of the blame seems to have been voiced by the head of
> the wrecking firm who must recognize there was criminal
> carelessness on his own part, or the bark would not have
> capsized. Had Farley listened to the clamor of the crowd and
> tried to put out through the wreckage another tragedy would
> have occurred.[31]

Thus, both a hero and a villain seem to have emerged from the tragedy, the former in the person of Captain Farley and the latter in the person of Fisher, the salvor. At the same time Captain Westphal increasingly appeared as a shadowy figure, a minor tyrant who drove his men hard to achieve the results that the salvor wanted, but who as master of the ship had permitted the unwise removal of the permanent ballast that was to jeopardize the lives of all aboard.

Although his fictional captain is not particularly likable, author Jack L. Graves is somewhat ambivalent on the subject of how the community actually perceived the real Captain Westphal. He recalls hearing a rumor that the captain had a drug dependency problem, an assertion difficult to prove. He also remembers allegations that when the captain departed the area he left behind a number of unpaid bills, somewhat easier to prove.[32] Perhaps the strongest conclusion that can be inferred from the established facts regarding the captain's character is that Westphal altered his public statements from time to time to suit his immediate purposes.

Regardless of his behavior, however, Captain Westphal projected a romantic image of a German sea captain. Newspaper photographs of him give him the look of someone who might have been sent out by central casting as an authentic U-boat commander. Apparently he did subsequently serve in World War One, remaining in the merchant service. According to his daughter, a woman with the interesting name of Mimi Fischer, he served as captain of the 3,800-ton German steamer *Walküre* which was seized by the French at Tahiti early in the war, only to be sunk when the German cruiser squadron raided that port under the command of Admiral Graf Spee.[33] In 1916 the ship was raised by an enterprising American investor, John A. Hooper of San Francisco, reflagged as an American ship named *Republic*, and sold to a Chilean firm for an enormous profit.[34] Somewhere along the way, Westphal was imprisoned and later escaped. Some years later Mimi Fischer tried without success to sell her father's story to a book publisher or movie producer.[35]

In retrospect it appears that to the people of the north coast of Oregon the *Mimi* incident had served as a forerunner to the intrigues of World War One. Perhaps the result turned out much like the result of the war, in that the wrong people—the innocent—died, and those responsible for the disaster—the salvor and the captain—lived.

〜

The final word of the *Mimi* story may not yet have been written. During the writing of this book William Klein, a former resident of the Nehalem Bay area, came forward to report that a few years ago he saw from the air what he took to be the hull of the barque off the Nehalem spit in the same location where she was last seen in 1913.[36] A local photographer who specializes in aerial views of the coast, Don Best, reports that he has not encountered the wreck, but speculates that it could have been re-buried by the same kind of winter storm that had uncovered it a few years ago.[37]

Perhaps the ghost-like qualities of the *Mimi* that had terrified her chief mate in 1913 have endured, and now she haunts the site of her loss, waiting to be seen again and to taunt her salvors.

Chapter Six

The Mystery of the *Francis H. Leggett*

Maritime historians and writers are always on the lookout for little-known disasters that have unique features not common to most sinkings, strandings, or collisions. In fact, the genesis of this chapter was an item recounting just such a disaster which appeared in a long-defunct San Francisco newspaper, the *Call-Post,* on 19 September 1914. That item briefly reported that the American steamer *Francis H. Leggett* had collided with the Japanese cruiser *Idzumo* off the Oregon coast, and that seventy-eight people were lost in the ensuing sinking. Given that set of circumstances, the makings of a great never-before-told sea story were immediately evident.

Later, when further research revealed that the *Leggett* had probably not collided with the Japanese cruiser but had foundered in a storm, the story lost some of its allure. However, once it was established that the cruiser had indeed played a cryptic role in the strange drama, and that the steamer had been a victim of weather and other circumstances that she should have overcome, it was clear that the story still had that unique touch that set it apart from run-of-the-mill maritime mishaps.

One compelling aspect of the story was the death toll, which was later established as more than sixty-five, a figure that cannot be expressed more precisely, since casualties on coastal ships were hard to determine accurately because of last-minute passenger and crew changes. With that number of casualties, the sinking of the *Leggett* earned the ship the dubious distinction of being among the five most deadly West Coast maritime disasters of the twentieth century. This distinction was notable in that each of the four ships whose loss produced the most deaths, the *Rio De Janeiro, Valencia, Columbia,* and *San Juan,* was a true passenger liner carrying several hundred people, while the *Francis H. Leggett* was simply a small lumber ship that carried passengers—lots of them.

Another dimension to the *Leggett* story that added human interest and poignancy was the fact that only two men survived from a crew of about thirty and a passenger list of about thirty-nine. The official Wreck Report filed by the owners indicated that there were "31 so far as known" in the crew, and "36 so far as known" passengers.[1] Thus, the full story may never have emerged—only those aspects of it which were witnessed and later recalled by these two passengers who were plucked, half-dead, from the cold waters of the North Pacific.

To understand the uniqueness of this episode it is necessary to know something of the ship, and the niche her owners were trying to serve. It is also essential to understand the geographic and economic factors that prompted passengers to take long trips on small slow ships such as the *Francis H. Leggett* in the face of a very competitive shipping environment that included a number of comfortable, large, and fast passenger ships traveling up and down the Pacific Coast.

The *Leggett* was among the first steel-hulled vessels used in the Northwest lumber trade. She was not a traditional steam-schooner in design; rather she was a small freighter of a unique design resembling a tanker more than a dry cargo ship. Although she had earlier been classified as a cargo vessel, the official governmental directory, *Merchant Vessels of the United States,* listed her as a passenger vessel in the 1914 edition.

Within the coastal lumber trade she was well known and well regarded. Her cargo gear, utilizing two masts serving a large after hold and one on a smaller forward hold, was highly efficient. At Grays Harbor, Washington, she had once set a record for loading lumber when she was able to handle 1.475 million board feet in twenty hours time.[2]

The *Leggett* had been built at the Newport News Shipyard in 1903 for the Hammond Lumber Company. She was 258 feet in overall length, 41

This view of the *Francis H. Leggett* shows how she looked with a full deck load of lumber. (Courtesy of the San Francisco Maritime National Historical Park)

feet in beam, and 19 feet deep, measuring out at 1,606 gross and 975 net tons. With oil-fired boilers, she was powered by a triple expansion reciprocating steam engine mounted aft which produced 1,000 shaft horsepower and drove her at ten knots.

It is not clear how she acquired her name. Francis H. Leggett was a wealthy wholesale grocery merchant in New York City with no apparent ties to the West Coast.[3] Perhaps he had invested in some of the C. A. Hammond lumber, railroad, or shipping enterprises. The ship had been acquired from Hammond in 1912 by the Hicks-Hauptman Company of San Francisco, but for more than a year had been operated under a charter by the McCormick Steamship Company of San Francisco. This company made extensive use of small ships in passenger service; in fact, some of the firm's smaller ships carried as many as seventy passengers on short coastal runs.

⬿

Accounts of the sailing of the *Leggett* from Grays Harbor on Washington's southwest coast were characterized by the same confusion that surrounded the entire final voyage of the ship. Most of the area newspapers fixed the departure as late morning on Thursday 17 February 1913, but the survivor most widely quoted in later newspaper stories claimed it was on Wednesday morning and the other survivor recalled it as Wednesday evening.

In any case, the ship was under the command of Captain Charles Maro, about thirty-five years of age and recently married, a veteran of service on four other McCormick ships.[4] The *Leggett* was bound non-stop for San Francisco, about 560 miles to the south, with a final destination of San Pedro in southern California. In addition to her passengers she was carrying a cargo of 1,400,000 board feet of fir lumber including railroad ties, as part of a large deck load which was a standard feature on lumber ships. The ship was insured for $175,000 and her cargo for $11,161.[5]

The point of departure, Grays Harbor, is a large bay about forty nautical miles north of the mouth of the Columbia River. It contains two deepwater ports, Aberdeen and Hoquiam. The former is at the point where the Chehalis River first opens into the bay, and the latter is six miles further west along the north shore of the bay. Like all the harbors on the north Pacific coastline, Grays Harbor is a "bar port" which requires that ships cross a shallow sand bar in entering, an operation that can be extremely dangerous when heavy seas and swells are breaking.

About half the passengers who boarded the *Francis H. Leggett* for this trip were residents of Aberdeen and Hoquiam. The other half were from Seattle, about 105 land miles to the northeast.[6] These people had traveled to Grays Harbor by train to catch the ship, perhaps to save on the total distance they would cover at sea. Ships leaving Seattle must go north through Puget Sound to the Strait of Juan de Fuca, then round Cape Flattery, before heading south in the open ocean. The distance by sea to the mouth of Grays Harbor from Seattle is about 215 miles, almost a half day's run for the fastest passenger ships of that era.

However, in choosing to travel on a slow lumber ship from Grays Harbor rather than a fast passenger ship from Seattle, the traveler had to weigh the disadvantages against the advantages. A ten-knot lumber ship would require fifty-seven hours for the passage to San Francisco from Grays Harbor, while a fifteen-knot passenger ship would reach the Bay Area from Seattle, a distance of about eight hundred nautical miles, in about fifty-three hours. Moreover, a twenty-knot passenger ship such as the *Great Northern* in 1915 would soon cut the longer run to forty hours, beating the speed of passenger trains. Comfort, of course, would also be far greater on the larger and faster ship, including both that assured by the less violent motion while in rough seas and that provided by the amenities found aboard.

Cost, then, would seem to be the only reason why a Seattle passenger would choose the slower trip from Grays Harbor. However, considering that the San Francisco fare was as low as fifteen dollars, first class, on all ships of the Pacific Coast Steamship Company,[7] and fifteen dollars first class, and ten dollars second class, on the *Admiral Farragut, Buckman,* and *Watson* of the Alaska Pacific Steamship Company, predecessor of the Admiral Line,[8] it is hard to imagine how low the fare on the *Francis H. Leggett* must have been in order to attract passengers, particularly since a railroad fare from Seattle to Grays Harbor would have to be added to the total cost for passengers taking that route. One of the survivors reported that his ticket from Seattle had cost fourteen dollars for first class, but that he had been told by the agent that since the seas were stormy the passengers were being sent to Grays Harbor by train to catch the ship.[9]

Vessels that were primarily passenger ships did not normally call at Hoquiam or Aberdeen. Consequently, people from that area could travel south by sea only on lumber ships; fares on such ships were not advertised in metropolitan newspapers, but were probably about 75 percent of Seattle fares. Travelers from Grays Harbor could also go overland to Portland or Astoria to catch a passenger ship. Portland fares were often advertised, generally running about a third less than Seattle fares. In 1913 fares on the *Rose City* from Portland to San Francisco were advertised as low as ten dollars first class and six dollars second class, in both cases including berth and meals,[10] The North Pacific Steamship Company matched that fare on the *Roanoke,*[11] but the first-class fare on the small wooden-hulled *Santa Clara* of the same line inexplicably was fifteen dollars.[12] The two large liners of James H. Hill's railroad-based steamship company, the *Northern Pacific* and the *Great Northern,* in 1915 would offer tourist-class passage from Portland for fifteen dollars and eight dollars in third class.[13] In any case, why a large number of passengers, particularly those from Seattle, traveled from Grays Harbor aboard the *Leggett* in preference to larger ships or passenger trains remains a mystery.

⌒

The ship encountered no difficulty in crossing the bar in leaving Grays Harbor on Thursday morning. However, a southeast gale that would reach sixty knots was beginning to blow, and storm warnings were posted northward from Point Arena, California. The ship was soon laboring heavily as she worked her way down the Oregon coast. The then-current *Coast Pilot*, the mariner's guide to the lore of the sea in that locale, also known as the *Sailing Directions for the North Pacific*, said this about weather on the North Pacific coast: "September is a quiet month. Storms are infrequent. Occasional storms occur toward the close of the month and rainfall is heavier on the Oregon and Washington coasts."[14] The *Francis H. Leggett*, it seems, had the bad luck to encounter one of those occasional early storms.

On Thursday evening the *Leggett*'s chief radio operator, eighteen-year-old C. J. Fleming, reported to a shore station that the ship was passing the mouth of the Columbia River, and this position was reported in the shipping columns of newspapers on the West Coast. While no indication of trouble appeared in the message, the ship was obviously making very little speed in that it had taken nine hours to cover the distance from Grays Harbor. This was the ship's last contact with the outside world. From this point on, the story is known only through the recollections of the two survivors, Alexander Farrell of Seattle, who was twenty years old at the time, and George Poelman, a twenty-three-year-old Canadian.

By Friday noon, 18 September, it was clear that the ship was in serious trouble. She had made only sixty miles since passing the mouth of the Columbia, and was being pounded savagely by the heavy seas. The deck cargo had begun to come apart. In an effort to improve the ship's stability Captain Charles Maro ordered that the railroad ties in the deck load be jettisoned. During this operation the passengers were ordered to their cabins. It is not clear what happened next, but somehow Captain Maro may have disappeared, perhaps swept overboard according to some accounts.[15] However, one of the survivors later recalled seeing him on the stern just prior to the end; "he seemed dazed, and stood looking at the deck."[16] The other survivor whose initial recollection led to speculation about the captain's disappearance later thought he was "aft with the passengers."[17] In any case, Captain Maro was not acting as the captain of the ship during her final moments. The command of the vessel was then assumed not by the chief mate, but by one of the passengers, Jens Jensen, a licensed ship master.[18] According to a survivor report, Captain Maro had asked Captain Jensen to assist with the passengers during the crisis while he, Maro, remained responsible for the navigation of the vessel;[19] their locations aboard ship, however, did not bear out this arrangement.

Jensen had made the shipping news early in 1914 as master of the schooner *Nokomis* which had grounded on Clipperton Island, hundreds of miles off the coast of Mexico. After the captain, his crew, and his wife and two small children had spent several months as castaways on this desert island, the second mate of the vessel and two seamen had set out in a damaged boat for Acapulco, 700 miles away. After a remarkable seventeen-day voyage, for the last three days of which they had neither food nor water, these men managed to reach their goal and to alert authorities to the plight of the remaining people on the island. The Navy despatched the cruiser *Cleveland,* which was able to rescue the rest of the crew and another group of stranded Mexicans and bring them back to civilization. The Jensens had returned to San Francisco aboard the *City of Sydney* of the Pacific Mail Line on 10 July, only six weeks before the ill-fated trip of the *Francis H. Leggett.*[20]

After taking his wife and family to her parents' home in Olympia, Washington, Captain Jensen was anxious to resume his career, and to overcome the stigma of losing a ship. Captain Maro of the *Leggett* kindly offered him a complimentary passage to San Francisco, where Jensen was hoping to find another berth as master or mate of a sailing vessel.[21] Why he apparently assumed command of the *Leggett* in her moment of peril was unknown, but perhaps he wanted to repay Maro for his faith in him. Perhaps, too, he saw an opportunity to vindicate himself for an earlier mistake—in the same fashion as did the central character of Joseph Conrad's classic sea story *Lord Jim.* Regardless of motive, Jensen handled himself admirably during the final moments of the *Francis H. Leggett.*

Around three o'clock that afternoon a huge wave crashed into the *Leggett*, ripping open a hatch and causing the vessel to develop a severe list. The new captain ordered the vessel abandoned. According to the survivor, Alexander Farrell, two boats were launched. In one were about thirty people including two women, and the other contained only four women and their husbands. As Farrell recalled: "It was at that moment that the only excitement occurred. As the second boat was being prepared some men rushed for it, but Captain Jensen made them stand back, saying he would shoot the first man who stepped aboard until all the women were cared for. As soon as the small boats struck the water they capsized and all in them were lost."[22]

Shortly after the boats were launched the ship rolled over and floated bottom up in the water. Many of the passengers were not on deck and thus had no chance to escape. Farrell had been on the bridge and was thrown into the water. As he recalled, "I went down with the suction—how far I cannot say—but it was a long way, and as I came to the surface I saw the vessel's bow stick out of the water and then gradually sink." Farrell was eventually able to cling to a railroad tie. He thought that there were perhaps thirty people in the water at that moment, but soon only five people were in sight: the radio operator, an oiler, and three women.[23]

Poelman, too, was thrown into the water, from the stern of the ship, and was also able to cling to a pair of railroad ties. He recalled that at least everyone in the cold water seemed to be wearing a life jacket.[24] At this point, with the ship sinking rapidly, and each person in the bone-chilling water struggling to survive, the sequence of events becomes difficult to reconstruct.

An SOS message containing her position had been sent out from the ship during her final moments upright, but no shore stations or merchant ships received this message. The only ship receiving it was the Japanese cruiser *Idzumo* which was operating off the Oregon coast. Accounts of her role in the events that followed differed significantly. One indicated that after some delay the cruiser sent a message to shore stations with a rather imprecise location for the sinking, this in an effort to be helpful without giving away her own position.

The beach at Nehalem Bay was strewn with railroad ties and lumber after the sinking of the *Leggett*. (Courtesy Tillamook County Pioneer Museum)

World War One had started early in August of 1914, and the Japanese had entered the war several weeks later. Since two German cruisers had earlier been on the west coast and were generally unaccounted for at the moment, the *Idzumo*'s captain had been understandably reluctant to give away his location. Curiously, the press was largely supportive of the Japanese reluctance to get involved in the rescue.[25]

Another account of the *Idzumo*'s action, however, has the cruiser more fully involved. A dispatch datelined San Francisco and quoting "advices received from Vancouver" indicated that the warship had reported her actions by radio as follows:

> About 2 o'clock Friday afternoon the *Idzumo* heard an SOS from the ill-fated steamer which gave the position about twenty miles south of the Columbia River. The cruiser was about 200 miles away from this location at the time, and the commander, knowing that he could not reach the ship in time to render assistance relayed the SOS to any ships which might be in reach of the ship. He then proceeded toward the place designated by the *Leggett*'s operator at full speed, but did not arrive there in time to give any assistance.[26]

Inasmuch as the *Idzumo* was known to have contacted the Japanese consul in Vancouver, the story released to the press could have been edited favorably by the consular staff.

The radio procedures of the *Idzumo* raise further questions. The steam schooner *Norwood*, which later reported she was only twenty-five miles from the *Leggett*, heard a strong nearby transmission from the Japanese cruiser; the message said "SOS, WSB [the call sign for the *Leggett*] sank at 2 o'clock."[27] When the SOS was sent, presumably containing the location, why did the *Idzumo* not acknowledge its receipt to the sinking ship?[28] Why did she omit the location in relaying the message, and then not answer any further inquiries? If the cruiser had thought the *Leggett*'s transmission was too weak to be heard elsewhere, why did she not simply repeat the message, including the location of the sinking? Why was the *Idzumo* the only ship or station that heard the *Leggett*'s SOS?

Moreover, two accounts indicate that the *Idzumo*'s Friday afternoon message to the shore station came at 3:15 P.M.[29] or 3 P. M., according to the *Norwood*'s radio operator,[30] reporting the time of the sinking as 2:00 P.M. This time discrepancy might suggest that the cruiser had more direct information about the event than she readily acknowledged. This possibility is accepted in *The H. W. McCurdy Marine History of the Pacific Northwest*, the standard maritime history of the area, which alleges that the cruiser had sighted the sinking lumber ship, and had the opportunity to pick up victims in the water but did not do so. Marshall's *Oregon Shipwrecks* repeats this allegation.[31] These accounts were written many years later, and, although presumably were based on the most reliable sources that were available, cannot be confirmed.

Another question concerns how the story of the collision between the *Idzumo* and the *Leggett* was started. Perhaps the mere proximity of the cruiser was responsible. Rumors about cruisers of the belligerent nations being off the north coast, and even rumors of great battles being fought by these warships, were abundant during the first few months of the war, and the public was quick to associate any maritime mishaps with the presence of these ships. The specific rumor apparently came from a wire-service story, datelined Seattle, appearing in the Portland *Oregonian*. It said:

> In connection with the report of the sinking of the steam schooner *Francis H. Leggett*, S. Takahashi, Japanese consul here, said tonight he had been notified through the Marconi

wireless station that a vessel had been sunk off the Columbia River, and through the same agency had heard rumors that the sinking of the vessel had come about through a collision with the Japanese cruiser *Idzumo*.[32]

The true role of the *Idzumo* in this incident has never been critically examined, primarily because the records of the Imperial Navy have not been available. Although the Japanese ship presumably was searching for German cruisers when she came upon the *Leggett*, the one such ship known to be on the West Coast, SMS *Leipzig*, had been detected a week earlier by British authorities as she departed the Gulf of California, The German cruiser then captured a British tanker on 11 September 1914, at a point about 1,800 miles south of where the *Idzumo* encountered the *Leggett* a week later.[33] It is not clear whether the British ship was able to send a radio message. Thus, the *Idzumo* may or may not have been aware of the presence of the *Leipzig* far to the south a week earlier.

The *Idzumo* continued to play the role of an *agent provocateur* who could not be trusted in her relationship with American authorities. Later in World War One, despite denials by the Japanese government, she was present when the Japanese cruiser *Asama* went aground at Turtle Bay in Baja California, a violation of Mexico's neutrality. At the onset of World War Two she was moored at Shanghai, and provided the major firepower to cover Japanese Marines who overran the American gunboat *Wake* and destroyed the British gunboat *Peterel*.[34]

An interesting sidelight to the *Idzumo* story surfaced during the writing of this book when the eldest son of the *Leggett* survivor George Poelman reported that his father after being pulled from the water was asked if a Japanese ship had sunk the lumber ship. In saying "no," he became aware that a false answer could have provoked a serious international incident.[35]

⌐

Another mystery of the *Leggett* is how the rescue ships were able to locate the site of the poorly-reported foundering. First on the scene was the Associated Oil tanker *Frank H. Buck,* bound from Monterey to

Portland. Her captain, George B. Macdonald, reported that his radio operator had picked up the *Idzumo*'s radio message at 4 P.M., alerting the tanker to the possibility that there might be survivors in the water ahead. At about 11 P.M. third officer Gibbs on the bridge heard a cry through the windy darkness. When Captain Macdonald reached the bridge he heard what he later described as "a call for help from a pair of powerful human lungs and charged with all the terror one human voice could carry." The ship was stopped, searchlights were illuminated, and George Poelman was located in the water. The ship maneuvered alongside him, and quartermaster Lars Eskildson swam to him with a lifeline. The two men were then pulled from the water.[36]

The *Buck* then launched a boat to search for other survivors. Alexander Farrell was found at about midnight, after he had been in the water almost nine hours. The tanker then sent the first radio message which accurately reported what had happened and where. In the meantime the Portland-bound passenger liner *Beaver* of the San Francisco & Portland Steamship Company arrived on the scene, and took Farrell aboard. The transfer was effected by the simple procedure of tying a line around him and hoisting him out of the lifeboat and aboard the ship through a side port.[37]

The tanker *Frank H. Buck* which rescued the survivors of the *Leggett* needed a bit of help herself on occasion. (Courtesy of San Francisco Maritime National Historical Park)

These two rescue vessels were an interesting study in contrasts. The *Frank H. Buck* was fresh from the builder's yard, beginning a career that would soon take her to Europe as a Navy tanker in World War One, during which time she would survive a surface encounter with a German U-boat. She would then go on to a decade of service on the West Coast, in the course of which she would survive several groundings before succumbing to a fatal one near San Francisco in the mid 1920s.[30] The *Beaver* was also relatively new, dating from 1910. In 1913 she had acquired a measure of notoriety in colliding with the Norwegian steamer, *Selja*, off Point Reyes in California, sending the freighter to the bottom.[39] She, too, would soon be acquired by the Navy for World War One service, but would spend the rest of her career as a submarine tender in that service, never again functioning as a merchant ship.

McCurdy indicates that the *Buck* and the *Beaver* heard the message from the *Idzumo*, but since that message reportedly contained no position for the sinking it is not clear how the ships knew where to begin searching. Fortunately, however, the *Leggett* had been close to the main north-south steamer track, so in time the two ships must have encountered large amounts of lumber in the water, enough to be readily apparent even at night.

Other ships had joined in the search, including the steam schooners *Daisy Putnam* and *Norwood* and the Standard Oil tanker *El Segundo,* but found no survivors and, perhaps because of the roughness of the sea, no bodies. After spending several hours on the scene, the *Beaver* and *Frank H. Buck* gave up the search and proceeded north, encountering debris in the water for several hours. Captain Mason of the *Beaver* reported that the scene of the disaster was thirty miles northwest by north from Yaquina Head Light which is near the coastal city of Newport.

That location is about seventy-five miles south of the mouth of the Columbia, somewhat farther south than the other reports placed the sinking, and shows charted depths of two hundred to three hundred fathoms. It also appears to be somewhat outside the regular trackline between the Columbia Lightship and Cape Blanco, the westernmost point of Oregon and the main turning point on the coast. That location might be explained by the fact that the *Leggett* had been pounded by southeasterly gales which would have set her to the west. Her two rescue vessels were probably also somewhat west of the track.

The morning after the sinking of the *Leggett*, while en route to the mouth of the Columbia River the captain of the *Frank H. Buck* sighted the *Idzumo*, southbound off the Tillamook County coastline, thus providing the only visual evidence that the cruiser was reasonably close to the scene of the sinking—albeit somewhat later.[40] When the *Buck* eventually reached the Columbia bar on the morning of 19 September she was forced to wait for the seas to calm before attempting to cross en route upriver to Portland where the survivor George Poelman would be met by officials of the steamship company. The *Beaver* also took extra time in reaching Astoria at noon on Saturday with the other survivor, Farrell.

Relatively little information about Poelman appeared in subsequent newspaper accounts. He was reportedly from the Winnipeg area, but since he had come to Canada from Holland only three years earlier and spoke limited English he was not interviewed as extensively as was Alexander Farrell. Farrell, however, proved to be good copy for the reporters, coming across in interviews as a keen observer as well as a believer in the essential goodness of humans. In the case of a rapid foundering, there is little time to observe acts of heroism, or of cowardice. Farrell saw no cowardice during the sinking, and much that was good. He later singled out Captain Jensen for his consistent heroism, and the radio operator Fleming who had voluntarily relinquished his hold on the railroad tie he shared with Farrell to let a woman have a better chance of survival. Eventually, neither Fleming nor the unidentified woman whom he had helped could stay afloat, nor could the other three people who were close by Farrell.[41]

Farrell obviously enjoyed his contacts with the press, and in subsequent interviews professed to know much more about what went on aboard the *Leggett* during her final moments than he had reported in earlier statements. He also benefitted financially from his brief fame;

One of the two survivors of the *Leggett* was George Poelman, a young Canadian who clung to a railroad tie eight hours before being rescued. (Courtesy of family of George Poelman)

to supplement money which was collected for him by the passengers of the *Beaver*, he made an arrangement with the *Oregon Journal* to sell newspapers in front of the *Journal* building in downtown Portland as a personal fundraiser.[42]

The question must be asked: why did this ship sink? She was modern, adequately powered, in familiar waters, on a routine voyage which she had often made before, loaded within her established limits—and yet she sank, and quickly. The weather at the time of the *Leggett's* loss was unseasonably bad, but not catastrophic. The *Buck* was able to launch her boat in that location, something that could not have happened in truly mountainous seas. Shipping columns in newspapers observed that northbound ships were late in arriving at Portland, but there were no other marine casualties reported during the storm. As is the case when operating conditions are marginal, some ship masters opted for prudence while others took risks. At Coos Bay, for example, the day after the loss of the *Leggett* most small ships remained bar-bound by the storm, but the captain of the small passenger ship *Nann Smith* sailed for San Francisco with no less than sixty-four passengers aboard—and encountered no trouble.[43]

Inevitably, the question of mechanical problems arises in the case of a foundering. One newspaper charged that, according to what the chief engineer had told an engineering service at Grays Harbor, the *Leggett* had experienced steering gear problems on her previous trip to that port, and had to be steered by the emergency tackle rigged to the rudder.[44] However, even though Farrell repeated the charge of a steering failure in a later interview,[45] this allegation failed to arouse much follow-up interest among the media or the public.

Some speculation has suggested that the speed at which the *Leggett* sank was not characteristic of a ship filled with lumber, and that therefore she must have broken apart. Certainly the sheer weight of her lumber cargo added to the weight of the vessel must be considered in accounting for her inability to stay afloat, in spite of the offsetting buoyancy of that cargo.

Determining the weight of the cargo can be achieved in several ways. Shipping columns of the newspapers had reported that the cargo of the *Leggett* consisted of 1,400,000 board feet of fir lumber, well within the 1,500,000 board feet which was considered the capacity of the vessel. Since by definition a board foot is one twelfth of a cubic foot, this load would occupy 116,667 cubic feet. Using .56 as the specific gravity of fir wood (as per Charles Desmond's book *Wooden Shipbuilding*), the weight of the cargo can be computed as 1,820 tons. Yet the wreck report filed by the ship's owners with the Lifesaving Service reported the weight of the cargo as "about 2,375 tons," presumably long tons, which might suggest that the load was as large as 1,825,000 board feet.

Captain Harold D. Huycke, a northwestern maritime historian and shipmaster with experience in the lumber trade, disregards specific gravities and computes cargo weight on the basis of 1000 board feet, weighing, in the case of well-seasoned fir, 1.4 long tons (equivalent to a specific gravity of .60).[46] On this basis, 1,400 units of 1,000 board feet would weigh 1,960 tons.

What would these weights do to the draft of the ship? On a freighter of this small size, it would take about twenty tons to change the draft of the ship one inch, a factor known in the trade as "tons per inch immersion." With the weight computed by specific gravity the ship would increase her draft 91 inches, by the company's computations 117 inches, and by Captain Huycke's method 98 inches. By the most extreme of these computations, the draft would have changed nine feet and nine inches. Although we do not know the draft of the ship, her depth, according to the shipyard that built her, was nineteen feet from keel to main deck. If she had a light draft of six feet to keep her screw in the water, the increased draft in the company's own scenario would have left a freeboard, or distance between water and main deck, of only about three feet, a bit marginal even for a lumber ship.

One of the revered authorities on seamanship, Captain Felix Riesenberg, in his standard text first published in the 1920s, offers a rough approximation of what a ship can carry as 2.5 times her net tonnage.[47] On this basis, the *Leggett* could carry 2,437 tons, a bit more than what the owners said she was carrying. However, this rule of thumb applies to measured below-deck space, and deck cargoes would be in excess of its limits.

Thus it seems fair to say that the *Leggett* was well loaded but not overloaded. Whether she had ample stability is another matter. If too much weight is placed high in a vessel, the center of gravity moves upward, and the righting arm—the force acting to restore a rolling ship to equilibrium—is reduced. Apparently, in attempting to jettison the deck load, Captain Maro had been trying to reduce the topside weight and to improve the ship's stability. Furthermore, if that load had moved horizontally under the impetus of heavy seas, a list could easily develop, and a listing ship is more vulnerable to forces tending to capsize her than a ship in stable equilibrium. In Farrell's expanded recollections of the accident he indicated that a strong starboard list persisted even after the deck cargo was gone.

Even if she capsized, however, she would not necessarily sink, at least not immediately. The considerable buoyancy of a lumber ship would tend to retard her sinking. Since, however, the *Leggett* went down quickly, the theory that she broke up appears to be a plausible explanation for her loss.[48] Farrell's earlier recollection of the bow of the ship jutting upward out of the sea might confirm that the vessel was in at least two pieces at this point, although his later comments do not mention this possibility.

∽

With the physical cause of the disaster now reduced to a plausible hypothesis, it is appropriate to assess the human impact of the sinking of the *Leggett*. There was fairly general agreement among newspaper accounts as to the number and names of the victims. Some disagreement occurred in the identification of the ship's mates. Two newspapers identified Ole Green as chief mate, L. Pederson as second mate, and T. Jordfeldt as third mate, while another paper had Pederson as chief mate, Jordfeldt as second, and F. Meyers as third. The dissenting paper also claimed that the mate's wife was aboard, an assertion made in several other papers as well, along with the captain's wife.[49] However, no additional person with a name corresponding to that of any of the officers appeared on the lists published in the newspapers.

Curiously, the name of the radio officers, C. J. Fleming and Henry F. Otto, do not appear on the lists of officers, but radio officers were sometimes considered employees of the commercial radio companies which licensed equipment and services to steamship companies.

On the passenger list in addition to Captain Jensen were members of a seagoing family: Mrs. Nelson Anderson of Aberdeen, wife of Captain Anderson of the schooner *Carrier Dove*, and her twelve-year-old daughter, Helen. Another family consisted of Mr. and Mrs. Homer D. Snediker and their son Raymond of Seattle; Snediker was identified as a former employee of the Bon Marché store. Another couple was identified as Mr. and Mrs. C. A. Parks of Seattle. Two women made up the balance of the female passenger list. One was identified as Rose Gomez from Aberdeen and the other, also from Aberdeen, was Tillie Ingals, each of whom was given the standard newspaper designation of that era, "colored," although both survivors described them as Mexican.

The most thoroughly identified victim among the passengers was C. A. Rohrbacker, a seventy-six-year-old insurance man and widower from Seattle who was on his way to visit a daughter in El Paso, and, over the objections of his son, had insisted on taking the longer route to California by sea because of his passion for ocean travel.

The newspaper accounts balanced out numerically, with parallel lists of names of passengers that, while often jumbled, were roughly comparable. On the basis of six different passenger lists in as many newspapers, it appears that there were thirty-nine passengers and thirty crewmen aboard who could be identified by name. Additional probabilities include the mate's wife who was widely reported to be aboard, as well as two alleged stowaways who seem to have gone unnamed and uncounted,[50] bringing the total of those aboard to seventy-two.

Little other information was provided concerning other passengers, although three men were identified as laborers from Seattle, another a longshoreman from Aberdeen, two loggers from Hoquiam, a railroad brakeman, a college student en route to school, and two French sailors off a schooner.[51] From what little is known of them, the passengers seem like a blue-collar group, one that at another time and place might have been encountered aboard a Greyhound bus, rather than a train.

One of the most curious aspects of the *Leggett* disaster was the wide distribution of the bodies of the victims. Bodies floated ashore all the way north from the central Oregon coast to Neah Bay at the entrance to the Strait of Juan de Fuca. One of the most unusual discoveries of victims occurred on Sunday, 27 September, when two bodies were found some distance apart on a Washington beach with evidence that they had each been lashed to a raft. They were identified as Henry F. Otto, the second radio operator, and John Johnson, a seaman traveling as a passenger. The coroner determined that the men had only recently died; in fact, the finders of the bodies had even attempted resuscitation. The coroner and various seafaring men in nearby Grays Harbor reckoned that the two men had constructed a raft which had kept them alive more than a week following the sinking on Friday, 18 September.[52] One can only shake one's head in disbelief upon hearing such an ironic and tragic story. This tremendous display of heroism and courage illustrates both the power of the human spirit and the unforgiving nature of the sea.

As a result of what is known about those aboard the *Francis H. Leggett*, it is possible to develop an empathy with the crew and the passengers of that ship that goes beyond that generated by most of the other disasters that are highlighted in this book. Because of the few survival options they were given, these people deserved better than they received.

Unfortunately, the transcript of the hearings held by the inspectors following this disaster cannot be found at either of the locations where it would be expected: the National Archives regional branches in Seattle, or San Bruno, California. So it is impossible to learn how the responsibility for this accident was ultimately assigned. According to the *Coast Seamen's Journal*, there was concern expressed at the time within the shipping community about the excessive size of deck loads. The same magazine also editorialized against the practice of using the weight of such loads as a substitute for the battens and strong-backs which are normally used to keep a hatch tightly closed and waterproof.[53] One of the two survivors, otherwise unidentified, seems to have confirmed this practice; he reported that the ship went down "like a rock, the hatches having not been put on before leaving port."[54]

In one sense, the absence of acceptable findings in this case is unfortunate, since the whole affair involved so many unresolved issues. In another sense, however, it may be just as well that there are loose ends remaining that could not be tied up in administrative hearings. The intense human dramas in this story simply could not have been be recaptured in front of the inspectors with any more significance than that conveyed in the accounts which the survivors and the rescuers had already related to the world through news interviews. Similarly, the unresolved aspects of the incident, including the cause of the sinking, the role of the *Idzumo,* and even why so many people chose to travel aboard this ship—these things are perhaps now best left to further constructive speculation rather than hastily and awkwardly put behind us simply for the sake of that elusive goal of closure.

Chapter Seven

The *Santa Clara*: A Beach Too Crowded

The steamer *Santa Clara* was unique in several respects. First, she was a passenger ship built in the Pacific Northwest, a rarity in itself. Second, she was built of wood, certainly not the preferred material in passenger ship construction, but the material with which many northwestern shipyards were the most comfortable. And third, she was built to fill a particular niche, but seemed to have trouble in finding and filling that niche.

This unusual ship was the product of the White Shipyard at Everett, Washington, in 1900. Doomsayers had an opportunity to predict a dark future for her when her keel was broken on her original launching, requiring that she be rebuilt.[1] Built as the *John S. Kimball* for the Kimball Steamship Company and subsequently operated by the Dollar Line as the *James Dollar*, she was conceived as a ship to serve the smaller ports of the West Coast, providing low-cost passenger service that could compete with railroad transportation. She was small, only 223 feet in overall length, 38 feet in breadth, and 24 feet in depth. Her gross tonnage was 1,558 and her net tonnage 1,200. She was powered with a reciprocating steam engine that was rated at 900 horsepower.

Although she competed against steam schooners for passengers in the smaller ports, the *Santa Clara* was not of that breed, either in appearance or in her trade. She was clearly a small passenger ship that carried cargo, and her hull appearance, with her short foredeck and long deckhouse, accentuated that role. Unlike many of the passenger ships built by the shipyards in Philadelphia for the West Coast, she had a fairly high bridge structure on top of the deckhouse as well as a high stack and high freeboard. This verticality contributed to an image of stockiness.

In the official directory known as *Merchant Ships of the United States* she was described as having a crew of twenty-four, a remarkably small number to provide service to the fifty or so passengers she was capable of carrying. A bit of quick arithmetic shows that with four deck officers, four engineers, two radio officers, six seamen, and six unlicensed personnel in the engineering department, that level of staffing would leave only two positions available for the entire steward's department. Although somewhat more than that minimum crew were aboard in 1915, the existence of that prescribed crewing level suggests that the *Santa Clara* was authorized to provide what today would be called "no frills" service.

She may have provided "no frills" safety as well. She apparently carried six lifeboats, but with her low level of manning that would allow only an officer and one deckhand to each lifeboat, and only about two men per boat to row. However, in all fairness to the ship, those may have been better ratios than existed in such passenger ships as the *Queen* and *Valencia*.

In her fifteen years of service she had apparently belonged to at least seven different companies: Kimball Steamship, the Dollar Line, Alaska Pacific Navigation Company, the "Big Three," C. P. Dodge, Northwestern Steamship, and North Pacific Steamship Company. It is apparent that finding the proper niche for the ship had not been easy. She had borne the name *Santa Clara* for the last ten of those years, apparently to commemorate an earlier steamer by that name, a pioneer in the North Coast lumber trade in the mid-nineteenth century.

She had experienced several major crises during her fifteen years of service. In 1907 en route between Seattle and Alaska she sprang a leak off Cape Flattery and was forced to return to port in a flooded condition.[2] In 1910 she survived a grounding off Table Rock near Cape Mendocino on the California coast,[3] and the same year struck the Humboldt Bay bar at Eureka and had to be towed into port with her decks nearly awash.[4] In 1911 entering the Golden Gate in fog she struck a rock off Point Bonita and was subsequently towed into port and beached in shallow water.[5] Thus she had experienced a considerable amount of wear and tear for a coastal vessel.

∽

She left Portland on Monday morning, 1 November 1915, under the command of Captain August Lofstedt. He had gone to sea twenty-six years earlier at age fourteen, originally serving in Scandinavian sailing ships before switching to steam, and had come to the north coast in about 1911, settling in Portland with his wife and four children. He had been captain of the larger and more prestigious *George Elder,* but when that ship had been taken off the Pacific Northwest run six months earlier he was transferred to the *Santa Clara.*[6] Now, his current command was en route to San Francisco with an intermediate stop at Coos Bay on the southern Oregon coast (where the major city was then generally known as Marshfield), and another at Eureka on the northern California coast. Aboard were approximately forty-eight passengers and thirty-two crewmen. The purser later said, "According to my count, there were forty-nine passengers and forty-four crew aboard the *Santa Clara,*"[7] but his crew figure seems unrealistically high.

She was operating under the flag of North Pacific Steamship Company, which had a total of three ships in service between Portland and several California ports, including some of the smaller ports in the Golden State such as Eureka, Monterey, Port San Luis, and Santa Barbara. She was equipped with wireless, and, in spite of her wooden hull, in all respects appeared to be an appropriate ship for the trade in which she was employed.

Like the passengers on the *Francis H. Leggett,* those on the *Santa Clara* seemed to be working class or lower middle class people, conscious of the need to save money on transportation whenever possible. However, Coos Bay, where most of the passengers were headed, had not yet been connected by rail to Portland, so there was no choice in mode of travel. Although Coos Bay had rail lines going inland to bring out lumber and coal, the connection with the mainline of the Southern Pacific at Eugene which was being built from the north had not been completed; that would come in 1916, providing for the first time an alternative in travel time and in cost. Thus, for now the only means of travel in and out of the area remained coastal steamers, and the *Santa Clara*, even with her maximum nine and a half knot speed, may have been the best of the lot.[8]

The weather had been typically blustery and unpleasant as the *Santa Clara* worked her way down the Oregon coast, but the skies had cleared and only a light southerly wind was blowing as she approached Coos Bay.[9] The passengers were looking forward to the port visit as a homecoming for many, and as a respite from seasickness for all. When the ship arrived off Coos Head moderately rough seas were running, and the bar was breaking at times. It was apparent that this would not be an easy trip across. It was then 4:30 in the afternoon, which in November meant that daylight would last only another hour at most. Time became important to the captain.

The bar at Coos Bay has always been treated with respect by mariners. One source estimates that at least sixty ships have come to grief in the entrance channel.[10] This channel had been provided with a protective rock jetty on the north spit in the 1890s, but the south side jetty was not completed until 1928. Consequently, the *Santa Clara* in 1915 faced the potential danger of a sand spit on the south side, inshore of which was the rocky bluff of Coos Head. The approach to the harbor is tricky; crossing the bar is effected on a heading a bit south of east, and then the channel swings sharply to the left on a north-northeasterly reach.

As she made her approach toward the entrance channel several seas slammed into the *Santa Clara*, spinning her off course. The helmsman tried to bring her back, but reported to the captain that she was not answering the helm properly. Captain Lofstedt blew a four-blast danger signal to alert any traffic that the ship was having difficulty maneuvering. Simultaneously, the ship touched heavily on a sand bar, but lurched ahead and cleared the shoal.[11]

The captain recognized that the steam-driven steering gear was not functioning properly. This vital part of the *Santa Clara*'s equipment had previously been subject to problems, and Lofstedt should have been prepared to shift to manual operation of the steering engine in an emergency such as this. Instead, he put the engine in reverse in the hope of returning to deeper water, but this maneuver failed to check the drift of the ship toward the spit on the south side of the entrance. When the ship touched the spit the captain gave her a thrust ahead with the engine to put her ashore, and the bow of the *Santa Clara* rode up onto the spit, where Lofstedt thought she would be safer than if she continued to be bounced about at the mercy of the seas with no steering control. Shortly, however, she was lifted off the sand by a wave on the rising tide which carried her farther to the south, eventually impaling the ship on a ragged rock near Coos Head.

With the ship's bottom now ruptured and the engine room rapidly flooding, the captain quickly ordered his wireless operator to send an SOS message. This man was either E. L. Reimers or O. E. Goodwin, each of whom was a shipboard radio operator carried in compliance with an updated 1910 law requiring radio equipment with a range of at least one hundred miles on American passenger ships. With the adoption of amendments to this law in 1912 such ships were required to have two operators if they engaged in voyages of more than two hundred miles and were certificated to carry at least fifty passengers. The *Santa Clara's* radio transmitter operated with one kilowatt of power on 710 kilocycles.[12]

At the time the SOS radio message was sent, lighthouse keeper Dunstan at the Cape Arago lighthouse telephoned the Coast Guard station to report the accident he had just witnessed, and to recommend that no approach from seaward be made as part of the rescue attempt. This lighthouse is not at Cape Arago, but on a rocky islet two and a half miles north. It occupies a commanding location with an excellent view of the approaches to the Coos Bay bar. It had once been the site of a lifesaving station, but that station had been shifted to Charleston, east of Coos Head.

Another report of the accident came in a radio message to the authorities ashore from a nearby ship, the outbound steam schooner *Adeline Smith*, that had witnessed the erratic movements of the *Santa*

Clara. Thus word of the accident was spread simultaneously from at least three sources, and help was soon on the way.

Rather than wait for this help, however, the captain ordered the lifeboats launched from the ship as she settled onto the seemingly precarious perch where the seas had deposited her. To facilitate embarkation into the boats he ordered that male passengers go to the upper deck, and women and children to the lower deck. Life preservers were distributed to passengers and crew, and the embarking of passengers into the boats was handled in an orderly fashion with no sign of panic.

Six boats were eventually launched, although press reports and interviews account for the activities of only about four. The first boat to be launched contained about a dozen women and children with members of the crew at the oars. The boat successfully cleared the side of the ship, and was making its way to the shore, a few hundred yards away, when it appeared to strike a rock in the surf line. A number of those who were in this boat were drowned in the surf, although some were pulled from the water by men who arrived at about the same time in the second boat.

Apparently this is what happened in the case of the Dunn family from Butte, Montana. All three members of this family, Bridget, the mother, Roy, the grown son, and Marguerite, the younger daughter, left the ship successfully in the early boats, but the boat in which the mother and daughter had been placed swamped at the beach. Roy Dunn in the following boat made a frantic effort to save both of them, as the second boat reached the beach ahead of the boat with the women in it. However, his mother disappeared from view before he could help her. As he explained, "She seemed to go down at once. I saw my little sister, so I waded out and swam in the breakers and got hold of her and brought her ashore. I saved her, but I could not save my mother."[13]

Another of the passengers in the first boat was Alice Church, a young woman from Marshfield. "I was put into the first lifeboat with about twenty others," she said later. "But we had not gone far before the boat was swamped. I didn't see any of the others after that."[14]

C. Phillips, the chief steward, recalled what happened after the first boat was upset in the surf: "The next two boats got away all right. In

The wooden coastal passenger ship *Santa Clara* was being savagely pounded in the surf when this picture was taken. (Coourtesy of Coos County Historical Society)

one of these we put an old man who was crippled, his wife, and a little child. The reason they were not in the first boat was that they remained in their stateroom and we did not find them until after the first boat left."[15] These people must have been the Crowleys, the only couple aboard who were listed as having an infant child with them. While Mrs. Crowley would survive the accident, Mr. Crowley's name did not appear on either the death list or the list of survivors. The thirteen-month-old child was identified as among the dead.

There were still women to be evacuated when it was time for the third boat to be launched. One of the passengers, W. T. Noyes who was bound for Eureka, found two seasick women in their cabin, Mrs. D. T. Ballard of Sedro Woolley, Washington, and her daughter, Lucille. He made sure they were in that departing boat, and they subsequently reached shore safely. Noyes later was washed overboard, but swam ashore with the aid of an oar for flotation.[16]

Another hero was not as lucky. Robert Shearer, a winch driver on the *Santa Clara*, after arriving safely at the beach, had gone into the surf to help others. After rescuing two small children he went back to a swamped lifeboat to help a woman in distress, but neither he nor the woman were seen again.[17]

During the evacuation of the passengers the lumber-laden *Adeline Smith*, under the command of Captain B. W. Olson, stood by in the channel to render whatever assistance she could, but there was really no opportunity to provide aid from another vessel. Later, Olson came ashore to assist with the operation of the breeches buoy, a skill he had perfected several years earlier when he rescued the crew of a lumber schooner by that means in about the same location.[18] The seagoing hopper dredge *Michie* of the Army Corps of Engineers also stood by, but could not get close to the *Santa Clara*. The Coast Guard rescue party, heeding the advice from the lighthouse keeper, made no attempt to approach with a boat, and instead made their way by land to the scene of the accident.

As darkness came the abandon-ship operation continued. Although the seas were moderating, a cold rain began to fall, adding to the misery of those survivors on the beach who sought warmth and comfort, and to those who assisted in the rescue. The stretch of beach where the boats and individual survivors had landed was about twenty miles from Marshfield at a spot called Bastendorff Beach. There, a summer dwelling had been pressed into service as a rescue center.

Some of the early newspaper accounts erroneously associated this location with Shore Acres, but the nearby house by that name which was owned by a local lumber magnate was a mansion, not a cottage, by Oregon coast standards. Its grounds survive today as a state park noted for its gardens. Other accounts describe the structure used by the survivors as located at Mussel Beach, and as "a small cabin on the beach built by young boys as a club house." This designation seems to fit the small and sparsely furnished structure better than does that of house or cottage.

Even though local people had brought food and clothing to the scene, in the darkness there was no way that individual survivors could know where to turn for help when they found themselves on the beach in an exhausted condition. Bonfires were lighted by local residents along the bluffs ringing the shoreline, but the heavy rain subdued the light from these fires.

The final boat was launched from the stranded ship to bring the captain and the remaining crewmen ashore. Fifteen men were in this boat when one end hung up in the falls, an accident sometimes called "cockbilling," and the boat capsized shortly after it entered the water. Chief Engineer Deshar, Chief Mate Tessel, and four others swam to the shore, not an easy accomplishment even with the buoyancy provided by a lifejacket. As the chief mate explained, "...Captain Lofstedt was the last to go. Just as our boat was being lowered she upset from the davits and I did not see Captain Lofstedt after that. The sea was moderating when I began to come through the surf."[19]

With respect to survival skills, it is interesting to speculate how any mariners on the northwest coast could have learned to swim. Certainly, the cold water of the ocean beaches of the area provided no opportunity to develop such ability, so the men who learned to swim must have done so in the back bays and inland lakes whose waters were warmed enough by the sun to make swimming tolerable. Mariners of this era were not known for their swimming ability, and thus life jackets were doubly important to them. Unlike some of the other shipwrecks of the Pacific Northwest, there was no problem with life jackets aboard the *Santa Clara*, either in quantity or quality, and this fact would increase the survival rate aboard the little ship.

Although two crewmen from the upset boat were drowned, the captain and six others managed to get back aboard the *Santa Clara*. Once back on the ship, the captain and the remaining crewmen, with no lifeboat now aboard, had to look for other means of escape. They soon broke out the Lyle gun, set it up just abaft the funnel, and began to fire it. On the second try they were able to put a line across a tree on the bluffs above the beach, and that line was subsequently found by the Coast Guard crew which had struggled to the area by team and wagon, arriving at 9:00 P.M.[20]

This crew brought with them a line-throwing gun, lines, tackles, and breeches buoy. Immediately the Coast Guardsmen began rigging the breeches buoy, and at 9:30 P.M. a sailor named Carlson was the first crewman from the *Santa Clara* to come ashore via this rescue route. He was soon followed by the five other crewmen. Captain Lofstedt, in the best tradition of the sea, was then the last to leave the ship.[21] The evacuation of the ship was thus completed about six hours after the vessel had originally struck, but the difficult tasks of locating and helping survivors on the beach, as well as determining who had survived and who had not, remained ahead.

Unfortunately, the purser had lost his passenger list while coming ashore in one of the boats. Apparently another copy must have existed, however, because within a day the newspapers were printing the passenger list along with the list of survivors and those known to be dead. The passenger list provided by the steamship company contained the names of forty-seven passengers; the survivor and death toll list compiled by newspapers with those names totaled about the same number. Numerous inconsistencies existed between the two lists, but through resourceful pairing up of names which had some common elements the mis-matches could be markedly reduced.

To the forty-seven names on the official passenger list should be added at least one other name, the fourth member of a family traveling aboard, only three of whom were on the passenger list. Six passengers were recognized as having died in the wreck which should have left forty-two survivors, but only thirty-five passengers were accounted for in Coos Bay, leaving seven unaccounted for. Some of the missing group, however, may not have boarded the ship at Portland or at Astoria where it had stopped briefly, although it is equally possible that some were actually lost as a result of the wreck.

The tally which was made at Coos Bay of identified survivors also included eight to thirteen additional names which were not on the passenger list, as well the body of one victim not on the original list. (The range of additional names reflects problems in counting, such as the case of three women who were reported at one time to have survived the wreck, and at another time to have never been aboard.) At the lower range these additional names, together with those of the thirty-five identified survivors and six victims from the passenger list, would agree roughly with the figure of forty-nine thought to be aboard. However, some of the extra people may actually have been crew members, a determination which was hard to make since no crew list ever appeared in the newspapers, even though thirty-two different individuals were named as crewmen in various stories—including five who were dead or missing. Also, some of the eight to thirteen people not on the passenger list might conceivably have been imposters, wishing to benefit from the largesse shown survivors by the local community.

In any case, the firm number of casualties identified by name appeared to be twelve. The official report of the accident filed by the local inspectors of the Steamboat Inspection Service would later confirm that the total loss of life was twelve, seven passengers and five crewmen.[22] However, the maximum possible number of casualties could be as high as nineteen if those persons unaccounted for are presumed lost, or even higher if there were others not on the passenger list who also became victims.

This identification problem has been noted in earlier publications, including Gibbs' classic book on West Coast shipwrecks which has always carried the death toll in the *Santa Clara* disaster as sixteen to twenty-one, while the other shipwrecks in his book have generally carried a fixed total, albeit one open to adjustments in many cases. It has been suggested that the death toll at Coos Head could never be established definitively because some of the people who had survived the accident may have gone home from the beach and never reported to anyone. With 85 percent of the passengers destined for Coos Bay, that explanation makes sense. The problem was so pressing that the local newspaper, the Coos Bay *Times*, even ran stories asking survivors to check in with the authorities if they had not done so already.[23]

One account provides a suggestion of how those missing people may have left the scene:

> Some survivors who were in good condition hiked out on a forest trail through rain, fog, and darkness in order to get to town, some eighteen miles away. Most, if not all of them, probably got a ride in one of the cars they met on the road from Charleston to Sunset Bay. Tom Wasson was one of those who made several trips to town in his car, carrying women and children. His wife, and others who lived in the vicinity of the wrecked ship, helped out at the cabin on the beach.[24]

In the event it did happen that way, the reported toll of the missing would, of course, be inflated. On the other hand, if there were bodies that were never found, the number of casualties would have been understated.

On the day following the shipwreck, while tugs and small craft cruised along the surf line looking for bodies, men walked up and down the beach for the same reason, poking into driftwood and behind rocks. Ironically, with the sea now calm the wreck of the *Santa Clara* was largely out of the water at low tide, and could almost be reached by walking out on the relatively flat beach. Photographs of the scene confirm these conditions. Those officials with reason to visit the wreck found the staterooms dry and in good condition. From all appearances everyone could have stayed aboard, and been able to reach shore leisurely the next day, hardly getting their feet wet en route. Instead, an undetermined number of people were now dead. It was easy to speculate that Captain Lofstedt may have made the same mistake that Captain Johnson of the *Valencia* had made in launching boats too soon, particularly at night.

During the next few days a debacle took place that was to embarrass the community. The ship's cargo, valued at about twenty-five thousand

At low tide the curious and the greedy, intent on looting, began to approach the ship as she rested on the beach. (Courtesy of Coos County Historical Society)

dollars, contained considerable merchandise for the Christmas trade. After initially making sure that no looting would take place, the company officials then announced that in the absence of insurance, the adjustment of which would have tied up the cargo, local merchants were invited aboard to salvage their portion of the cargo. In the words of a local newspaper reporter, ". . . bedlam and chaos broke loose at the beach and the wreck yesterday when the pirates and the merchants together went aboard the *Santa Clara* to broach the cargo."[25] Hundreds of people made an orgy out of looting the ship during the next few days.

Some of the looters, in an effort to get at cargo stowed in a lower hold, tried both dynamite and fire to speed up the process. Eventually, the ship caught fire, and sustained considerable damage. During all of this freelance salvage operation, no one exercised any responsibility for the cargo. Neither county authorities nor the U.S. Marshal in Portland believed that they had any jurisdiction. The local newspaper editor observed that this was "one of the most famous cases of looting on the marine records. . . . Had the *Santa Clara* and her cargo and people been lost in the wildest part of the world the owners of the goods aboard would have had no less protection than they did within half a mile of the entrance of Coos Bay."[26] The local district attorney also expressed regrets over the looting, and citing precedent in admiralty law noted that "the disposition of goods found on or beneath the sea, or thrown upon the shore, is usually a fair index of the degree of civilization reached by the people within whose domain such property is found."[27]

One bright spot in the looting process occurred when someone found a dog in a crate in the hold, an Irish setter named Erin Kildare which belonged to a local doctor. The dog had been shipped home to his master after spending time in Portland. Upon being released the dog leaped overboard and swam to shore where he was reunited with his former caretaker who had been anxiously waiting on the beach.[28]

The community mourned the victims with a memorial service a few days after the accident which concluded with the singing of "Nearer My God to Thee."[29] Her deckhouse already destroyed by the fire, the ship broke up quickly during the days ahead, and soon there was only a jumble of wooden planks on the beach to remind the world of the passing of the SS *Santa Clara*. The most official memento salvaged from the wreck was the ship's whistle, which for many years thereafter was a fixture at the Weyerhaeuser Lumber Company mill at Coos Bay.

Life went on for the living, and for those responsible for the care of the dead. Within a week of the accident, five survivors of the *Santa Clara* and the bodies of several victims sailed south aboard the tiny steamer *F. A. Kilburn* which carried eighty passengers to Eureka and San Francisco.[30] The survivors quite possibly would have preferred to go by train, but transportation in and out of Coos Bay was still the exclusive domain of the steamship.

ᔓ

The subsequent investigation of the accident focused on the problem with the steering gear. In spite of the pressures from the *Valencia* investigation in 1906 to relocate inspectors regularly, B. B. Whitney was again in charge of the deck department aspects of the investigation, and was joined this time by Harry C. Lord who was responsible for the engineering aspects of the inquiry. Inasmuch as the steering engine was a piece of equipment over which each department aboard ship shared responsibilities, both inspectors carried equal weight in the determinations of the inquiry. The hearings took place in two locations, with Captain Lofstedt appearing before the northwestern inspectors at Portland, and the balance of the crew testifying before the California inspectors at San Francisco.[31]

Testimony made clear that the *Santa Clara* had two back-up systems for steering in case of a failure of the steam-powered engine. One was a manual system, in which a steering wheel on the main deck at the stern of the ship could be linked directly to the geared quadrant in the steering engine flat directly below. This quadrant was attached directly to the rudder post, and as it moved so did the rudder. This manual system, with no machine or hydraulic assistance, could at times require considerable physical effort to steer, but it had no related components which could fail.

The other system was a last-resort method, making use of what was called relieving tackle. It consisted of fairleads in the hull through which wires could be led from pad eyes on the rudder itself to the

This view of the *Santa Clara*, impaled on a rock below Coos Head, personifies the dangers of the Oregon coast. (Courtesy of Coos County Historical Society)

drums of winches on deck. It enabled the ship to be steered by a man at each drum taking up or easing out wire on the drum, thus pulling directly on the back edge of the rudder and changing its angle. This procedure could also be used if a ship had lost a rudder and had jury-rigged some kind of improvised rudder from hatchboards or some other material. It was obviously used only when a ship was *in extremis*, but when her crew still had enough time to do the complicated rigging which was required.

Although electric and hydraulic steering systems later supplanted steam steering engines, these arrangements for manual steering and emergency steering by winch remained much the same for merchant ships for many decades after this time. During this time shipboard emergency drills often called for shifting steering control to the after station.

In the case of the *Santa Clara*, the use of the manual steering system, with guidance from a compass which was provided at the after steering station, would have been the viable alternative to using the faulty steam steering engine directed from the bridge. At the hearing in

Portland Captain Lofstedt explained what was wrong with that steering engine:

> I would state that the steering gear has been bucking frequently which the whole crew on board can testify to, and the chief engineer had it to pieces time after time, but it did not seem to get any better. It seemed like that whenever the ship got into rough water, where there was a pressure on the rudder, the engine had not power to put the rudder over to starboard or port, as the case might be.[32]

When this explanation eventually was forwarded to the office of the Steamboat Inspection Service in Washington, DC, the supervising inspectors there asked for further explanation of the defect in the steering engine. The local inspectors replied that all they knew about it was in the statement provided by the captain. Again, as in earlier investigations into the causes of maritime disasters, it was easy to sense the lack of acuity shown by the local inspectors in trying to identify the cause of the wreck.

One witness from earlier voyages, a second mate who had served on the *Santa Clara* in the spring of 1914, deposed that the bucking problem existed at that time, but was not considered serious. The ship was running between San Francisco and San Pedro at that time, a run that would have generally provided better weather than that found on the North Coast. He also remembered no steering casualty drills, but he had served aboard for only two months.[33]

The inspectors determined that the steering engine had "bucked a number of times while running down the Columbia River on this last trip," and that on earlier trips the engineers spent considerable time in trying to make it work satisfactorily. The cause of the problem, in the professional opinion of the inspectors, was to be found in the valves of the engine which "were in a leaky condition, thus affecting its power by admitting steam to both sides of the pistons, a condition that could be bettered only in a machine shop or such place where there were adequate facilities for doing such work."[34]

Since this had not been done, and since the engine had been kept in service, with the ship's master fully aware of the problem, the inspectors concluded he was responsible for the loss of the vessel and the lives of those who died. At the end of the hearing, Captain Lofstedt pleaded guilty to a charge of negligence in having failed to use the hand steering gear.

The outcome of such a plea was normally the suspension or revocation of the license of the officer at fault by the inspectors. In early December 1915, inspectors Whitney and Lord of the Steamboat Inspection Service, in a gesture that acknowledged that the accident could have been prevented by the correction of a known defect, predictably revoked the license of Captain August Lofstedt.[35] It was not the end of his career, however; he rebuilt his tarnished reputation by working several years on tugs and dredges, and subsequently became a Columbia River bar pilot, a position he held for a quarter of a century.

Apparently the inspectors assumed no responsibility for the accident themselves, even though they had established the fact that the defect in the steering engine had existed for at least a year and a half, during which time the ship would have been subject to an annual inspection by the Steamboat Inspection Service.

The loss of the *Santa Clara* was a hard blow for the North Pacific Steamship Company. Two years later, with the loss of the *Roanoke* off the central California coast, the company was left with a single ship and very limited prospects. In 1919 the company was absorbed by the Admiral Line, and the role of the little niche steamship company that had sent genuine, albeit diminutive, passenger liners to the smaller ports came to an end. The North Coast had claimed yet another victim.

Chapter Eight

J. A. Chanslor: Tanker in Trouble

The tanker *J. A. Chanslor* was not the kind of ship one would expect to encounter in a book on major maritime disasters. Unlike the unlucky *Rosecrans,* which had been converted to a tanker from a cargo/passenger vessel, the *J. A. Chanslor* had been built from the keel up as a modern tankship. Such vessels in their first two decades of service on the West Coast had acquired excellent reputations for reliability and safety.

Built by the Newport News Shipbuilding Company in 1910, she was a fine example of the new built-for-the-purpose tankers that were becoming major players in the distribution of petroleum products from California refineries to locations over the entire length of the West Coast. Her proportions were ample for that era, with dimensions of 378 feet in length, 52 feet in beam, and 30 feet in depth. With a gross tonnage of 4,938 and a net tonnage of 3,121, she approached in size a group of mass-produced tankers being built by the U.S. Shipping Board in 1919, the same year the *Chanslor* found herself in peril. With a reciprocating steam engine rated at 2,000 horsepower, she was, in all respects, a thoroughly modern ship.

In keeping with the practice of tanker operators, the ship had been named for a prominent figure in the oil industry. In this case, the honoree was a southern California oil man, J. A. Chanslor, who owned an independent oil company and may also have been on the board of Associated Oil, the owner of the ship. Associated Oil was the predecessor

The *J. A. Chanslor* of the Associated Oil Company was a modern tanker with a good safety record before her accident at Cape Blanco. (Courtesy of San Francisco Maritime National Historical Park)

company of Tidewater and its well-known "Flying A" logo on the West Coast.[1]

Unlike steamship companies which could be readily started and terminated, tanker operators were generally major oil companies in business for the long haul, literally and figuratively. Unfortunately, however, maritime historians have sometimes paid little attention to these firms as ship operators. The status of the marine fleet of each of these companies as an adjunct to another primary purpose, the processing and sale of petroleum products produced by the company, has probably been responsible for the neglect they have experienced at the hands of these traditional historians. However, in the coastal waters of the United States these companies were major players in maritime commerce, both in the number of ships they operated and in the tonnage they carried.

On the West Coast, in addition to Associated Oil, tankers were operated by a number of other companies, including Standard Oil of California, Socony-Vacuum, Union Oil, Richfield, Gulf, and Texaco. Initially these ships carried refined products north, but soon, following a general trend in the oil industry, refineries were built at northern sites some distance from the source of production. This resulted in tankships going north from California carrying crude oil to refineries in Portland and Puget Sound, a trade that required frequent tanker voyages.

In one of the ironies that seem to characterize disasters, while the news of the grounding and breakup of the *Rosecrans* on the Columbia bar with a loss of thirty lives still dominated the marine news of the West Coast in January, 1913, the *J. A. Chanslor* made the shipping columns a few days later by going aground in the Columbia River near Astoria. After a thousand tons of oil had been pumped out into barges, the ship was refloated and proceeded on her way upriver to Portland.[2]

∽

In December 1919 the *Chanslor* was off Cape Blanco, Oregon, under the command of Captain A. A. Sawyer. Sawyer had been chief mate of the Associated Oil Company's tanker *Frank H. Buck* in 1914, and had commanded the lifeboat launched from that ship to rescue survivors of the *Francis H. Leggett,* which had foundered off the northern Oregon coast in heavy seas. The *Frank H. Buck* and her captain, George B. Macdonald, went on to an outstanding career in the Navy during World War I, but it is not clear whether Sawyer also remained with the ship during this time.[3]

Although some of the shipwreck books indicate that the *Chanslor* was northbound with a cargo of thirty thousand barrels of oil loaded at Goleta, near Santa Barbara, she was actually southbound in ballast from Portland to San Francisco. The round trip from southern California to Portland had not been without difficulty. The *Chanslor* had reached Portland with a cargo of fuel oil on 14 December after an arduous trip up the Columbia during which she was trapped for a day by ice near Longview, Washington.[4] After pumping out at the tanker terminal at Linnton she departed about 8:30 A.M. on Wednesday 17 December, bound down the ice-cluttered river for the open sea. She cleared the bar with no trouble and reported her position at 8 P.M. that day as fifteen miles south of the Columbia River. That was her last radio report.

The following afternoon, on the lonely stretch of coastal waters off Cape Blanco in Oregon, Captain Sawyer found himself trying to outmaneuver widespread fog. A year earlier one of the pioneer tankers of the West Coast, the *George Loomis* of Standard Oil of California, had vanished completely between Cape Mendocino where she was last seen and Coos Bay, her destination, and was never heard from again.[5] Recalling that mystery must have given pause to any tanker captain passing through these waters.

Tanker captains, like those of steam schooners, have often shown a tendency to shorten the point-to-point mileage of coastal trips by rounding the headlands as close as possible. This may be what the *Chanslor* under Captain Sawyer was doing on 17 December 1919. As noted earlier, the Oregon coast lacks turning points where a few precious minutes can be shaved off the elapsed time of the voyage, so if any shaving is to be done it must be done at Cape Blanco.

Cape Blanco is home to the most westerly lighthouse in Oregon, and second only to Cape Flattery as the most westerly lighthouse of the contiguous forty-eight states. The cape itself is a wind-swept promontory, with a few trees on its lee side. The light structure is not only the oldest lighthouse on the Oregon coast, dating from 1870, but the highest above the sea, with the elevation of its base at 245 feet, plus the fifty-nine foot height of its tower, giving it a visibility of twenty-two miles. Curiously, it has no foghorn, an adaptation made because the height of the station tends to dissipate the sound from the signal.

Although there is no large reef projecting seaward from Cape Blanco, there are numerous clusters of rocks along the adjacent coast that represent hazards to navigation for ships rounding the cape too closely, particularly on the south side. Most mariners respect the need to be well offshore when rounding the cape, and surprisingly few ships have grounded there. Apparently Captain Sawyer had intended to be five miles off, a conservative enough distance, but he had not counted on being set toward the shore. As he observed later in newspaper interviews, "We were right on our course at noon on Thursday, and at 6 P.M. we were wrecked on a rock five miles off our course. A strong cross-current, unobserved, had caused the mischief."[6]

The captain's statement suggests that he had a reliable noon position from which to navigate by dead reckoning through the fog he would encounter in the afternoon. The troublesome "mischief" of being set badly off course had occurred in sea conditions that were not particularly rough at the time, at least for ships. For lifeboats, which would soon become the only hope for the crew, the state of the sea was a different matter. Furthermore, the unusually cold air would later compound the "mischief" as the weather began to deteriorate.

As a result of the unanticipated conditions, the *J. A. Chanslor*, off course and surrounded by the dusk and fog, hit an offshore rock north of Cape Blanco, and quickly split into two pieces. The forward section of the hull, from the bow aft through the midship house, had enough buoyancy to stay afloat briefly. The after section, containing the engineering spaces and most of the accommodations for the crew, sank quickly.

Photos of the wreck site later showed the bow of the ship above water about a half mile from shore in a broad bight of the ocean which had several rocky islets within it. The location appeared to lie between Gull Rock, a mile north of Cape Blanco, and Castle Rock, which is a half mile farther north and east.[7] Local sources identified the site to the media as Blacklock Point, and provided a homey flavor to the story by pointing out that the "nearest neighbors are the Hughes brothers,

This photograph of the bow section of the *Chanslor* was taken from the nearby beach. After the ship broke up, the stern disappeared quickly. (Courtesy of the Curry County Historical Society)

dairymen, who live under the lee of Cape Blanco."[8] The Portland *Oregonian* noted that it was the same location at which the *South Portland* in October of 1903 went aground with a loss of twenty-two lives.[9]

There were about forty men aboard the *Chanslor*, although some accounts place the number nearer fifty. The crew list subsequently published in the San Francisco *Chronicle* listed thirty-nine shipboard billets by the name of the incumbent, but indicated that several changes may have been made just before sailing. The most unusual feature of this crew list was that the ship's engine-room crew seemed larger than normal, with six firemen, three oilers, and three watertenders. Those twelve men made up a total that was double the number of certificated personnel normally carried in the engine rooms of steamships of that size and complexity.

With the evening meal completed in the dining area on the stern, the deck crew members on watch and the mates who lived amidships had returned to the deckhouse below the bridge. At that hour probably every man in the crew was awake, normally a beneficial factor in determining how many crewmen survive accidents. Captain Sawyer described what happened next:

> When the *Chanslor* struck she seemed to part amidship, almost at once. The bow rested on the rock, but the stern and after half of the hull dropped away and disappeared. None of the men in the engine-room had a chance to escape alive. Only the men forward were enabled to reach the lifeboat, which we launched with ten men aboard, among them First Officer W. H. Weeks, Second Officer Oliver F. Norton, Third Officer E. Rose, and Steward Frank Cashen. It was dark, but we could see the Cape Blanco light.[10]

These guarded observations by the captain, made within the next two days, were noticeably short on specific details of how the ship had been navigated before striking the rocks. Nothing was said about the ship's speed, courses steered, whether soundings had been taken, the use of lookouts, and whether any forewarning existed. The reference to the visibility of the light from Cape Blanco also raises the question as to whether that same visibility had existed earlier, when it would have been useful in preventing the ship from getting so close to the shore.

The one lifeboat that had been successfully launched drifted through the night. In the morning two additional men who were found nearby floating with the aid of a plank were pulled aboard, making a total of a dozen survivors at that point. One of these men soon died, however. As quartermaster William Merkel, one of the three ultimate survivors, described this part of the drama:

> We came in sight of the two sailors Friday. They had evidently been floating about all night, but they had stuck out with a fierce determination, but only to die on our hands afer we had taken them into the lifeboat. Their support was a staging that was used on the *Chanslor* by painters, and when the ship went down they found this refuge after having been down in the water and floating and swimming about on coming to the surface.[11]

The stage described by Merkel is a plank a dozen or so feet long with two cross bars underneath and perpendicular to it from which it is suspended by lines from above. The cross bars hold the stage away from the surface of the hull or deckhouse while sailors sit or stand upon it as they paint.

Because of the quartering of deck officers in the midship section of tankers, all the deck officers of the ship were clustered in this one lifeboat, along with a few men from other departments whose duties, or survival instincts, had taken them to the midship section of the ship when the ship struck the rock.

⌒

According to newspaper accounts, the accident had occurred suddenly and apparently without any sense of pending danger existing aboard the ship. However, an account published many years later by Monroe Upton, who in 1921 had been a shipmate of the survivor William Merkel on another Associated Oil tanker, claims that Merkel had been the lookout on the bow of the *Chanslor*, and had cried out "White water ahead!", a warning that was disregarded because it was at variance with the plotted position of the ship.[12] At the time of the accident a local newspaper had reported that Merkel did issue such an alarm, and that the captain was then en route to the bridge.[13]

Although not required to do so by law, Associated Transportation Company, the shipping division of Associated Oil, had installed low-powered radio equipment aboard its ships, enough to meet the needs of coastal service. The *Chanslor*'s transmitter used a frequency of 860 kilocycles and a power of one kilowatt, giving it a range of one hundred to five hundred miles.[14] However, there had been no opportunity to send any kind of distress message. In fact, although on tankers of that era the radio room and the operator's quarters were normally amidships, the ship's radio officer, Fred E. Tambaugh, was apparently still lingering on the stern of the vessel after supper. Thus, the ship's radio sat unused through her moment of crisis.

Tambaugh was no stranger to shipwrecks, nor to the section of the coast where the *Chanslor* was now aground. He had been radio operator on the *Sinaloa* when that vessel was wrecked off Cape Blanco in June 1917, and on that occasion had been rescued by the Coast Guard.[15] The *Sinaloa* was salvaged, and returned to service.

Not only did no radio message leave the *Chanslor*, but there were no visual emergency signals sent toward the shore from the ship. There had barely been enough time for the men amidships to get into the lifeboat. The seas had picked up, and although the boat was successfully launched with no resultant casualties, getting safely ashore in it would be a real challenge. As Captain Sawyer explained, "We rowed toward shore at first, but soon realized that there was no chance to land on the rocks in the rough sea, and so turned oceanward. We fired rockets in the hope of attracting attention, but without avail."[16]

Again there are significant differences between newspaper accounts and local recollections concerning whether anyone at Cape Blanco Lighthouse or elsewhere ashore became aware of the plight of the ship and her crew for the next twenty-four hours. The newspapers generally reported that the keeper of the Cape Blanco light eventually saw the wreck late Friday afternoon and made out the identity of the ship, after which he notified the Coast Guard at Bandon.[17]

However, a local source told a different story. Patrick Masterson in a history of the Port Orford area claimed that the wreck was sighted on Friday morning, 19 December, by members of the Hughes family who owned the ranch which fronted on the ocean near the mouth of the Sixes River. By this account, they immediately notified James Hughes, keeper of the Cape Blanco light, who in turn notified authorities in Port Orford and in Bandon.[18]

Deputy Sheriff Howard W. Jetter and three men from Port Orford then took a double-ended surfboat overland to the mouth of the Sixes River, where it was launched. A breaker upset the boat in the surf line, capsizing it. Jetter drowned, and the other men washed ashore, exhausted but alive. A telephone message was subsequently sent from the Hughes ranch to Captain Robert Johnson of the Coast Guard station in Bandon, telling him of the accident to the surfboat.[19] Presumably, by this time Johnson already knew about the wreck of the *Chanslor*. However, no reference to this fatal rescue attempt appears in most newspaper accounts.

Bandon was the location of the nearest lifesaving station at the mouth of the Coquille River, about seventeen miles north of Cape Blanco. Although as distances go along the Oregon coast that station was reasonably close to the wreck scene, all that a rescue crew from that location could now have hoped to do was to find the ship's boat and tow it across the narrow bar at that port, itself a very dangerous maneuver. It should be noted at this point that although rescues from the shore were now a responsibility of the U.S. Coast Guard, the old nomenclature of the Lifesaving Service prevailed; thus, officials with the courtesy title of "captain" at the lifesaving stations did not hold that rank in the Coast Guard.

Captain Johnson recognized that the Coquille bar was impassable at that time for his powered lifeboat. So he and his crew set out overland toward the Hughes Ranch over roads described as very bad, but ultimately were unable to launch their boat and render any assistance. Because no boats had been launched from shore, the community of Bandon was critical of Captain Johnson and his Coast Guardsmen for their ineffectiveness as rescuers. Johnson became defensive, pointing out that his station was seriously undermanned and that most of his men were green recruits. After he accosted and threatened two of his critics, he realized that he had overreacted, and subsequently presented himself before a municipal judge who fined him five dollars for creating a disturbance.[20] Eventually the Coast Guard made an internal investigation of the Bandon station, the results of which have not been located.

In the meantime several ships had diverted from their courses to search for survivors of the wreck. These included the steam schooner *Johanna Smith*, and the passenger ships *Rose City, Admiral Schley*, and the *City of Topeka*, which had figured in the search for survivors of the *Valencia* thirteen years earlier. None of these ships met with success.[21]

Captain Sawyer's description of the ordeal in the lifeboat continued:

> Friday morning we found ourselves several miles out and some distance north of the wreck. We hoped a passing vessel would see us, but none did. Toward night I observed that the men were dropping away from the boat, one by one, from exposure. It was bitterly cold, and they had been working continuously for twenty-four hours to keep the boat afloat in the mountainous seas.
>
> As darkness approached I saw that to stay out another night meant certain death for all of us, so I ordered an attempt made to find a landing place. We rowed along for some distance, and must have passed the Coquille's mouth not more than a mile or so out, but we could see nothing of the harbor entrance in the thick weather.
>
> When we ran into the first line of breakers we headed straight for the beach. An enormous breaker struck the boat and sent it flying end over end and clear of the water. Every man was thrown out. All wore life preservers, but some drowned afloat because heavy breakers were constantly breaking over our heads. It was only by sheer luck that anybody emerged alive.
>
> After I was washed ashore I fell asleep from exhaustion and lay in the sand for a number of hours. When I awoke it was raining heavily. I saw a light some distance away and made for it. After walking several hours I arrived at Bandon. It seems to me quite impossible that any of our men who failed to get ashore yesterday can still be alive.[22]

Indeed, no one but the men in the boat did survive, and only two of those among the captain's original eleven companions in that boat were alive after the pummeling they encountered in the surf. One was Earl W. Dooley, a messman, who had joined the ship only a few days earlier at Linnton, the tanker terminal near Portland. The other was the quartermaster, William Merkle.

Dooley explained how he, as a member of the steward's department, was fortunate enough to be in the lifeboat launched from midships:

> We were creeping along in the fog and the ship struck the reef about six o'clock Thursday night. The distress signal sounded at once and all was excitement. I rushed to the forward deck to find a means of escape, but the ship had broken in two and the after portion was sinking in no time. On the forward deck there were about ten of us, as nearly as I can remember, but most of the engineers, stewards, and oilers and sailors were aft and went down with that part of the vessel.[23]

Apparently several of the men aft recognized the seriousness of the situation and rushed forward along with Dooley in time to reach midships before the catwalk between that area and the stern was destroyed. Dooley later indicated there were two oilers in the boat that got away. He continued with his account of the escape in the lifeboat:

> All day Friday we were driven northerly in a bitter cold wind and heavy rain. We did have a few sea biscuits, but no water. When darkness came Friday night we were about all in, and after dark sighted shore and heard the breakers roaring. It was then we decided to take our chance in trying to run the breakers.[24]

The boat had come ashore about four miles north of Bandon at a point called Whiskey Run Beach, where a small stream with that name empties into the ocean.

Dooley's account of the boat being buffeted in the surf follows closely that of Captain Sawyer. When questioned about his background, Dooley told reporters he had no real home address, but lived wherever employment took him. Union officials, when asked by newspaper reporters about the names and addresses of other crewmen who may have joined the ship at Portland, confirmed that seamen commonly had no home address on file with their employment records.

Newspaper accounts differed widely on how the survivors reached safety once ashore. According to the account in the *Oregonian,* the quartermaster Merkel had been in the best condition of the three men in the boat. Aware that Captain Sawyer had been badly bruised in coming ashore, Merkel, with the help of Dooley, half-buried Sawyer in the sand to keep him warm, after which he struck out alone for Bandon. Merkel arrived there at about 7 P.M. on Friday, bringing the first word of the survivors, after which the Coast Guard went out to look for the other two men.[25] This explanation differs from Captain Sawyer's account in the *Chronicle* in which he spoke of sleeping "a number of hours" before walking "to Bandon," presumably by himself,[26] and from the version reported in *The Western World* of Bandon which had the captain sleeping for an hour and walking to the lighthouse, across the river from Bandon.[27]

The latter paper reported that Merkel was the first survivor to reach safety, arriving at the Coquille River lighthouse near the north jetty in early evening with the first word of the shipwreck. Somewhat later Dooley and Captain Sawyer arrived together at a nearby house on the north side of the harbor entrance.

When he reached safety Captain Sawyer was admitted to the hospital in Bandon and put under sedation. He had received a fractured rib, was suffering from exposure, and was expected to develop pneumonia from his congested lungs. Dooley, too, may have been hospitalized, while Merkel was looked after by concerned townspeople.

Beach patrols at Bandon had reported seeing two men in a life raft off the mouth of the Coquille River, and that one of the men appeared to have jumped into the water in an attempt to reach the shore. However, no bodies were found in this location following the reported sighting, so it was not clear what happened to these men.[28]

At the time that the metropolitan newspapers abandoned their coverage of the disaster, five or six days after it had occurred, only four bodies had been recovered, all of which were from the group of men who had been on the midship section of the vessel. The bodies were identified as those of C. Pfantzsch, the ship's boatswain; W. H. Reese, the chief mate; Edward A. Rose, the third mate; and Adolph Hohne, a seaman. The confusion that often surrounds names of shipwreck victims was present in this case as well, in that Reese was identified as the chief mate but Captain Sawyer spoke of a man named Weeks as his mate. Perhaps the interviewer had heard "Weeks" for "Reese" from the lips of the sedated captain.

The survivors agreed that the hero of their experience in trying to reach shore was Adolph Hohne, who was one of the occupants of the lifeboat when it overturned in the surf. Described as the most physically fit of any of the men, he was seen swimming back and forth between men who were fighting for their lives in the water, getting them back into the boat only to have it overturn again. This rescue effort was maintained until a wave smashed Hohne against the boat, breaking his jaw. He subsequently drifted away, and his body was later found on the beach.[29]

Among the crew who perished were several men who were relatives of well-placed men ashore. One was Francis Jackson, second assistant engineer, whose father, C. S. Jackson, was publisher of the *Oregon Journal*, Portland's other daily newspaper. Another was M. J. Jones, who was thought to be aboard as a replacement for one of the engineers on the crew list; he was the brother of Hugh B. Jones, marine superintendent for Associated Oil, owner of the ship. Special efforts were made by the well-to-do families of these two men to find their bodies, but to no avail. As was the case in most shipwrecks involving loss of life, other less-affluent families also sent representatives to locate bodies of loved ones, again with no results. Some of the same confusion as to who was aboard that characterized other coastal shipwrecks also followed the loss of the *Chanslor*.

The forward part of the hull of the ship moved around somewhat during the days following the accident, generally working its way further inshore. Local sources report that the ship's black cat clung to the protruding mast for many days. For sixty years this mast was visible at low tide, before finally disappearing completely about 1980.[30]

As in the case of most shipwrecks by grounding, a certain amount of looting took place before the wreck broke up. One of the prizes taken from the captain's cabin was a table inlaid with silver. Perhaps the most visible piece of memorabilia from the *Chanslor* was the lifeboat salvaged from Whiskey Run; it was brought to Bandon and placed on a bluff overlooking the Coquille River lighthouse, where it remained for many years.[31] If anything else remains of the ship today, divers can look for it in the location listed in the new books on wreck diving; one such book even provides the loran coordinates with which to locate the site electronically.

The accounts of the tragedy in metropolitan newspapers seem remarkably unimaginative. Except for the two semi-celebrities, Jackson and Jones, no one in the crew, alive or dead, received much attention from the journalists. Even Captain Sawyer remained an obscure figure; no mention was made of his heroism on the *Frank Buck*, his earlier career, or his service in the war. The "investigative journalism" of that era seems generally to have been interested in the personal ironies and tragedies of shipwrecks, particularly when passengers were involved, but rarely looked deeply into conflicts or imperfections in performance of duty. Officials, whether ship captains or investigating inspectors, were taken at their word, and their years of service was always translated into exemplary performance in the eyes of the press.

The grounding of the *J. A. Chanslor* represented a difficult case in which to determine what went wrong. Blame, however, was a simpler matter. On the surface it appeared that if ever there was a clear-cut case where responsibility for disaster lay on the shoulders of the ship's master, this would seem to be it. Under the orders of the captain, the ship appeared to have been steered on a course that took her onto the rocks.

The question of whether more men could have been saved is not as clear-cut as is the assignment of blame. It seems possible that additional lives could have been spared had a number of men on the stern raced forward to the midships section while that escape route was still open. Apparently, at that time tankers were not required to have another set of lifeboats at the stern of the vessel, a regulatory gap that was closed thereafter, when federal law was amended to mandate an additional set of lifeboats on the stern section of any tanker. However, photos of the *Chanslor* show a second set of lifeboats on the stern, so the ship did provide an escape route for the men who were aft at the time of the accident. Why the boats were not launched remains a mystery, although Dooley did allude to the possibility that an after lifeboat may have reached the water.

Like the *Rosecrans*, the other Associated Oil tanker described in this book, the *Chanslor* left only three survivors. Among these three on the latter ship, however, was the captain, the one man who knew what had transpired on board during the ship's last hours. The imprecise statements made by Captain Sawyer after the accident may have been limited by his exhaustion and poor physical condition, but they also may have reflected his interest in protecting himself. In the end, facing the prospect of being stigmatized as a captain who abandoned ship and survived while most of his crew died for lack of a chance to escape, he might as well have been candid in describing what took place aboard his ship.

The key to the cause of the disaster lay, of course, in what the ship did during the six hours between noon and the time she hit the rocks. Presumably, visibility at noon was good enough to provide Captain Sawyer with a position he trusted, but apparently no later fixes were possible, fixes which could have indicated a drift to the left from the course line. Dooley's reference to "creeping along in the fog" suggests that the captain may have reduced the speed of the ship as fog was encountered, but, in spite of the grapevine that exists aboard ships, in his position as the crew messman this man could not have had any direct knowledge of the ship's speed.

Also, it is unlikely that Sawyer, in believing that he was passing well offshore of Cape Blanco, would have taken the precautionary step of taking soundings. This is because the continental shelf is at its narrowest along the Oregon coast at this point. The fifty-fathom curve, marking too great a depth from which to obtain soundings readily with a sounding machine equipped with a lead line, is only about five miles offshore, the same distance that Sawyer felt he was putting between the ship and Cape Blanco.

Assuming that the ship had not slowed down, she had made perhaps fifty-two miles since noon, and had apparently been set five miles toward the shore during that time. With the wind and seas on her starboard bow, and riding high in the water from having no cargo, the ship could easily have worked her way inshore to the point of grounding. This result would have required making good a course only five and a half degrees to the left of her projected course. Wind and current, poor steering, and/or increased compass error could readily have combined to produce this result, particularly in the absence of any visual clues that could have been used to correct the ship's course as she steamed ahead. While the five and a half degree departure from the course would have been meaningless in mid-ocean, along the coast it took on life-and-death proportions.

Unfortunately, no record could be located of any official inquiry that may have been held regarding the circumstances of this disaster. Newspaper coverage of the story stopped within a few days, and contained no reference to pending investigations. However, early in February of 1920 the inspectors announced that such an investigation had been postponed because of the illness of Captain Sawyer.[32] Although a recent search of several newspapers for early 1920 failed to turn up the results of this investigation, Patrick Masterson, the author from Port Orford, professed to know the fate of the captain. He indicated that in Portland in March of 1920 the inspectors found Sawyer "guilty of failure to properly navigate his vessel," and suspended his master's license for two years.[33]

Thus, the saga of the *J. A. Chanslor* was finally resolved, albeit unsatisfactorily for everyone. The standards of the sea, calling for retribution for poor performance of duty, had been upheld, but the price of that redress had been thirty-six lives.

Initially it appeared that the hull of the ship might survive. Although the ship was being pounded regularly by heavy seas, a formal effort was soon organized to salvage what was left of the *Chanslor*. In late January of 1920 the San Francisco firm of Pillsbury & Curtis telegraphed the sheriff at Bandon to announce that they had acquired the rights to the wreck from the underwriters, and that they intended to salvage it for the estimated fifteen thousand dollars in gear which remained aboard. George Forty of Port Orford was designated as the local representative, and Captain Alex Scott, who had placed the required line aboard as proof of non-abandonment of the wreck, was identified as the salvor.[34]

A month later another announcement was forthcoming, this time that Captain Lebeus Curtis, a marine surveyor in San Francisco and apparently the same man who had represented the underwriters at the wreck scene, and Dan Hanlon, an Oakland shipbuilder, had entered into an agreement with the underwriters to float the intact portion of the hull and to rebuild the ship. As their salvage vessel, these entrepreneurs began to convert the twin-screw steam schooner *Homer* which had been built at Bandon, a ship that would go on to a long career in salvage work.[35] However, by the end of March, after a further inspection of the tanker, Curtis announced that the hull was filling with sand, and that the salvage effort had been abandoned.[36] The *J. A. Chanslor* was now left to erode away irretrievably and ignominiously on the Oregon coast.

Chapter Nine

The *South Coast*:
Vanished Ship, Vanished Era

The steamer *South Coast* was one of the first of a unique breed of vessel built on the north coast of California and in the Pacific Northwest, known as the steam schooner. Although that designation later came to be loosely used for any small vessel in the lumber trade, it originally meant a vessel that had either been converted from or evolved from a lumber schooner. It was not until 1888 that the first steam schooner was built with an engine installed.[1]

The classic steam schooners had their deckhouse and engineering plant aft, leaving a long foredeck which provided entry through hatches into cargo holds and also provided open space onto which deck loads of lumber could be loaded. They generally retained the ability to carry a fore-and-aft sail from their mast and boom. For many years such ships were built of wood, but later some had steel hulls, particularly when larger lumber ships with midships deck houses were built.

The SS *South Coast*, dating from 1887, was one of the classic steam schooners in design and construction. She was originally configured with two masts, having the second mast near the after end of the deckhouse. That mast, which supported a boom carrying a fore-and-aft sail, was later removed, leaving only the mast at the break of the forecastle which served the cargo boom on the foredeck.

The small size of the *South Coast* and her classic steam schooner lines are evident in this picture taken at a "doghole" on the northern California coast. (Courtesy of San Francisco Maritime National Historical Park)

This little ship had survived many years of service up and down the West Coast before she vanished at sea in 1930, leaving behind a number of traces of her loss but no real clue as to what had happened to the ship. To this date, no one knows her fate. Ships normally do not vanish, and in the Pacific Northwest that concept is as valid as any other truism about ships. A few ships, however, did disappear completely. As James A. Gibbs, the preeminent expert on West Coast shipwrecks, has noted, "Authorities say the North Pacific is not as rough as the North Atlantic, but countless ships have mysteriously disappeared without a trace in North Pacific waters." Most of these vessels listed by Gibbs in his *Shipwrecks of the Pacific Coast* disappeared during the nineteenth century. A few, however, have managed to vanish in more recent times.

Cape Flattery is used as the point of departure on ocean voyages from Puget Sound and the Strait of Juan de Fuca, and through many decades it has also been the point of no return for several vessels. The British Navy's sloop HMS *Condor* in 1900 has already been mentioned in earlier pages, and another ship, the American collier *Matteawan*, while bound for San Francisco vanished with all hands a year later in the same area.[2] Many years later, when ship-to-shore radio communication was standard aboard large ships, the Chinese-owned and British-registered *Haida* vanished in 1937 with twenty-seven men aboard,[3] and in 1952 the steamer *Pennsylvania* of the States Line, an ex-World War II Victory ship, disappeared outbound from Cape Flattery when a crack developed in her hull, forcing her crew of forty-six men to take to the lifeboats, in which they vanished completely.[4]

These ships were outbound for foreign ports, and can only be presumed to have met their end in nearby coastal waters while storms of record were raging. Coastwise voyages were shorter, and virtually all such trips ended in the arrival of the ship at her destination. There were significant exceptions, however. One occurred in 1907, a bizarre episode which began when the small gas schooner *Bessie K.* loaded cedar lumber at Port Orford and put out to sea, bound for San Francisco. Four days later her hull was sighted, bottom up, off Bandon. The seven men in her crew never were seen again, alive or dead. The hull was sighted several times in the months ahead until it grounded off Swatow, China, eighteen months later, the lumber still in her hold.[5] A similar case was that of the four-masted schooner, *Susie M. Plummer*, which was found off Cape Flattery in November of 1909, dismasted and abandoned, with all of her boats gone and no sign of her crew.[6]

Another long-lost ship was the venerable Standard Oil tanker *George Loomis* which went missing off the California-Oregon border in 1918 with no clue to the fate of her eighteen-man crew.[7] So little is known about the fate of this ship that she had to be ruled out as a possible subject for inclusion in this book.

It is one of the ironies of studying the history of maritime disasters that the disappearances of ships, which ought to represent the most inherently interesting of all such events, seldom are reported or even mentioned in the standard shipwreck books. This omission, of course, occurs because these unique events provide no *corpus delicti*, no proof of what has occurred. Although in the case of the *South Coast* there was evidence that the ship's deckload and her deckhouse had become detached, there was still no indication as to the fate of the hull of the ship and the men aboard her. Thus her story has never been properly told.

Another ship lost earlier in the same waters as the *South Coast* was the small tanker *George Loomis* of Standard Oil Company of California. (Courtesy of Chevron Corporation)

To say that the *South Coast* was a familiar ship along the West Coast may be somewhat inaccurate. After forty-three years of service her name was recognized by many in the industry, but perhaps her origins and history were not as well known. Inasmuch as Washington, Oregon, and California all have geographical areas designated as the "South Coast," it is impossible to know for which area this particular steam schooner was named. However, since there was a South Coast Steamship Company operating steam schooners to southern California at one time, and this California-built ship was acquired by that line, it seems likely that the company felt that the ship was named for the California South Coast.

The *South Coast* would have to be regarded as one of the smaller steam schooners, measuring out at only 301 gross tons, with dimensions of only 132 feet long, 32 feet in beam, and 11 feet in depth. Built at the Charles G. White yard in North Beach in San Francisco, she was powered by a reciprocating steam engine of only 190 horsepower which propelled her at about nine knots.

In spite of these size and power limitations, the little ship became something of a jack-of-all-trades. In 1888 she towed a harbor ferry boat from San Francisco to San Pedro, one of the first towing jobs undertaken by a steam schooner.[8] In the late 1890s, along with dozens of other West Coast ships, she spent time as a gold-rush ship in Alaska. In fact, in 1898 she convoyed a group of stern-wheel river steamboats to Alaska, serving as a collier, towboat, and repair ship to this strange armada.[9] Late in her career she experienced the indignity of having tanks built on her deck to enable her to operate as a gasoline tanker between San Francisco and Crescent City, California.[10]

She had her share of brushes with disaster, but seems to have had better-than-average luck in surviving them. In 1890 at Fort Bragg, California, she was blown aground in a gale, but was successfully pulled off the beach, repaired, and put back into service.[11] In these early years her captain was James S. Higgins, celebrated among steam schooner skippers because he was an ordained minister who often prayed over his ship and crew.[12] Perhaps his request for divine intervention helped to keep the little ship afloat during her early years.

An interesting story surrounds Captain Higgins and his relationship to the ship. He was not only her master, but was also her owner, the man who had placed the order with the shipyard for her construction. Several years after she went into service Higgins drowned when he fell overboard. In the settlement of his estate, the *South Coast* was sold to the J. R. Hanify Company, an operator of steam schooners. That company put the ship into the Alaskan trade when the Klondike gold rush started. Later, after her days with the South Coast Steamship Company, Hobbs Wall & Company, an affiliate of the Hammond Lumber Company, bought the ship for use in its lumber operations.[13]

In mid-morning of Tuesday, 16 September 1930, the *South Coast* departed Crescent City, California, under the command of Captain Stanley Sorenson of San Francisco. She was bound for Coos Bay, Oregon, with a 250-ton load of cedar logs, the third such voyage she had made in recent weeks under a charter. A crew of eighteen men was aboard.

Because of the short runs on which the ship was engaged, the full complement of officers which was mandatory on longer runs was not required for this voyage. On deck, the captain had two mates with whom to share the watches, while in the engine room the chief engineer had one assistant engineer. A full complement of eight able-bodied seamen and a winchman completed the deck department, suggesting strongly that the ship's crew was responsible for loading and unloading cargo.

In the engine department there were three firemen to tend to the steam boilers. A cook and a galleyman comprised the steward's department. The ship had no radio equipment, so no wireless operator was aboard. Thus, the ship's complement was about as lean as it could be while still providing enough men to work cargo. One report indicated that there were also several longshoremen aboard the *South Coast* at the time of her demise, but no names of these men appear in any of the newspaper reports.[14]

Rather typically, the ship's crew was heavily Scandinavian. Only four native-born American citizens were aboard: the two engineers, a fireman, and the galleyman. The others had been born in Norway (7, including the captain), Sweden (3), Denmark (1), Finland (1), Germany (1), England (1), and Ceylon (1, apparently British). Their ages ranged from twenty-five to sixty-seven, again a fairly typical distribution for that era and that type of ship.[15] The first indication of trouble for the ship came when the steel freighter *Lake Benbow*, owned by the Ford Motor Company, reported by radio that at 3 P.M. on 17 September she had encountered an empty lifeboat with SS *South Coast* stenciled on the bow. The location was given as latitude 42 degrees 15 minutes north, longitude 124 degrees 52 minutes west. This location was well offshore of a point about half way between Brookings and Gold Beach. At about the same time the tanker *Tejon* of General Petroleum Corporation, Captain Sven Tornstrom commanding, reported that she had encountered an area of debris floating in the water. Her message said: "Numerous logs floating over large area. Also ship's deck house and other wreckage. Position about thirty miles southwest of Cape Blanco, Oregon." Some accounts indicate that the *Tejon* picked up a metal lifeboat which she found at the scene, but this seems an unlikely action for a passing ship, particularly for a tanker which generally would not have had large booms with which to lift a boat.[16] A Belgian ship, identified as the *Carilel*, also radioed in late afternoon that she had passed part of the deck house of the *South Coast*, as well as two square windows floating in the water.[17]

Immediately upon receipt of these messages, the lumber company sent one of its ships, the steam schooner *Elizabeth*, north from San Francisco to assist in the search. The U.S. Coast Guard also ordered its seagoing tug *Cahokia* north from Point Arena on the California coast, to be responsible for all search and rescue efforts.[18] This ship was 141 feet in length, larger than the steam schooner for which she would soon be searching. Heavy fog prevailed as the search began.

When the *Elizabeth* arrived at Crescent City officials of Hobbs Wall decided to terminate her role in the search, opting instead to send out an aircraft in search of the *South Coast*. However, the fog delayed any flights from that craft for some time, so the bulk of the search was conducted by the Coast Guard ship.

The news of the missing ship cast a long shadow of gloom over a special event in San Francisco that was scheduled to feature the rich history of the *South Coast*. This event, at which four hundred people were expected, was the annual banquet of the Propeller Club, a well-known organization within the steamship industry. As the San Francisco *Chronicle* reported on the event's ties to the ship,

> Because of her history she was chosen as the subject of a sketch to have been presented last night at the second annual banquet of the Propeller Club at the Commercial Club.
> For weeks a number of members of the club spent their evenings rehearsing a farce entitled "Twenty Minutes Before the Mast on the Lumber Steam Schooner *South Coast*," depicting the humor and rough life on a lumber carrier.
> When news of the finding of the wreckage reached the club the banquet became a perfunctory affair, all interest being centered on the fate of the old steamer.[19]

No encouraging news reached those attending the banquet, however, and hopes began to fade even more when nothing promising was reported the next day.

The Coast Guard ship *Cahokia* spent the first night of her search lying to at a point eighteen miles off the mouth of the Rogue River, immobilized by the heavy fog prevailing in that vicinity. Subsequently, she found two empty lifeboats from the *South Coast*. One of these boats was wooden with a square stern; the other was a metal double-ender. Neither boat was provisioned with food and water; each boat also lacked oars. Eventually, the *Cahokia* shelled these two boats and sank them.

Similarly, she located the pilothouse containing the ship's nameboard which the *Tejon* had spotted earlier. She then shelled that structure until it broke up and sank.[20] These procedures were fairly standard at the time in destroying derelicts as hazards to navigation, but they also destroyed any opportunity to gain additional clues from the physical evidence as to what had happened to the ship.

Assisting the *Cahokia* in her search for clues to the disappearance of the *South Coast* were additional Coast Guard vessels, including a powered surfboat from the lifesaving station at Bandon, and the cutter *Red Wing* from Astoria. When weather permitted, the airplane hired by the lumber company joined the search, but no further physical evidence was found during a seven-hour reconnaissance. Further tragedy was averted when the pilot had to make an emergency landing on the beach north of Brookings at the end of the long flight.[21] After six days the search was called off.

The fact that the debris was found well offshore suggests that the *South Coast* was not trying to pass Cape Blanco close aboard. It would perhaps have been natural for a ship visiting two adjacent coastal ports such as Eureka and Coos Bay, a distance of only about 175 nautical miles, to have kept close to the shore, but this apparently did not happen in this case.

During the search, as additional debris was found, all kinds of theories were put forth as to what might have happened to the ship. One explanation was that the *South Coast* had been in a collision, but no ship had reported any such event and no other ship was reported missing. Furthermore, after a few days, when ships without radios would have had a chance to reach port and make their reports, that hypothesis no longer had any validity. Other suggested theories included hitting an offshore rock pinnacle, or capsizing, possibly from a shifting of the deck load.

Alternative scenarios which might have been advanced, but apparently were not, were fanciful to the point of virtual impossibility. These included some kind of act of barratry in destruction of the vessel by the captain and crew (who then went where in what?), an act of piracy (by whom, for what end?), and some sort of dangerous encounter while engaged in extra-legal activity such as rum-running.

One other more plausible explanation involved a boiler explosion, an event which was now so infrequent on steam vessels that the idea was difficult to evaluate. The Steamboat Inspection Service had been founded in 1852 to investigate the then-frequent boiler explosions that occurred on steamboats, but improvements in boilers and in engineering competence had made boiler explosions a rarity. However, some compelling evidence arose in support of this theory when a group of Gold Beach residents came forth to describe a flash of blue light followed by an explosive sound about fifteen miles offshore which they saw and heard on the night the ship disappeared.[22] The charted depths in that location are one thousand to fifteen hundred fathoms.

Ralph Myers, manager of the steamship department of Hobbs Wall, agreed that it was difficult to know what had happened: "The weather was not unduly rough and it is hard to account for an accident that would sink the vessel. If the deck load shifted and had to be jettisoned, carrying part of the deckhouse with it, the hull of the steamer may still be afloat, even if helpless."[23] No such derelict hull turned up, however, and further searching, including by the aircraft, provided no additional clues to the fate of the ship.

In a curious coincidence, a year earlier a pilothouse had figured in the aftermath of another West Coast ship disaster. Following a collision with a tanker, the steel-hulled passenger ship San Juan sank in three minutes off the central California coast with enormous loss of life. Within a few days her wooden pilothouse floated to the surface, thus establishing that it did not take a blow to the structure itself to dislodge such a deckhouse.[24]

The fact that the seas had not been stormy, plus the reality that the boats had gone adrift with no one remaining in them, added to the mystery of the *South Coast*. The lifeboats might have provided the best clue as to what had happened, but no one knew how to read the clue. For many years on most merchant ships, launching a lifeboat into the water was completed either by an automatic mechanism that released or unhooked the rings on the boat from the hooks on the falls coming down from the davits, or by a manual releasing mechanism using a toggle or lever. Lifeboats, unlike life rafts, which sometimes have automatic releasing systems responsive to water pressure, do not have releasing systems that operate when the boat goes under water. Thus a lifeboat adrift from a ship is presumed to have been launched by human hands whether released automatically or manually, but not set free through flotation or through a pressure release.

However, early lifeboat installations using radial davits sometimes had open hooks at the bottom of manila boat falls, and these hooks would probably separate from the rings on the boats should slack come into the falls, as it would if the boat were buoyed up by water. Steam schooners such as the *South Coast* may have retained such a simple lifeboat system into their latter days, making it impossible to determine how the lifeboats were released. Much would depend on how thoroughly the boats were "griped" to the deck. The whole issue of how the lifeboats were released is the kind of question that could have been answered at the time by investigators, but was not investigated or explained. The *Cahokia* reported evidence that the battered boats had not been launched, but did not indicate how that conclusion was reached.[25]

Contemporary descriptions of the *South Coast* suggest that she carried three boats, the two sighted and investigated by the *Cahokia* plus one more, possibly the one reportedly picked up by the *Tejon*. Some sources reported that a third boat, a metal one, had indeed been aboard; this boat was never found, giving rise at the time to the hope that some of the crew were safe in that boat and eventually would turn up somewhere—a hope that soon vanished.

Within the scope of the two most plausible theories, capsizing and hitting a rock, launching boats seemed possible. Indeed, precedent for such action exists earlier in this book in the case of the *Francis H.*

Leggett, which managed to put boats in the water when she capsized, and the *J. A. Chanslor,* which successfully launched one boat when she struck a rock pinnacle.

The capsizing theory, however, draws one back to the fate of the lumber ship *Francis H. Leggett.* In that case, the fact that the ship was steel meant that considerable negative buoyancy was at work against the positive buoyancy of the lumber cargo in the hold and on deck. In the 1930 case of the wooden-hulled *South Coast* the question must be raised again: can a wooden ship with a cargo of lumber actually sink within a few days? Curiously, this question does not seem to have been addressed seriously by maritime historians.

Water-logged wooden vessels in time lose their buoyancy, of course, becoming in effect no more buoyant than steel vessels. With the *South Coast* being forty-three years old that possibility must be considered. As Newell and Williamson report in *Pacific Lumber Ships,* "some of the ancient craft placed in the lumber trade were so decrepit that a cargo of pingpong balls couldn't have kept them afloat in any kind of a blow."[26] It is worth noting that the reputation of the *South Coast* around Coos Bay was that of an old water-logged vessel, close to, if not already in, an unseaworthy condition.[27]

As noted previously, the absence of an investigative capability in 1930, such as that we now expect from the Coast Guard and the National Transportation Safety Board, made it difficult to look for clues as to what went wrong aboard the ship. For example, burned or singed lumber from the cargo or from the pilothouse might suggest the possibility of a fire or explosion. The lifeboats might contain clues as to whether they were ever occupied, such as whether the oars had been unlashed, or whether they had been launched properly. In the boats found by the *Cahokia* there were neither oars nor supplies, a fact that raised as many questions as it resolved. Likewise, if the boats had not been lowered, as determined by the Coast Guardsmen, what alternative scenario had been played out? Did the boats come free as the ship sank, or had the boat falls been cut to release them? Likewise, the pilothouse and the wheel it contained might have contained clues as to what course was being steered or what speed had been rung up.

The absence of bodies was another curious circumstance of the loss of the *South Coast*. The other physical evidence strongly suggested that the ship may have met a violent end, but no bodies were picked up amidst the debris in the water or on the beaches of southern Oregon, where patrols were established for this purpose. Inasmuch as the *Francis H. Leggett* had foundered well offshore and at least a dozen bodies from that disaster had later washed ashore on Oregon and Washington beaches, it seems reasonable to expect proportionately the same results for the *South Coast*.

Not only did no comprehensive investigation of this nature take place, but no investigation of any type occurred. The local inspector for the Steamboat Inspection Service, Frank Turner, announced: "We cannot hold a hearing unless someone who was aboard the ship or witnessed the accident is here to testify."[28] That attitude must have seemed cold and callous to the families of the missing seafarers.

At the time of this accident the Steamboat Inspection Service and the Bureau of Navigation were still two separate agencies in the Department of Commerce, but in 1932 they would be merged into the Bureau of Navigation and Steamboat Inspection, which in 1936 became the Bureau of Marine Inspection and Navigation, later to be absorbed into the U.S. Coast Guard. However, the procedures for investigating casualties varied little from year to year as these name changes were made, and the investigations rarely showed acute analytical skill in resolving difficult questions.

Newspaper stories reported on the grief of the families of only a few of the crew of the *South Coast*, in part because the lumber company did not even have addresses for twelve of the crewmen. Those who were identified as having bereaved relatives included the captain who left a wife and stepson, the ship's cook who left a wife and grown children, and the assistant engineer who left a son.

The most ironic story concerning victims was that of Pontus Stambourg, the fifty-six-year old second mate who left a wife in San Francisco. Stambourg held a master's license and was waiting to assume command of a ship that was being overhauled at the Union Iron Works. In the tight employment market that prevailed in the 1930s in the West Coast shipping industry he had taken the job aboard the *South Coast* as an interim position until his new command was ready.[29]

The rootlessness and loneliness of the lives of many of the seamen could be inferred from the fact that no one knew or cared where two-thirds of the members of the crew lived ashore. It could also be glimpsed through the addresses of some whose housing arrangements *were* a matter of record: A. J. Tallaksen, the chief mate, and W. J. Baird, the chief engineer, each of whom gave home addresses that were residential hotels in San Francisco.[30] For such men, life aboard ship may have been a more fulfilling social experience than life ashore. While one can readily sympathize with men who were forced to live without any family ties ashore, it is sometimes difficult to recall that the world of work in 1930 often required men to go where the work was, regardless of where home, in the fuller sense, might be. It is equally difficult to remember that "none" was a common statement on next-of-kin declarations made by seamen.

Physical condition, age, and pure luck among those on board determined who survived a disaster. Those factors also established the fine line between what became a shipwreck in fact and what remained a mystery—a ship that was overdue and presumed lost. In the case of the *Francis H. Leggett* the survivors were a pair of passengers, and had they not survived to tell their story that ship would have become one of the mysteries of the sea. On the central California coast three half-dead crewmen drifting in a lifeboat from the foundered *Roanoke* were the only means by which the world learned about the sinking of that ship.[31] In each case, a few hours more and all survivors might have perished, leaving behind another unsolved mystery of the sea.

⌐

As with other vanishing ships, when the entire crew of the *South Coast* was lost, the ship upstaged the death of nineteen good men, and became the mystery herself. What could have happened to her? Perhaps the most difficult aspect of examining the disappearance of a ship is the lack of a basis for comparison. On the entire Pacific Coast only a few ships have completely vanished, making it difficult to generalize about the circumstances that these events might have had in common. In the pre-radio era there was in most cases no way of even knowing at what point in the voyage the mishap to the vessel took place. Thus generalizations about locations of the disappearances have been nearly impossible, a fortunate circumstance in one sense, in that no Bermuda Triangle speculation has developed along these lines. However, allegations regarding magnetic anomalies affecting compasses occasionally have been put forth as the basis for the loss of ships through grounding.

As a greater scientific knowledge of the physical behavior of the sea has developed in recent years, better explanations of earlier disappearances are now possible. Such phenomena as tsunamis, "rogue" waves, and wind shear and micro-bursts can cause localized effects which may go unnoticed a short distance away. Oregonians need only be reminded of the infamous and largely cloudless "Columbus Day Storm" of October 1962 to agree that narrow bands of brief, violent, and unpredicted weather can and do occur. Eighty-two years earlier, in May of 1880, the great fishing boat disaster off the mouth of the Columbia took the form of a one-hour storm of hurricane-strength winds which sank several hundred boats and took more than three hundred lives, leaving behind seas which rapidly returned to the same calm state that had existed before the strange weather phenomenon occurred.

Geophysical phenomena are also characteristic of the offshore zone of the Oregon coast. A major fault line in the area has been responsible for significant earthquakes in the past. Two schooners off the northern California coast in 1895 witnessed a violent explosion of water that lasted about two minutes, after which the sea returned to its normal state.[32] Obviously, some kind of geophysical activity had taken place on the ocean floor. Another West Coast schooner of that era was struck by a small meteor while en route to Honolulu.[33] Thus weather, seismic activity, and even extraterrestrial events are among the natural forces that could have played a role in the loss of the *South Coast* in 1930. Perhaps the Bermuda Triangle syndrome should not be completely discounted after all!

Although no formal inquiry was made by the inspectors from the Steamboat Inspection Service, the existence of insurance on the vessels called for a general review of the circumstances surrounding the disappearance of the *South Coast*. In the casualty report filed with the Coast Guard by Hobbs Wall & Company, the value of the vessel was described as twenty thousand dollars and the insurance on the hull as ten thousand dollars.[34] While these were not large amounts, the underwriters would still have been interested in knowing what happened before authorizing payment of the claim.

Speculation immediately after the incident did not favor any single explanation of the disappearance of the ship, nor has the subsequent speculation proposed any logical resolution of the mystery from among the various possibilities. However, there are some theories to which it is difficult today to accord any great credence. There was no major storm at the time; this, together with the absence of bodies, seems to rule out any weather-induced foundering such as that encountered by the *Francis H. Leggett*. Similarly, the lack of another ship seems to rule out collision, and the nonexistence of known underwater hazards as far offshore as the debris was found works against, but does not rule out, the notion of the ship striking a submerged reef. In each of these last two cases there should also have been bodies in the water or in the lifeboats. What, then, is left?

There are, of course, those highly unlikely possibilities which were alluded to above, what might be called today the X-theories—meteorological, seismic, or extraterrestrial. These extreme explanations, however, would still have to account for the problem of the missing bodies and the intact wheelhouse. The one remaining possibility with any plausibility would appear to be a devastating explosion. Yet that explosion would have to be so intense as to mangle bodies, rendering them unable to float, and yet not so severe as to destroy the reasonably intact wooden deckhouse and the boats.

There is an old syllogism, variously attributed to Sherlock Holmes and other fictional detectives, that, after one has eliminated all the probable explanations, what remains as the improbable must be the answer. Unfortunately, in the case of the *South Coast*, identifying any additional explanations of her loss, however improbable, seems as difficult today as it was in 1930.

Chapter Ten

The *Iowa*: Crossing the Bar

The story of the SS *Iowa* is not one of the great romantic sagas of Pacific Northwest maritime history, nor is it full of heroic, ironic, or poignant moments in the fashion of some of the other stories in this book. Instead, it is a story of an ugly blunder that cost the lives of every man aboard the ship. It is also a reminder that even in the fourth decade of the twentieth century, when great strides had been made both in accident reduction and in rescue techniques, the sea remained as unforgiving as it had always been.

The story is distressingly modern in another aspect, in that the wreck was followed by enormous amounts of litigation, far more than all the other shipwrecks described in this book had produced collectively.[1] Fortunately, there were no passengers and their families to bring legal action. However, militant seamen, a new breed fresh from the West Coast strikes of 1934 and 1936, were posthumously, through their survivors and their unions, exercising their rights to better protection from the perils of the sea, with the steamship company singled out as the target of these proceedings.

The *Iowa* was a product of the shipbuilding program of the United States Shipping Board in World War One. Like most of the ships turned out by the Emergency Fleet Corporation, the shipbuilding branch of the Shipping Board, she was completed well after the end of the war, and made her mark as a peacetime between-the-wars ship. She was completed in 1920 at the Western Pipe and Steel yard in South San Francisco, one of a type generally referred to as a West or West Coast ship, all of which bore that geographic prefix in their names.

She had originally been the *West Cadron*, and had been operated in trans-Pacific service for the Shipping Board under that name by the Columbia Pacific Shipping Company. In 1928 this entity became the States Steamship Company, and the name of the ship was changed to *Iowa* in keeping with the line's policy of naming its ships for states. She had acquired a reasonably good record, the only conspicuous blemish on her reputation being a collision in Japan in 1934 that took her out of service for several months for repairs.[2]

The ships of the States Line had one unique identifying feature. Painted on their stack was a swastika. Although today that symbol is identified almost exclusively with Nazi Germany, in the mid 1930s it was a well-established symbol of good fortune in many cultures including that of American Indians, and it was widely used in jewelry and ornamentation. The Oklahoma National Guard of that era wore the swastika as a shoulder patch.

Like her sister ships, the *Iowa* was of 5,724 gross and 3,564 net tons, and was 411 feet long, 54 feet in breadth, and 27 feet in depth. This class of ship was of the "three island" design, having a raised forecastle, poopdeck, and midship house. Propulsion machinery consisted of a triple expansion reciprocating engine of 2,800 horsepower.

On the evening of Saturday, 11 January 1936, the *Iowa* completed loading at the Weyerhaeuser dock at Longview, Washington, and at 7:45 P.M. departed downriver toward the sea, beginning a long voyage that would take her to the East Coast. Her captain was Edgar L. Yates, a veteran captain with the States Lines, who was making his first voyage in the ship. Conning the vessel was the river pilot, Stewart V. Winslow of Portland.

The ship was crewed in the pattern that would prevail into World War II. The deck department consisted of three mates, a boatswain, carpenter, six able-bodied seamen, and three ordinary seamen. The

The steamer *Iowa* of the Portland-based States Line was lost with all hands on the Columbia River bar in 1936. (Courtesy of Oregon Historical Society)

engine department was comprised of a chief engineer, three assistant engineers, a deck engineer, three oilers, three firemen, and a wiper. The steward's department was made up of a steward, two cooks and three messmen. The radio operator rounded out the thirty-three-man crew. Eleven of the crew were from the Portland area, eight were from Washington state, four gave California addresses, nine were from other states, and one gave no address.[3]

The *Iowa* was loaded with about 6,945 long tons of general cargo, a total that apparently included the deck load of 1,446,000 board feet of lumber on the forward well deck to a height of fourteen feet, and 918,000 board feet of lumber to the same height in the after well deck. The hatches had been left clear so that additional cargo could be loaded into the holds at San Francisco. Her draft at Longview had been 17′ 7″ forward and 26′ 5″ aft, for a mean draft of twenty-two feet.[4] In seawater the draft would have been about half a foot less.

The river pilot was dropped at Astoria at about 11:50 P.M. The weather at this time was rainy, and storm warnings were flying. The wind on the bar was reported as force 9 to 11 on the Beaufort Scale, which would correspond to forty-one to sixty-five knots or nautical miles per hour. The last ship to have crossed the bar outbound had been the Japanese-flag *Kosei Maru* at 10 P.M.; the last of three inbound ships had entered the river by 9 P.M. The bar pilots of those ships all reported rapidly increasing wind.[5] By chance, one of these pilots was August Lofstedt, whose license had been suspended for losing the *Santa Clara* in the surf at Coos Bay in 1915.

Captain Yates, who had pilotage for the area and had crossed the Columbia bar more than two hundred times, declined the services of a bar pilot, and elected to take the ship over the bar himself. The sixty-eight-year old Captain Yates was originally a British mariner and had held a master's license under that flag before being licensed in the United States. He had sailed for twenty years under the American flag, first for the Oriental Navigation Company and since 1928 for the States Line.

Under Yates' conn the ship proceeded to sea, but immediately encountered the effect of a westerly swell, southerly wind, and ebbing tide, which produced very rough conditions on the bar and slowed the ship to about four knots of speed. Through his telescope a Coast Guard observer at Cape Disappointment Lighthouse watched the slow progress of the *Iowa* as she fought her way seaward. He reported later that the ship seemed to pick up speed after buoy 10, a mile or so south of the lookout station, and that everything seemed under control. At buoy 6, off the end of the south jetty, the ship appeared to hesitate, but apparently set a southwesterly course for the lightship.[6]

Squalls began to reduce visibility, but at about 2:45 A.M. it appeared that the ship was drifting to the north toward Peacock Spit. However, no distress signals were apparent. The last time the lookout ashore saw the lights of the ship was just before 3:30 A.M. when he went outside to punch the clock at the edge of the cliff, a few yards away. At that time, in his words, "a hell of a squall came by." He could no longer see the lights of the ship, which had been bearing 240 degrees from the lookout when last observed. This line of bearing placed her near Peacock Spit where the depths were no more than twenty-five feet.[7]

At 4 A.M. the watch at the lighthouse was relieved, and by 4:30 the oncoming watch had sighted the ship within the waters of the Peacock Spit area. The position of her lights indicated that no evasive course change had been made. At about the same time the radio station at Astoria called the lighthouse to report that an SOS had been received from the *Iowa* indicating that she was aground on Peacock Spit. This

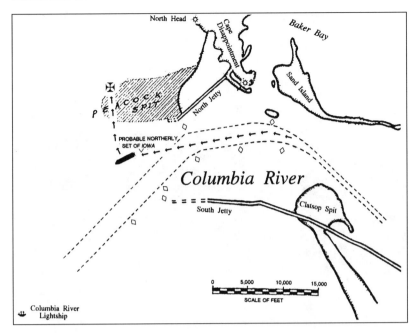

This map, a composite of newspaper versions and coastal charts, shows how the *Iowa* left the mouth of the Columbia and was driven north onto Peacock Spit while still heading out to sea.

message had first been heard at 3:50 A.M. by a Coast Guard vessel, the *Chelan,* one of the "Lake" class 250-foot cutters, which was at sea assisting another ship in distress off to the south. The *Chelan* relayed the message to another cutter, the 165-foot *Onondaga,* moored at Astoria. Within two hours, that ship was underway for the wreck site.[8]

An amateur radio operator later reported that he had listened to the *Iowa* that night and had heard her operator chatting with the shore stations, noting that while the weather was rough nothing was amiss. Shortly before the SOS was sent the ship's operator had sent a weather report to the Coast Guard. This may have been the same message sent at 3:12 A.M. when the ship reported that she had left the Columbia River at 1:00 A.M., bound for San Francisco, and ended the transmission "I have nothing further for you."[9] Thus it seems clear that as the *Iowa* lurched out the channel her crew had no sense of impending danger.

The Coast Guard cutter en route to the stranded *Iowa* encountered extremely heavy seas once she made the turn below Cape Disappointment and headed for the open ocean. She would spend several hours reaching

All that could be seen of the *Iowa* after her grounding was her bridge and masts, shown here from a Coast Guard vessel which visited the wreckage. (Courtesy Lincoln County Historical Society)

the scene of the disaster, only a few miles away. In the meantime at the observation station at the lighthouse a small group of Coast Guardsmen and their families had gathered to watch the drama unfolding before them. With radio contact to the *Iowa* lost, the radio station at Astoria requested that the lookout station attempt to contact the ship by signal light. When a general call was sent by blinker, a feeble light appeared on the freighter, but it was soon blotted out by a passing squall. Although it was still quite dark, a flag hoist signal was then sent, resulting in some flags being hoisted aboard the stricken ship, but no one at the lookout station could make out the message.[10]

With the coming of a gray dawn the activities aboard the ship could be faintly seen through the telescope. The last sign of life on board was apparently the emergence of a figure on deck who was seen making his way toward the foremast, only to be swept away in full view of the observer by a giant comber which broke over the ship. Shortly thereafter the funnel and the pilothouse washed away, and before long the bulk of the ship disappeared into the raging sea with only her masts still above water.[11]

En route to the *Iowa*, the cutter *Onondaga,* under the command of Lieutenant Commander R. Stanley Patch, took a beating as she bucked the heavy swells breaking on the bar. The waves battered two of her lifeboats, smashed a ventilator, bent a stanchion, snapped off a davit, loosened a three-inch gun from its mount, and ripped canvas dodgers and boat covers to shreds. One wave passed over the vessel and dumped water through an open companionway into the quarters below. One of the officers of the *Onondaga* later estimated that the waves were as high as seventy-five feet.[12]

In spite of this hammering, the cutter was eventually able to clear the channel, and swing north along the western edge of Peacock Spit. There she found the freighter, and after getting within fifteen hundred yards of the wreck, Commander Patch saw no signs of life aboard. He kept the *Onondaga* in the area long enough to be sure that no survivors were in the water, and that nothing more could be done. The cutter then returned to Astoria at 3:45 that afternoon. The disaster, and its related rescue effort, had now ended with the death of the captain and his crew of thirty-three men.

⤳

The aftermath phase of the accident, together with its resultant rancor, began immediately. The first group of six bodies was found on Sunday by the Coast Guard small craft which reached the scene as soon as weather permitted. Large search crews, including Coast Guardsmen and men from the nearby Civilian Conservation Corps camps, covered the adjacent beaches where another body was found a few days later, and an eighth body drifted ashore near Ilwaco ten days after that. Several of the bodies were lightly clad, suggesting that the men may have been asleep when disaster struck.[13]

Because the ship was home-ported in Portland, a number of the next-of-kin of the lost men descended on Astoria and Ilwaco, and there were heart-rending stories in the newspapers about the vigils maintained by these close relatives. The usual stories of premonitions or partying which caused lucky crewmen to miss the ship were also carried by the press. One element of other shipwrecks was lacking, however: the ambiguity about who had been aboard. Since the ship had departed from the area where she was home-ported, the company had excellent records of those aboard.

Aerial reconnaissance was provided by a Douglas amphibian aircraft from the Coast Guard station at Port Angeles, Washington, which made a number of passes over the scene of the wreck and the nearby coast, but was unable to locate either survivors or bodies. Another aircraft flew a newsman and photographer from the Portland *Oregonian* over the scene.[14] Although the presence of these aircraft supplied a modern touch to the proceedings, their use provided no significant benefit in understanding the nature of the accident.

For many days following the wreck the residents of the coast north of the mouth of the Columbia enjoyed lucrative beach combing, as all kinds of food, lumber, appliances, and other general cargo washed up on the beaches. Since vehicles have always been allowed on this stretch of beach, the beachcombers were able to utilize cars, trucks, and wagons to haul away large quantities of their booty. All sorts of stories of the largesse enjoyed by local people through the loss of the *Iowa* appeared in the press in days to come, including the story of the local rancher who fed his scrubby cattle a gruel made from the abundant flour, thus nourishing his herd to prime condition.

It was only a matter of a few days before the first calls for an investigation were made, and the first legal actions were taken. Predictably, the Bureau of Marine Inspection through inspectors Frank Edthofer and John H. Nolan announced on Wednesday 15 January that since there were no survivors, there would be no investigation.[15] That same day, the Portland Central Labor Council, through a radio address by G. O. Hunter, its vice-president, called for a federal investigation of the disaster.[16] Captain Vance Trout, port captain for the States Line, said the company would welcome such an investigation.[17] The following day the Coast Guard began its own internal investigation of how its operations had been conducted.

The *Oregonian* reported on Friday 17 January that five maritime labor unions, responding to the announcement that there would be no official inquiry into the wreck of the *Iowa*, were beginning their own investigation to force such an inquiry. In the same issue, the government inspectors were quoted as saying that they would welcome anyone coming forward with any information on which a hearing might be based.[18] Apparently thirty-four dead men did not yet represent sufficient justification to the local inspectors.

On the following day, the first lawsuit was announced, that of the widow of Alfred Kreiger, the chief mate of the *Iowa*. Many of the charges later brought concerning the seaworthiness of the *Iowa* had been conveyed by Kreiger to his wife in a farewell telephone call from Longview, in which he had expressed a premonition of danger because he knew that the captain intended to take the ship across the bar that night.[19]

On the day after the filing of the lawsuit, a flurry of announcements was forthcoming. One, from Oregon Governor Charles H. Martin, announced that he had contacted the United States Secretary of Commerce to seek a federal inquiry. In turn, the Department of Commerce announced that J. B. Weaver, chief of the Bureau of Navigation and Steamboat Inspection, would be sent to Portland for that purpose.[20]

Even the local inspectors, Edthofer and Nolan, felt compelled to issue a statement, clarifying their earlier announcement about no investigation; they now said that they were referring only to the wreck itself, but they had already been interviewing people relative to the condition of the ship and the judgment of the captain. Captain Nolan asked that all persons who might have knowledge pertaining to the wreck communicate with his office. He concluded with the rather peculiar statement that "all evidence we've assembled so far is to the effect the weather was favorable when the *Iowa* headed into the Pacific."[21]

Despite their reluctance to get involved, the inspectors did move ahead promptly on an inquiry, and by 20 January were engaged in the fact-finding portion of the investigation. In charge was J. B. Weaver, director of the bureau, assisted by Captain Walter Fisher, supervising inspector for the bureau's Pacific coast headquarters in San Francisco, along with the local inspectors Nolan and Edthofer. Eleven witnesses were questioned. Four were described as Columbia River pilots (three of whom were identified by newspaper accounts as bar pilots, not river pilots), two were officers of the Columbia Lightship, and one each were the commanding officer of the *Onondaga*, the port captain for the States Line, a cargo official of the steamship company, a surveyor for the Board of Marine Underwriters in San Francisco, and the aunt of the *Iowa*'s chief mate in whose behalf a legal action against the company was pending.[22]

In March a letter was sent to the Secretary of Commerce summarizing the inquiry, along with twenty-four attachments. Extant copies of this letter are not signed, nor do they contain a letterhead or any clue to the agency originating the correspondence, but the writer is identified as "Director," and his initials are WWS. He concludes his report with these opinions:

> I believe that when the IOWA left Astoria and proceeded to sea conditions were such that without information concerning conditions on the bar the master believed that he could take his vessel to sea; that a rapid change in weather conditions and the state of the vessel relative to load and trim combined to prevent the vessel from making headway and it was impossible to maneuver and bring the vessel back to a safe anchorage. I am of the opinion that had the master received advance information concerning conditions on the bar he would have anchored his vessel inside and awaited more propitious weather.[23]

The writer of the letter goes on to recommend better radio messages concerning bar conditions, improved lighting on the buoys, the establishment of an observation station on the North Jetty, better information on local weather, required use of a "competent" bar pilot, and greater attention to the draft and trim of vessels crossing the bar.

The reference to "competent" bar pilots reflected the pressure that existed with respect to compulsory use of the full-time pilots from the association, as opposed to letting masters with pilotage endorsements for the bar take their own ships in and out. During the inquiry several interesting facts dealing with the use of pilots emerged. One was that only about 27 percent of the ships crossing the bar used the professional pilots, and hardly any Portland-based ships were in that group. That statement was countered by another which noted that no professional pilot had lost a ship on the bar since 1879.[24] However, on this issue of pilotage, the inspectors had to equivocate; their call for a "competent" bar pilot could not be interpreted as a call for compulsory use of professional pilots without repudiating the existing licensure of hundreds of masters who had earned pilotage credentials through the very procedures which the Bureau of Marine Inspection had created and supervised.

The recommendation regarding greater attention to the draft and trim of vessels reflected the concern expressed in the investigation over the *Iowa's* fore and aft profile, or trim. She was "down by the stern" perhaps more than normal loading would have called for, necessitated by leaving one hundred thousand cubic feet or 2,500 measurement tons open forward for her San Francisco cargo. This drag gave her excessive draft aft, and it also thrust her bow rather high in the air, providing a sail against which the southwesterly winds exerted torque, pushing the ship toward the north.

With the official inquiry out of the way, the court cases could now begin in earnest. At this point it becomes difficult to follow the proceedings through newspaper accounts, but eventually the various actions begin to show up in the pages of law books, particularly in *American Maritime Cases*. The 1936 volume of that publication notes that:

> On March 12, 1936, the States Steamship Company, as owner of the steamship *Iowa*, filed a petition for exoneration from and limitation of liability for loss, damage or injury resulting from the wreck of said steamer. On the same date the court approved an appraisal of the wreck of the *Iowa* and her pending freight in the sum of $10,624.76, and made and entered an order approving the stipulation of the petitioner in the sum of $10,624.76. The court also issued the usual injunction and restraining order.[25]

Attorneys for the seamen moved to except the jurisdiction of the court (the U.S. District Court, District of Oregon) and to vacate the finding, but were overruled.

By 1938 the case had expanded to include other plaintiffs in addition to the estates of the deceased seamen. These new participants included several firms which had suffered cargo losses. At this point the case was reheard by a Commissioner appointed by Judge James A. Fee. This man was Robert F. Maguire, whose efficient handling of the case was to bring clarity to a number of the confused issues. Over the course of twenty-eight daily sessions and thirteen evening sessions Maguire heard enough testimony to fill thirty-two volumes totaling 5,160 pages, and studied 116 exhibits. As staggering as these totals may seem, the case was reduced to a remarkably clear and cogent fourteen pages in the 1938 *American Maritime Cases*, and that summary represents the most comprehensive report extant of what happened to the *Iowa*.[26]

States Steamship Company sought exoneration from all liability, claiming that when the vessel left Longview she was in all respects seaworthy and that her loss was not occasioned by negligence of which the owners were aware. The plaintiffs countered that the ship was not seaworthy, and that the owners were liable. Ten specific faults were alleged:

1. That the ship lacked a communication system between the pilot house and the emergency steering station and between the pilot house and the steam steering engine room.

2. That the ship was loaded and permitted to leave Longview in bad trim.

3. That the *Iowa* was dangerously loaded and that she had an excessive drag by the stern and a correspondingly excessive freeboard forward.

4. That the steering gear was inefficient and out of order.

5. That its engines and motive plant were inefficient and would not develop its rated horsepower.

6. That the owners had failed to furnish the Master with the latest Local Notice to Mariners.

7. That the compasses were out of order and showed deviations so gross as to render them an unsafe guide with which to set and carry proper courses.

8. That the owners failed to give Captain Yates orders not to cross the Columbia River bar on the night in question.

9. That the *Iowa* did not have sufficient power to enable it to meet conditions of wind and current that might be reasonably expected.

10. That the owners did not furnish or direct the Master to obtain a bar pilot before crossing the bar.[27]

Special Commissioner Maguire responded to each allegation in turn. With respect to communication with the emergency steering station Maguire noted that technically the company was in violation of a new regulation mandating such a system that went into effect on 1 January 1936, but that no causal connection existed between this circumstance and the loss of the ship. With respect to the slight list which the ship had in coming down river, he found that it was also immaterial. On the matter of the ship's trim fore and aft, the Commissioner reviewed the advantages and disadvantages of a stern drag in crossing a storm-swept bar, and concluded that the ship was not made unseaworthy by the high freeboard and the deep draft aft.

The next two issues were somewhat more difficult to settle because of their technical nature. The ship's steering gear, a Benson telemotor system which was not in wide use at that time, had been somewhat unreliable during the two previous years, and a number of repairs had been effected in various ports. Maguire waded through much technical testimony and ultimately concluded that there was no evidence to show that the system had not been working properly on the trip from Longview to the dropping of the river pilot at Astoria.

Again, on the question of the ship's engines the Commissioner was required to evaluate considerable technical testimony concerning problems in the low-pressure cylinder of the main engine. Throughout the entire *Iowa* episode the issue of her lack of power had been raised, an issue that has been difficult to understand today inasmuch as her engine was rated at 2,800 indicated horsepower, 300 horsepower more than the larger World War II Liberty ships were later provided. Although Maguire did not speak directly to this question, he was again able to conclude that, although some problems had existed in the past, there was no evidence indicating that the ship was experiencing those problems as she crossed the bar.

On the matter of the failure of the company to provide the latest Notice to Mariners to the ship Maguire presented arguments on both sides relative to this responsibility, and ultimately turned to recent case law for his answer. "With considerable hesitation and doubt," he wrote in his decision, "the Commissioner has reached the conclusion that the doctrine announced in that decision would include local notices to mariners, at least so far as to make it the duty of the owner to place aboard his ship the current local notices affecting the waters in the vicinity of the home port, and that he has no right to rely upon the Master to himself obtain the local notices. Further than this the Commissioner feels that the rule should not go." Maguire went on to find that the *Iowa* was indeed unseaworthy in that it was not furnished the local notice of 6 January 1936, which advised that buoys 1 and 2 were missing, and that buoy 10 was reported extinguished.

This finding seemed something of a reversal of form for the otherwise pragmatic Commissioner, in that the absence of the buoys and the buoy with no light was moot—the *Iowa* passed buoy 10 with no trouble and never reached the offshore location of numbers 1 and 2. However, he later conceded that the state of those buoys had no causal connection with the wreck.

The question of unreliable compasses on the ship had been raised by only one person, and was countered effectively by the testimony of several former masters of the ship. Maguire was able to rule that the compasses did not contribute to any unseaworthiness of the ship.

On the eighth fault alleged by the plaintiffs, the matter of the company failing to direct the captain not to cross the bar, the Commissioner was given an opportunity to review the general relationship of owner to master within the shipping industry, as well as the practice within the States Line. The company's general guideline to masters was safety and not schedule, and the master was given the responsibility of determining what action to take in any situation requiring professional judgment.

Issues nine and ten had been incorporated into other findings, so it was now time for Maguire to announce his general findings:

> The Commissioner finds that the *Iowa* was properly and safely equipped, was sound and seaworthy except in the particulars

(1) that she was not equipped with means of communication between the pilot house and the emergency steering station and the emergency steering engine room, and (2) that the owners had not furnished the Master with a copy of the January 6, 1936, local notice to mariners. He further finds that her loss was not occasioned by any lack of seaworthiness. Inasmuch, however, as he finds that she was unseaworthy in the two particulars mentioned, he recommends that the petition for exoneration from liability be denied.[28]

In other words, the steamship company could be held liable.

The steamship company had anticipated that contingency, and had petitioned for limitation of liability. Generally speaking, the owner's responsibility for torts involving the ship is limited to an amount equal to the value of the ship and the pending freight. In the case of a wreck, no such value or pending freight exists, so liability is limited under laws amended in 1935 to sixty dollars per ton of the ship's gross tonnage. In the case of the *Iowa* the limitation would be $343,440.

Commissioner Maguire announced that in the question of limitation of liability it would be necessary to determine whether the ship was lost through negligence, an error of judgment, or the perils of the sea. Ultimately he concluded: "The Commissioner is forced to the conclusion that Captain Yates' action of putting out over the bar at the time he did was not a mere error of judgment but was in fact negligence. . . . He could have safely anchored and awaited moderation of the weather, but for some reason he concluded to take a chance and it was fatal to him, his crew and his ship. He was guilty of negligence which was the proximate cause of the *Iowa's* loss."[29]

On the question of the petition for limited liability filed by the States Steamship Company, Maguire ruled that the loss of the ship was not due to any negligence to which the company was privy, and recommended that the petition be granted. In a final case, heard in 1940, both sides sought exception to that finding, but Judge James A. Fee, who had appointed Maguire to serve as Commissioner in the 1938 hearings, reaffirmed Maguire's rulings and granted the petition for limited liability. Obscured by the legal language of the final ruling are clues as to whether any one of the human or corporate plaintiffs ever received payment from the limited liability funds.

The Cape Disappointment Lighthouse has witnessed a number of tragedies, including the loss of all hands aboard the *Iowa*. (Author's photo)

From beginning to end, the *Iowa* affair was complex and distasteful in all respects. Robert F. Maguire did a remarkable job in sorting it all out, and in assigning responsibility.[30] He acknowledged the difficulty in drawing the line between poor judgment and negligence, but he drew such a line because it had to be drawn in this case. Unfortunately, there was no way to include in his determination the fact that Captain Yates had almost made it, that he had covered perhaps 90 percent of the ground he needed to cover to reach both the safety of deep water and eternal vindication for his fateful decision.

Today the most significant reminder of the *Iowa* is a ring buoy bearing her name which hangs in the Visitors Center at the Cape Disappointment Lighthouse, a few miles from Ilwaco, Washington. Standing under that relic one can look out over the broad expanse of the Columbia River bar, and try to imagine what it must have been like on that savage night in January of 1936. From this magnificent setting a visitor can readily feel the words of Alfred Lord Tennyson's *Crossing the Bar* which are inscribed on an outdoor plaque overlooking the sea below. Tennyson requested that this poem be placed at the end of all editions of his poetry. It seems more than appropriate to place it at the end of this book as well.

Sunset and evening star,
      And one clear call for me!
And may there be no moaning of the bar,
      When I put out to sea,

But such a tide as moving seems asleep,
      Too full for sound and foam,
When that which drew from out the boundless deep
      Turns again home.

Twilight and evening bell,
      And after that the dark!
And may there be no sadness of farewell,
      When I embark;

For though from out our bourne of Time and Place
      The flood may bear me far,
I hope to see my Pilot face to face
      When I have crossed the bar.

⮌

Notes

Chapter One

1. Robert Hunt Lyman, editor, *The World Almanac and Book of Facts* (New York: New York *World*, 1923, 1930), p. 266 of 1923, p. 423 of 1930.
2. Giles T. Brown, *Ships that Sail No More: Marine Transportation from San Diego to Puget Sound, 1910-1940* (Lexington, KY: University of Kentucky Press, 1966), 172, citing *Annual Report of the Department of Commerce,* 14.
3. James A. Gibbs, *Shipwrecks of Juan de Fuca* (Portland, OR: Binfords & Mort, 1968), 184-85.
4. David H. Grover, "The Tragedy of the *San Juan,*" *Sea Classics,* January 1997: 46-55.
5. Edward A. Turpin and William A. MacEwen, *Merchant Marine Officers' Handbook* (New York: Cornell Maritime Press, 1944), 460.
6. Howard G. Chua-Eoan, "Going, Going ...," *Time,* 19 August 1991: 36.
7. See Chapter Three.
8. Gordon Newell and Joe Williamson, *Pacific Coastal Liners* (New York: Bonanza Books, 1959), 44.
9. James A. Gibbs, *Peril at Sea: A Photographic Study of Shipwrecks in the Pacific* (West Chester, PA: Schiffer Publishing Ltd., 1986), 36.
10. Gibbs, *Peril,* 95.
11. Gibbs, *Peril,* 63-64.
12. David H. Grover, "Danger on the Dredges," *Sea Classics,* February/March 1985: 48-49.
13. Gibbs, *Peril,* 103.
14. Gibbs, *Peril,* 77.
15. Nathan Douthit, *A Guide to Oregon South Coast History* (Corvallis, OR: Oregon State University Press, 1999), 128.
16. James A. Gibbs, *Sentinels of the North Pacific: The Story of Pacific Coast Lighthouses and Lightships* (Portland, OR: Binfords & Mort, 1955), 123.
17. Gibbs, *Sentinels,* 82-83.
18. The mistakes are explained in Gibbs, *Sentinels,* 75-76 and 79-80.
19. *Pacific Coast Pilot* (Washington, DC: U.S. Navy Hydrographic Office, 1909), 22.
20. Gibbs, *Sentinels,* 181.
21. Gibbs, *Peril,* 68.
22. *Register of the Commissioned and Warrant Officers and Cadets, and Ships and Stations of the United States Coast Guard* (Washington, DC: Government Printing Office, 1930), 95.
23. Seattle *Post-Intelligencer,* 29 March 1909: 8.
24. Portland *Oregonian,* 16 February 1913: II, 6.
25. *Pacific Ports Manual,* 7th edition, (Los Angeles, CA: Pacific Ports, Inc., 1921), 394.
26. These figures are derived from an examination of the San Francisco shipping publication, *The Guide,* for 1 July 1914.
27. Newell and Williamson, *Coastal Liners,* 33.
28. Brown, 12.
29. Quoted in Newell and Williamson, *Coastal Liners,* 42.

Chapter Two

1. Gerald M. Best, *Ships and Narrow Gauge Rails: The Story of the Pacific Coast Company* (Berkeley, CA: Howell-North, 1964), 100.
2. Sir Charles Russell, *Diary of a Visit to the United States of America in the Year 1883* (New York: 1910), quoted in Brown, 9.
3. Don Marshall, *Oregon Shipwrecks* (Portland, OR: Binford & Mort Publishing, 1984), 132, cites the forest fire as the source of the visibility problem, but James A. Gibbs, *Pacific Graveyard* (Portland, OR: Binford & Mort Publishing, 1993), 170, cites fog instead.
4. San Francisco *Chronicle*, 29 February 1904: 2.
5. Don Marshall, *California Shipwrecks* (Seattle, WA: Superior Publishing Company, 1987), 92.
6. San Francisco *Chronicle*, 29 February 1904: 2.
7. Details of the fire and subsequent events appear in the San Francisco *Chronicle*, 29 February 1904: 1-2.
8. San Francisco *Chronicle*, 29 February 1904: 2.
9. In the summer of 2000, during the writing of this book, the PBS television network ran a documentary on vaudeville in which "Bedella" was identified as an example of the eclectic nature of that kind of entertainment, in this case representing an Irish "coon song."
10. Seattle *Star*, 1 March 1904: 8.
11. Seattle *Post-Intelligencer*, 29 February 1904: 2.
12. Seattle *Post-Intelligencer*, 29 February 1904: 3.
13. Portland *Oregonian*, 29 February 1904: 3. The reporter's enthusiasm clouded his historical perspectives. It was the *Valencia*, sistership of the *Queen* and the subject of the next chapter, that had taken the Washington militiamen to and from the Philippines, and the *Queen* was homeported in San Francisco, not Seattle.
14. San Francisco *Chronicle*, 29 February 1904: 2.
15. The account of the hearing that follows is from the official transcript in Box 9, File 110, Record Group 41, Bureau of Marine Inspection and Navigation, National Archives, Seattle, Washington.
16. Seattle *Post-Intelligencer*, 29 February 1904: 1.
17. San Francisco *Chronicle*, 24 March 1904: 5.
18. San Francisco *Chronicle*, 26 January 1911: 1.
19. San Francisco *Chronicle*, 29 June 1918: 4.
20. San Francisco *Chronicle*, 10 January 1921: 1; 11 January 1921: 6.
21. San Francisco *Chronicle*, 20 June 1921: 1.
22. Brown, 71.

Chapter Three

1. Best, 121.
2. Seattle *Times*, 24 January 1906: 2.
3. James A. Gibbs, *Peril*, 189. The prominent historian of Army transports, Charles Dana Gibson, indicates, letter to the author, 4 August 2000, that the *Valencia* was time-chartered by the Army, meaning that the steamship company continued to crew and operate the vessel, on the San Francisco to Manila run. Under that type of charter she would not be designated as an Army transport.

4. Jack McNairn and Jerry MacMullen, *Ships of the Redwood Coast* (Stanford, CA: Stanford University Press, 1945), 112.

5. Gordon Newell, editor, *The H. W. McCurdy Marine History of the Northwest* (Seattle: Superior Publishing Company, 1966), 124, cited hereafter as *McCurdy*.

6. Newell and Williamson, *Coastal Liners*, 43.

7. Gibbs, *Juan de Fuca*, 167; James A. Gibbs, *Disaster Log of Ships* (New York: Bonanza Books, 1978), 107; Gordon Newell, *Ocean Liners of the 20th Century* (New York: Bonanza Books, 1963), 127. The last-named book has the ship leaving San Francisco on 11 January 1906, rather than 21 January 1906.

8. Seattle *Times*, 26 January 1906: 3.

9. Seattle *Times*, 26 January 1906: 3.

10. "Wreck of the Steamer *Valencia*," Report to the President of the Federal Commission of Investigation, 14 April 1906 (Washington: Government Printing Office, 1906), 9, cited hereafter as *Valencia* Report.

11. "Investigation of the Wreck of the U.S. Steamer '*Valencia*,'" 27 January 1906 (Washington: Department of Commerce and Labor, Steamboat Inspection Service, 1906), 576.

12. For diagrams of these currents see the Pilot Charts for the North Pacific, published monthly in earlier years by the Hydrographic Office of the U.S. Navy.

13. Gibbs, *Juan de Fuca*, 168.

14. Gibbs, *Juan de Fuca*, 168; Best, 121.

15. *Distances Between United States Ports* (Washington, DC: U.S. Department of Commerce, National Oceanic and Atmospheric Administration, 1993), T-31.

16. Gibbs, *Juan de Fuca*, 168.

17. Gibbs, *Juan de Fuca*, 167.

18. San Francisco *Chronicle*, 24 January 1906: 2.

19. Seattle *Times*, 28 January 1906: 3; Seattle *Times*, 2 February 1906: 1. The newspaper was genuinely confused at this point. The captain was identified by this paper as John Johnson, rather than O. M. Johnson, and was reported to have spent many years ashore at McKeesport, PA. In one edition the *Times* said this man was rescued, and in another that he died in the wreck. Still later, after rebuking the marine inspectors for licensing a man with such limited experience, the paper acknowledged that a mistake had been made, and that the man from McKeesport was not the captain of the *Valencia*. The San Francisco *Chronicle* properly identified John Johnson as a cook who survived the wreck.

20. San Francisco *Chronicle*, 23 January 1906: 2.

21. *Valencia* Report, 15.

22. San Francisco *Chronicle*, 30 January 1906: 1.

23. San Francisco *Chronicle*, 24 January 1906: 2.

24. *New York Times*, 25 January 1906: 5.

25. Seattle *Times*, 2 February 1906: 2.

26. Quoted in Gibbs, *Juan de Fuca*, 170. The hurricane deck mentioned by the boatswain is a term generally associated with coastal or inland vessels and refers to the uppermost deck.

27. Newell, *Ocean Liners*, 127. Stories about the *Titanic* have always mentioned this hymn.

28. Gibbs, *Juan de Fuca*, 176-77.
29. Manila line is measured by circumference. A five-inch line would have a diameter of about an inch and five eighths.
30. Gibbs, *Juan de Fuca*, 173.
31. Seattle *Times*, 26 January 1906: 1.
32. Testimony of Boatswain T. J. McCarthy at hearing before local inspectors, cited in Seattle *Times*, 29 January 1906: 11.
33. Jane King and Andrew Hempstead, *British Columbia Handbook* (Chico, CA: Moon Publications, 1998), 110-11.
34. This part of the story was told by Roby Daykin, younger brother of Phil Daykin who was in the rescue party from Carmanah Lighthouse. It appeared in the Victoria *Daily Colonist*, 4 October 1936, under the byline of F. M. Kelley to whom the story was told by the younger Daykin brother.
35. In an interesting parallel to the past, Native American boatmen still collect fees from hikers on this trail to transport them across the streams, even though the hikers have paid at least $95 for the privilege of hiking the difficult trail.
36. Daykin narrative.
37. Daykin narrative.
38. San Francisco *Chronicle,* 28 January 1906: 22.
39. Gibbs, *Juan de Fuca*, 174.
40. Gibbs, *Juan de Fuca*, 175.
41. Seattle *Times*, 27 January 1906: 2.
42. *Valencia* Report, 44.
43. Seattle *Times*, 2 February 1906: 2.
44. Seattle *Times*, 30 January 1906: 2.
45. Portland *Oregonian*, 26 January 1906: 4.
46. Seattle *Times*, 4 February 1906: 4.
47. Seattle *Times*, February 2, 1906, p. 13.
48. Seattle *Times*, 2 February 1906: 12.
49. Seattle *Times*, 1 February 1906: 9.
50. Seattle *Times*, 4 February 1906: 1.
51. "Investigation. . .*Valencia*."
52. James Mossman, ltr to the author, 19 July 2000.
53. A photograph of the monument appears in John Henry Frazier, "The Wreck of the *Valencia*," *Columbia, The Magazine of Northwest History*, Summer 1993: 23.
54. Frazier, 22.
55. *Valencia* Report, 3. Another member of that earlier investigating commission was Commander Cameron M. McKay, USN, who in World War One would serve as Commander-in-Chief of the U.S. Pacific Fleet. For the role of these men in the *General Slocum* investigation, see *Report of the United States Commission of Investigation Upon the Disaster to the Steamer "General Slocum"* (Washington, DC: Government Printing Office for the Department of Commerce and Labor, 1904).
56. Modern charts show the fourteen-foot shoal that prevents larger ships from entering Neah Bay. However, the author in 1954 served aboard a navy destroyer escort which regularly used the anchorage within the bay, while drawing twenty-one feet, the draft attributed to that class of ships in Morison's seminal history of the Navy in World War II.

57. *Valencia* Report, 38.
58. *Valencia* Report, 44.
59. *Valencia* Report, 53.
60. *Valencia* Report, 47.

Chapter Four

1. San Francisco *Chronicle*, 8 January 1913: 2.
2. Marshall, *Oregon Shipwrecks*, 118.
3. Marshall, *Oregon Shipwrecks*, 118n.
4. *Record* (New York: American Bureau of Shipping, 1898).
5. *Record* (New York: American Bureau of Shipping, 1900).
6. Charles Dana Gibson, letter to the author, 4 August 2000, citing *Report of the Quartermaster General, 1903* (Washington, DC: Government Printing Office, 1903).
7. William L. Worden, *Cargoes: Matson's First Century in the Pacific* (Honolulu: University Press of Hawaii, 1981), 25-26, 162.
8. Los Angeles *Times,* 13 March 1912: 4.
9. San Francisco *Chronicle*, 14 January 1913: 7.
10. Accounts of the *Rosecrans'* two California accidents appear in several of the standard shipwreck books, and also in St. John, Jeffrey, *Mysteries and Mishaps on California Coastal Steamers* (Napa, CA: Western Maritime Press, 1995). An earlier grounding in Alaska in 1900 is mentioned in *McCurdy*, 64.
11. The basic details of the accident on the Columbia River bar are reconstructed from undisputed facts in the accounts in the Portland *Oregonian* and San Francisco *Chronicle*.
12. Portland *Oregonian*, 9 January 1913: 5.
13. *Light List of the Pacific Coast, 1941* (Washington, DC: U.S. Coast Guard, 1941).
14. San Francisco *Chronicle,* 9 January 1913: 1. The observer was identified as Theodore Roberrage. It is not clear how he could have seen the anchors being dropped during darkness and foul weather.
15. Portland *Oregonian,* 26 January 1961: 26
16. Quoted in Gibbs, *Pacific Graveyard*, 41.
17. "Part VI: Seagoing Vessels of the United States with Official Numbers and Signal Letters," from the *Forty-fourth Annual List of the Merchant Vessels of the United States for the year ending June 30, 1912* (Washington, DC: Department of Commerce and Labor, 1912), 102-04. Cited hereafter as "Signal Letters."
18. San Francisco *Chronicle*, 9 January 1913: 1.
19. San Francisco *Chronicle*, 9 January 1913: 1.
20. Gibbs, *Sentinels*, 172.
21. Marshall, *California Shipwrecks*, 146.
22. Portland *Oregonian*, 9 January 1913: 5.
23. Portland *Oregonian*, 12 January 1913: 18.
24. Astoria *Daily Astorian*, 2 March 1988: 2.

Chapter Five

1. Schmidt's ownership of the three sailing vessels named *Mimi* is documented in a list maintained by Lars Bruzelius of the University of Uppsala in Sweden and displayed on his web site.

2. The reference to the *Mimi* replacing the grounded *Torrisdale* is in the Nehalem *Enterprise* for 13 February 1913, as quoted in the Nehalem *Fishrapper* for 9 February 1978. It also appears in *McCurdy*, 228.

3. This account appears only in an undated clipping from the Portland *Oregon Journal*, provided by the Oregon Maritime Center in Portland.

4. Portland *Oregonian*, 14 February 1913: 1; 15 February 1913: 7. The bulk of the coverage on the wreck was by the two Portland newspapers. The two Tillamook papers had surprisingly little to report except when the charges against the rescue crews were made later.

5. Portland *Oregon Journal*, 15 February 1913. Clipping, n.p.

6. *McCurdy*, 229.

7. Portland *Oregon Journal*, undated clipping, from Oregon Maritime Center.

8. Portland *Oregonian*, 22 February 1913: 12.

9. Jack L. Graves, *Flagg of the* Mimi (Garibaldi, OR: Garibaldi Books, 2000).

10. Portland *Oregonian*, 7 April 1913: 3.

11. Portland *Oregonian*, 7 April 1913: 3.

12. The story of the dream has been widely told. A useful account is in Marshall, *Oregon Shipwrecks*, 80.

13. Portland *Oregon Journal*, 8 April 1913: 1.

14. Portland *Oregonian*, 8 April 1913: 1, 4.

15. Portland *Oregonian*, 8 April 1913: 4.

16. Portland *Oregon Journal*, 8 April 1913: 1.

17. Portland *Oregonian*, 8 April 1913: 4.

18. Portland *Oregonian*, 8 April 1913: 4.

19. Portland *Oregonian*, 8 April 1913: 4.

20. Portland *Oregonian*, 9 April 1913: 6.

21. Portland *Oregon Journal*, 8 April 1913: 1.

22. Nehalem *Enterprise*, quoted in Nehalem *Fishrapper*, 6 April 1978.

23. Nehalem *Enterprise*, quoted in Nehalem *Fishrapper*, 6 April 1978.

24. Portland *Oregonian*, 9 April 1913: 6.

25. The Tillamook *Headlight*, 17 April 1913, ran letters from several of these men, and editorialized in support of Captain Farley. The *Herald* in the same community was generally critical of Farley. Neither paper did much investigative reporting, but relied instead on accounts in the *Oregonian*.

26. Portland *Oregonian*, 13 April 1913: 1.

27. Portland *Oregonian*, 15 April 1913: 16.

28. Portland *Oregonian*, 12 April 1913: 5.

29. San Francisco *Chronicle*, 17 April 1913: 15.

30. San Francisco *Chronicle*, 17 April 1913: 15.

31. *McCurdy*, 228.

32. Jack L. Graves, letter to the author, 1 November 2000.

33. Mrs. Mimi Fischer, letter to Captain Harold D. Huycke, 15 June 1956. According to *The Raising of the American Steamship "Republic"* (San Francisco: Paul Elder and Company, 1916), 3-5, the ship had been struck by German shells above the waterline, and was subsequently scuttled by the French authorities to prevent her falling into German hands.

34. *Raising . . . "Republic."*

35. Mimi Fischer to Captain Huycke.

36. William H. Klein, letter to the author, 27 December 2000.

37. Don Best, letter to the author, undated but January 2001.

Chapter Six

1. *Wreck Report*, filed by Hicks Hauptman Navigation Company with the U.S. Lifesaving Service, 1 October 1914.
2. Aberdeen *World*, 19 September 1914: 1.
3. *National Cyclopedia of American Biography* (New York: James T. White & Co., 1921), vol. ii, p. 114.
4. Portland *Oregonian*, 20 September 1914: 6.
5. *Wreck Report*.
6. Passenger lists appeared in the newspapers which covered the sinking, including the Seattle *Times*, Portland *Oregonian*, Aberdeen *World*, and Astoria *Astorian*.
7. Advertisement of Pacific Coast Steamship Company, San Francisco *Chronicle*, 17 September 1914: 14.
8. Advertisements of Alaska-Pacific Steamship Company, San Francisco *Chronicle*, 16 April 1913: 65; 18 April 1913: 17.
9. Portland *Oregon Journal*, 22 September 1914: 1.
10. Advertisement of San Francisco and Portland Steamship Company, San Francisco *Chronicle*, 12 February 1913: 14.
11. Advertisement of North Pacific Steamship Company, San Francisco *Chronicle*, 16 April 1913: 65.
12. Advertisement of North Pacific Steamship Company, San Francisco *Chronicle*, 2 November 1915: 13.
13. Advertisement of Great Northern Pacific Steamship Company, San Francisco *Chronicle*, 2 November 1915: 13.
14.. *United States Coast Pilot* (Washington, DC: Government Printing Office, 1910), 23.
15. Seattle *Times*, 20 September 1914: 1.
16. Statement of George Poelman, Astoria *Astorian*, 22 September 1914: 1.
17. Statement of Alexander Farrell, Portland *Oregonian*, 20 September 1914: 6.
18. Statement of Alexander Farrell, Astoria *Astorian*, 20 September 1914: 4.
19. San Francisco *Chronicle*, 20 September 1914: 37.
20. San Francisco *Chronicle*, 11 July 1914: 11. Some accounts indicate that it was the captain himself who made the small-boat voyage, but in interviews upon his arrival in San Francisco he made clear that it was the second mate, Gus Larsen, who took the boat to Acapulco.
21. *McCurdy*, 246.
22. Portland *Oregonian*, 20 September 1914: 6.
23. Portland *Oregonian*, 20 September 1914: 6.
24. Astoria *Astorian*, 22 September 1914: 1. This newspaper, in what appeared to be part of an ongoing feud with the Marconi Company, on 20 September 1914, p. 8, editorially accused the radio firm of withholding information of public interest from messages it transmitted regarding the *Leggett*, and inferred that the lack of such information may have hurt the chances of providing assistance to the sinking ship.
25. This attitude is reflected in a news item headlined "Japanese Cruiser Lauded" in the Portland *Oregonian*, 20 September 1914: 6.
26. Seattle *Times*, 20 September 1914: 2.
27 Aberdeen *World*, 30 September 1914: 7.

28. Portland *Oregon Journal*, 22 September 1914: 2. The survivor Farrell reported that the radio operator Fleming while in the water told him the message had been sent but not answered.

29. Portland *Oregonian*, 20 September 1914: 6.

30. Aberdeen *World*, 30 September 1914: 1.

31. *McCurdy*, 245; Marshall, *Oregon Shipwrecks*, 129.

32. Portland *Oregonian*, 19 September 1914: 1.

33. David H. Grover, *The San Francisco Shipping Conspiracies of World War One* (Napa, CA: Western Maritime Press, 1995), 38-39.

34. For details of the *Idzumo*'s role in Mexico later in World War One see David H. Grover, "Did Japan Attempt to Invade Mexico?: The *Asama Incident*," *Sea Classics*, April 1996. For the role of the same ship at the start of World War Two see David H. Grover and Gretchen G. Grover, "Night Attack at Shanghai," *Naval History*, Winter 1991.

35. Undated statement submitted to the author by Ralph John Poelman in April 2001.

36. Details of the *Buck*'s role in the disaster were provided in newspaper interviews with her master, Portland *Oregonian*, 21 September 1914: 1.

37. Portland *Oregonian*, 20 September 1914: 6.

38. St. John, 77-78.

39. St. John, 70-71.

40. Portland *Oregonian*, 21 September 1914: 3.

41. Farrell's recollections, and to a lesser degree those of the other survivor Poelman, were quoted extensively in all the news accounts of the sinking.

42. Portland *Oregon Journal*, 22 September 1914: 1.

43. San Francisco *Chronicle*, 21 September 1914: 5.

44. Hoquiam *Washingtonian*, 22 September 1914: 3. The San Francisco *Chronicle* reported, 20 September 1914, p. 1, that "Shipping men are of the opinion that the steamer with her high deck load got into the trough of the sea through the disablement of her engines or steering gear, and not having the seaway [proper speed and steering] received the full impact of the waves." This theory is weakened somewhat by a subsequent assertion that the deck load was so firmly lashed down that it added to the ship's tendency to roll dangerously in the troughs, whereas survivor testimony suggested that the load had been cut loose.

45. Portland *Oregon Journal*, 20 September 1914: 2.

46. Harold D. Huycke, letter to the author, 25 June 2000.

47. Felix Riesenberg, *Standard Seamanship for the Merchant Service* (New York: D. Van Nostrand Company, 1936), note, p. 21, citing *U.S. Shipping Board Bulletin*.

48. The Seattle *Times*, 19 September 1914, p. 2, without any attribution said, "The failure of the lumber to keep her afloat for several hours is believed to indicate that the vessel was broken in two."

49. Portland *Oregonian*, 20 September 1914: 1. The term "the captain's wife" may have been a misconstruction of "*a* captain's wife," since the wife of a schooner captain was on board.

50. The body of Mrs. Theodus Jordalt, wife of the third mate, was found near Gardiner, Oregon, according to a clipping from the Portland *Oregonian*, 4 October 1914. The presence of the stowaways was revealed in the Hoquiam

Washingtonian, 20 September 1914, p. 1. The recovered bodies of two men believed to have been stowaways from the *Leggett* were identified in the Portland *Oregonian*, 23 September 1914, as C. M. Walker and in the Aberdeen *World*, 22 September 1914, p. 5, as C. W. Caldwell. Caldwell's parents, however, claimed that he was a workaway, not a stowaway.

51. Aberdeen *World*, 19 September 1914: 6.
52. Aberdeen *World*, 28 September 1914: 6.
53. *Coast Seamen's Journal*, 21 October 1914: 5; *Coast Seamen's Journal*, 14 October 1914: 6.
54. Portland *Oregonian*, 21 September 1914: 3.

Chapter Seven

1. Coos Bay *Times*, 3 November 1915: 10.
2. Coos Bay *Times*, 8 November 1915: 21.
3. Marshall, *California Shipwrecks*, 147.
4. Coos Bay *Times*, 8 November 1915: 21.
5. Coos Bay *Times*, 8 November 1915: 21.
6. Coos Bay *Times*, 3 November 1915: 12.
7. Coos Bay *Times*, 3 November 1915: 11.
8. Her principal rival in this trade was the *Breakwater* of the Portland and Coos Bay Steamship Company, a busy ship that has been largely overlooked by maritime historians.
9. The weather and other circumstances of the disaster are described in the letter from the local inspectors, Bion B. Whitney and Harry C. Lord, to the Steamboat Inspection Service in Washington, DC, dated 3 January 1916.
10. Douthit, *South Coast*, 125.
11. Newspaper accounts, including statements by the captain, provide the details of the accident. The most voluminous accounts are in the Coos Bay *Times*.
12. The call letters, frequency, and power of shipboard radio stations of that era appear in *Signal Letters*, 102-05.
13. "Wreck of the *Santa Clara*," Chapter 11 of Nathan Douthit, *The Coos Bay Region, 1890-1944: Life on a Coastal Frontier* (Coos Bay, OR: River West Books, 1981), 127.
14. Seattle *Post-Intelligencer*, 3 November 1915: 1.
15. Captain Edward L. Skog as told to William L. Brown, "Coos Bay Tragedy: Shipwreck of the *Santa Clara*," Portland *Oregonian*, Magazine Section, 6 November 1938: 3. Skog was a former Coos Bay bar pilot.
16. Seattle *Post-Intelligencer*, 4 November 1915: 9.
17. Coos Bay *Times*, 4 November 1915: 16.
18. Coos Bay *Times*, 3 November 1915: 8.
19. Seattle *Post-Intelligencer*, 3 November 1915: 1.
20. Seattle *Post-Intelligencer*, 4 November 1915: 9.
21. Seattle *Post-Intelligencer*, 4 November 1915: 9.
22. Letter, local inspectors to Steamboat Inspection Service, Washington, DC, 3 January 1915. The date of the letter, written two months after the accident, should obviously be 1916.
23. Coos Bay *Times*, 4 November 1915: 16.
24. Douthit, *Coos Bay*, 127.

25. Coos Bay *Times*, 6 November 1915: 19.

26. Douthit, *Coos Bay*, 130, citing Coos Bay *Times*, 11 November 1915.

27. Douthit, *Coos Bay*, 131, citing Coos Bay *Times*, 12 November 1915.

28. Coos Bay *Times*, 3 November 1915: 11.

29. Coos Bay *Times*, 8 November 1915: 21.

30. Coos Bay *Times*, 8 November 1915: 22.

31. The details of the steering problem are set forth in letter, local inspectors Whitney and Lord, to Steamboat Inspection Service, Washington, DC, 7 February 1916. Correspondence pertaining to these hearings, but no transcript of the testimony, is contained in Box 13, Record Group 41, National Archives, Seattle.

32. Quoted in letter, local inspectors to Steamboat Inspection Service, Washington, DC, 7 February 1916.

33. Testimony of Louis Vallenga before inspectors Whitney and Lord, Seattle, WA, quoted in letter local inspectors to Steamboat Inspection Service, Washington, DC, 7 February 1916.

34. Letter, local inspectors to Steamboat Inspection Service, Washington, DC, 7 February 1916.

35. Portland *Oregonian*, 4 December 1915: 16.

Chapter Eight

1. The Associated Oil Company was originally formed by the Southern Pacific Railroad, which was converting its locomotives to oil early in the 20th century, and became a force in the California oil industry. See Frank J. Taylor and Earl M. Welty, *Black Bonanza* (New York: McGraw Hill, 1950), 118.

2. Portland *Oregonian*, 11 January 1913: 10.

3. The *Buck*'s wartime service is decribed in Lewis P. Clephane, *History of the Naval Overseas Transportation Service in World War I* (Washington, DC: Naval History Division, 1969), 4.

4. Portland *Oregonian*, 20 December 1919: 4.

5. *McCurdy*, 300.

6. San Francisco *Chronicle*, 21 December 1919: 1.

7. The most useful photo appears in Gibbs, *Peril*, 85, and is attributed to the Carl Christensen collection.

8. Portland *Oregonian*, 20 December 1919: 4.

9. *McCurdy*, 96. This incident was unique in that the captain, who was part-owner of the yacht-like ex-"banana-boat," departed in the first lifeboat. A coroner's jury subsequently found him guilty of criminal negligence.

10. San Francisco *Chronicle*, 21 December 1919: 1.

11. Portland *Oregonian*, 21 December 1919: 20.

12. Monroe Upton, *From the High Seas to Low Comedy* (Tucson, AZ: Living Desert Press, 1985), 148.

13. Bandon *Western World*, 25 December 1919: 1.

14. *Signal Letters*, 102-05.

15. Portland *Oregonian*, 23 December 1919: 4.

16. San Francisco *Chronicle*, 21 December 1919: 1.

17. Portland *Oregonian*, 20 December 1919: 1.

18. Patrick Masterson, *Port Orford: A History* (Wilsonville, OR: BookPartners, Inc., 1994), 117.

19. Masterson, 117. The deputy sheriff's name is spelled Jeter in the Portland *Oregon Journal,* as well as in the Gold Beach *Reporter.* The latter newspaper suggests, 29 January 1920, p. 5, that the men in this boat were intent on plundering the wreck, rather than looking for survivors.
20. Bandon *Western World,* 25 December 1919: 1.
21. San Francisco *Chronicle,* 21 December 1919: 1.
22. San Francisco *Chronicle,* 21 December 1919: 1.
23. Portland *Oregonian,* 21 December 1919: 20.
24. Portland *Oregonian,* 21 December 1919: 20.
25. Portland *Oregonian,* 21 December 1919: 20.
26. San Francisco *Chronicle,* 20 December 1919: 1.
27. Bandon *Western World,* 25 December 1919: 1.
28. San Francisco *Chronicle,* 20 December 1919: 1.
29. Portland *Oregonian,* 23 December 1919: 1.
30. Masterson, 118.
31. Masterson, 118.
32. San Francisco *Chronicle,* 7 February 1920: 7.
33. Masterson, 118.
34. Gold Beach *Reporter,* 29 January 1920: 5.
35. Portland *Oregonian,* 29 February 1920: 22.
36. *Coast Seamen's Journal,* 31 March 1920: 5.

Chapter Nine

1. McNairn and MacMullen, 17.
2. Gibbs, *Juan de Fuca,* 184.
3. Gibbs, *Juan de Fuca,* 187.
4. Gibbs, *Peril,* 203, 222.
5. Walter A. Jackson, *The Doghole Schooners* (Mendocino, CA: Bear & Stebbins, 1977), 34.
6. *McCurdy,* 166.
7. *McCurdy,* 300.
8. McNairn and MacMullen, 96.
9. *McCurdy,* 27. Details of this voyage are in "Log Book of Twelve Yukon Steamers on Trip from Seattle, Wash. to St. Michaels, Alaska," *Sea Chest,* vol. 23 (September 1989): 26-28.
10. McNairn and MacMullen, 72.
11. Marshall, *California Shipwrecks,* 132.
12. McNairn and MacMullen, 96.
13. San Francisco *Chronicle,* 19 September 1930: 3.
14. Portland *Oregonian,* 19 September 1930: 2.
15. Crew List Attachment, Record of Casualties to Vessels, filed by Hobbs Wall & Co. with the U.S. Coast Guard, 1 October 1930.
16. Portland *Oregonian,* 28 September 1930: 1.
17. Coos Bay *Times,* 20 September 1930: 3.
18. The *Cahokia,* named for the great mound-building Native American culture, had been built as the U.S. Shipping Board tug *Bayside* in 1921 and was immediately transferred to the Coast Guard, which retained her until 1936 when she was transferred to the Navy.
19. San Francisco *Chronicle,* 19 September 1930: 1.

20. The shellings were reported in the San Francisco *Chronicle*, 21 September 1930: 4. The *Cahokia*'s largest gun was a one-pounder, so sinking a lifeboat or a deckhouse was a major challenge for the vessel.
21. Coos Bay *Times*, 20 September 1930: 3.
22. Coos Bay *Times*, 20 September 1930: 3.
23. San Francisco *Chronicle*, 19 September 1930: 1.
24. Marshall, *California Shipwrecks*, 44.
25. Coos Bay *Times*, 20 September 1930: 3.
26. Gordon Newell and Joe Williamson, *Pacific Lumber Ships*, (Seattle, WA: Superior Publishing Company, 1960), 168.
27. Coos Bay *Times*, 20 September 1930: 3; Portland *Oregonian*, 18 September 1930: 6.
28. San Francisco *Chronicle*, 21 September 1930: 4.
29. San Francisco *Chronicle*, 19 September 1930: 3.
30. San Francisco *Chronicle*, 19 September 1930: 3.
31. Grover, "*Roanoke*," 24.
32. This phenomenon was witnessed from the schooners *Volant* and *C. T. Hill* as described in Jackson, 44.
33. Jackson, 32. The schooner was the *J. C. Ford,* which was eventually lost off Grays Harbor.
34. Casualty Report filed by Hobbs Wall & Co. with U.S. Coast Guard, 1 October 1930.

Chapter Ten

1. Actually, only one other legal action has surfaced in the accounts of the other eight shipwrecks in this book, the one that occurred after the *Valencia* disaster. In the face of the intense scrutiny of that event at the national level and the attention devoted to the victims, it seems unlikely that the claim for five thousand dollars damages by a survivor of the *Valencia* would have had much standing.
2. Portland *Oregonian*, 13 January 1936: 10.
3. Astoria *Astorian-Budget*, 13 January 1936: 4.
4. "Report of Investigation of the grounding and loss of the Steamer IOWA with all hands, about 4 A.M., January 12, 1936, on Peacock Spit, Columbia River Entrance," attached to letter, "W. W. S., Director" to the Secretary of Commerce, 29 March 1936, 3.
5. Report by "W. W. S.," 3-4.
6. *American Maritime Cases.* Baltimore: American Maritime Cases, Inc., 1938, pp. 614, 618-19. The lookout station at Cape Disappointment remains in use today.
7. *1938 American Maritime Cases,* 614, 621-22.
8. Report by "W. W. S.," 5.
9. Don McLeod, "The Wreck of the *Iowa*," Portland *Oregonian*, 24 July 1938, p. 4 of Magazine Section.
10. Portland *Oregonian*, 13 January 1936: 2.
11. Portland *Oregonian*, 13 January 1936: 2.
12. Astoria *Astorian-Budget*, 13 January 1936: 1; Portland *Oregonian*, 31 January 1936: 2.
13. Astoria *Astorian-Budget*, 13 January 1936: 4.

14. Portland *Oregonian,* 14 January 1936: 1, 4.

15. Portland *Oregonian*, 15 January 1936: 1.

16. Astoria *Astorian-Budget*, 15 January 1936: 1.

17. Astoria *Astorian-Budget*, 15 January 1936: 3.

18. Portland *Oregonian*, 17 January 1936: 4.

19. Portland *Oregonian*, 18 January 1936: 6.

20. Portland *Oregonian*, 19 January 1936: 1.

21. Portland *Oregonian*, 19 January 1936: 1.

22. Report by "W. W. S.," 2.

23. Report by "W. W. S.," 6.

24. Astoria *Astorian-Budget,* 15 January 1936: 3; Astoria *Astorian-Budget*, 16 January 1936: 8.

25. *1938 American Maritime Cases,* 1340, 1341.

26. *1938 American Maritime Cases,* 614.

27. *1938 American Maritime Cases,* 614, 621-22.

28. *1938 American Maritime Cases,* 614, 638.

29. *1938 American Maritime Cases,* 614, 639.

30. Maguire was a man of many accomplishments, including serving as the first president of the Oregon Bar Association, as Master in Chancery (equity) for the U.S. District Court in Oregon, and as a prosecutor for the International Military Tribunal in the Nuremberg war crimes trials. His obituary appears in the Vertical File on Biography at the Oregon Historical Society.

Bibliography

Books

Bascom, Willard. *Waves and Beaches*. Garden City, NY: Anchor Books, 1980.

Best, Gerald M. *Ships and Narrow Gauge Rails: The Story of the Pacific Coast Company*. Berkeley, CA: Howell-North, 1964.

Bowditch, Nathaniel, original author. *American Practical Navigator: An Epitome of Navigation and Nautical Astronomy*. Washington, DC: Government Printing Office, 1939.

Brady, Edward M. *Marine Salvage Operations*. Cambridge, MD: Cornell Maritime Press, 1960.

Brown, Giles T. *Ships That Sail No More: Marine Transportation from San Diego to Puget Sound, 1910–1940*. Lexington, KY: University of Kentucky Press, 1966.

Clephane, Lewis P. *History of the Naval Overseas Transportation Service in World War I*. Washington, DC: Naval History Division, 1969.

Desmond, Charles. *Wooden Shipbuilding*. New York: The Rudder Publishing Company, 1919.

Dicken, Samuel L., and Dicken, Emily F. *The Making of Oregon: A Study in Historical Geography*. Portland: Oregon Historical Society, 1979.

Distances Between United States Ports. Washington, DC: U.S. Department of Commerce, National Oceanic and Atmospheric Administration, 1993.

Douthit, Nathan. *A Guide to Oregon South Coast History*. Corvallis, OR: Oregon State University Press, 1999.

———. *The Coos Bay Region, 1890–1944: Life on a Coastal Frontier*. Coos Bay, OR: River West Books, 1981.

Gibbs, James A. *Disaster Log of Ships*. New York: Bonanza Books, 1978.

———. *Pacific Graveyard*. Portland, OR: Binfords & Mort, 1993.

———. *Peril at Sea: A Photographic Study of Shipwrecks in the Pacific*. West Chester, PA: Schiffer Publishing Ltd., 1986.

———. *Sentinels of the North Pacific: The Story of Pacific Coast Lighthouses and Lightships*. Portland, OR: Binfords & Mort, 1955.

———. *Shipwrecks of Juan de Fuca*. Portland, OR: Binfords & Mort, 1968.

———. *Shipwrecks of the Pacific Coast*. Portland, OR: Binfords & Mort, 1957.

Gorter, Wytze, and Hildebrand, George H. *The Pacific Coast Maritime Shipping Industry, 1930–1948*. Berkeley and Los Angeles: The University of California Press, 1952.

Graves, Jack L. *Flagg of the* Mimi. Garibaldi, OR: Garibaldi Books, 2000.

———. *"Now" Never Lasts: Stories of Garibaldi and Garibaldians*. Garibaldi, OR: Garibaldi Books, 1995.

Grover, David H. *The San Francisco Shipping Conspiracies of World War One*. Napa, CA: Western Maritime Press, 1995.

Holman, H. L. *A Handy Book for Shipowners & Masters*. London: The Commercial Printing and Stationery Co, Ltd., 1948.

Jackson, Walter A. *The Doghole Schooners*. Mendocino, CA: Bear & Stebbins, 1977.

Johnson, Robert Erwin. *Guardians of the Sea: History of the United States Coast Guard, 1915 to the Present*. Annapolis, MD: Naval Institute Press, 1987.

King, Jane, and Hempstead, Andrew. *British Columbia Handbook*. Chico, CA: Moon Publications, 1998.

Light List of the Pacific Coast, 1941. Washington, DC: U.S. Coast Guard, 1941.

Lyman, Robert Hunt, editor. *The World Almanac and Book of Facts*. New York: New York *World,* 1923, 1930.

McNairn, Jack, and MacMullen, Jerry. *Ships of the Redwood Coast*. Stanford, CA: Stanford University Press, 1945.

Marshall, Don. *California Shipwrecks*. Seattle: Superior Publishing Company, 1978.

———. *Oregon Shipwrecks*. Portland, OR: Binford and Mort Publishing, 1984.

Masterson, Patrick. *Port Orford, A History*. Wilsonville, OR: Book Partners, Inc., 1994.

Meyer, Jurgen. *Hamburgs Segelschiffe, 1795-1945*. Norderstedt, Germany: Chronik der Seefahrt, Verlag Egon Heinemann, 1971.

Morison, Samuel E. *History of United States Naval Operations in World War II,* vol. XV, Supplement and General Index. Boston: Little, Brown and Co., 1962.

National Cyclopedia of American Biography. New York: James T. White & Co., 1921.

Newell, Gordon. *Ocean Liners of the 20th Century*. New York: Bonanza Books, 1963.

———, ed. *The H. W. McCurdy Marine History of the Northwest*. Seattle: Superior Publishing Company, 1966.

———, and Williamson, Joe. *Pacific Coastal Liners*. New York: Bonanza Books, 1959.

———, and Williamson, Joe. *Pacific Lumber Ships*. Seattle: Superior Publishing Company, 1960.

Pacific Coast Pilot. Washington, DC: U.S. Navy Hydrographic Office, 1909.

Pacific Ports Manual, 7th edition. Los Angeles: Pacific Ports, Inc., 1921.

Parmenter, Tish, and Bailey, Robert. *The Oregon Oceanbook*. Salem, OR: Oregon Department of Land Conservation and Development, 1985.

The Raising of the American Steamship "Republic." San Francisco: Paul Elder and Company, 1916.

Riesenberg, Felix. *Standard Seamanship for the Merchant Service*. New York: D. Van Nostrand Company, 1936.

Rogers, Fred. *Shipwrecks of British Columbia*. Vancouver, BC: J. J. Douglas, Ltd., 1976.

St. John, Jeffrey. *Mysteries and Mishaps on California Coastal Steamers*. Napa, CA: Western Maritime Press, 1995.

Stange, G. Robert, ed. *The Poetical Works of Tennyson*. Boston: Houghton Mifflin Company, 1974.

Taylor, Frank J., and Welty, Earl M. *Black Bonanza*. New York: McGraw-Hill, 1959.

Timmerman, Tricia. *British Columbia: A Guide to Unique Places*. Guilford, CT: Globe Pequot Press, 2000.

Turpin, Edward A., and MacEwen, William A. *Merchant Marine Officers' Handbook*. New York: Cornell Maritime Press, 1944.

United States Coast Pilot. Washington, DC: Government Printing Office, 1910.

Upton, Monroe. *From the High Seas to Low Comedy: Memoirs of Radio Man*. Tucson, AZ: Living Desert Press, 1985.

Worden, William L. *Cargoes: Matson's First Century in the Pacific*. Honolulu: University Press of Hawaii, 1981.

Articles

Baily, Clarence H. "The Wreck of the *Valencia*." *Pacific Monthly,* March 1906.

Chua-Eoan, Howard G. "Going, Going . . . ." *Time,* 19 August 1991.

Drury, Aubrey, researcher. "John Albert Hooper." *California Historical Society Quarterly,* vol. 31, 1952.

Goddard, Joan. "Addressing Disaster—West Coast Life Saving Trail." *Resolution: The Journal of the Maritime Museum of British Columbia,* Autumn 2000.

Grover, David H. "Danger on the Dredges." *Sea Classics,* February/March 1985.

———. "Did Japan Attempt to Invade Mexico?: The *Asama* Incident." *Sea Classics,* April 1996.

———. "Riddle of the *Roanoke*." *Sea Classics,* August 1994.

———. "The Tragedy of the *San Juan*." *Sea Classics,* January 1997.

———, and Grover, Gretchen G. "Night Attack on Shanghai." *Naval History,* Winter 1991.

Henry, John Frazier. "The Wreck of the *Valencia*." *Columbia: The Magazine of Northwest History*, Summer 1993.

"Log Book of Twelve Yukon Steamers on Trip from Seattle, Washington, to St. Michaels, Alaska." *The Sea Chest,* vol. 23, no. 1, September 1989.

Wolferstan, Bill. The *Valencia* Tragedy: A Shipwreck that Killed 136 People." *Beautiful British Columbia,* Summer 1973.

Newspapers and Newsmagazines

Aberdeen *World*

Astoria *Daily Budget*

Astoria *Morning Astorian*

Astoria *Astorian-Budget*

Bandon *The Western World*

Coast Seaman's Journal

Coos Bay *Times*

Gold Beach *Reporter*

Guide, The

Hoquiam *Daily Washingtonian*

Los Angeles *Times*

Nehalem Bay *Fishtrapper*

Nehalem *Enterprise*

New York *Herald*

New York Times

Portland *Evening Journal*

Portland *Oregonian*

San Francisco *Call-Post*

San Francisco *Chronicle*

Seattle *Mail and Herald*

Seattle *Post-Intelligencer*

Seattle *Star*

Seattle *Times*

Tillamook *Headlight*

Tillamook *Herald*

Time Magazine

Washington Post

Victoria *Daily Colonist*

Government Documents

Investigation into the Causes of Fire on Steamship 'Queen,' *Saturday, February 27, 1904*. Hearing Before Captain B. B. Whitney and Mr. R. A. Turner, Composing the Local Board of Inspectors at Seattle, Washington, March 3, 1904. Record Group 41, Bureau of Marine Inspection and Navigation, National Archives, Seattle, Washington.

Investigation of the Grounding and Loss of the Steamer Iowa *with All Hands, about 4 a.m., January 12, 1936, on Peacock Spit, Columbia River Entrance.* Report of "Director WWS" to Secretary of Commerce, March 25, 1936. Record Group 41, National Archives, Washington, DC.

"Part VI: Seagoing Vessels of the United States with Official Numbers and Signal Letters," from the *Forty-fourth Annual List of the Merchant Vessels of the United States for the Year ending June 30, 1912*. Washington, DC: Department of Commerce and Labor, 1912.

Register of the Commissioned and Warrant Officers and Cadets, and Ships and Stations of the United States Coast Guard, January 1, 1930. Washington, DC: Government Printing Office, 1930.

Report of the United States Commission of Investigation Upon the Disaster to the Steamer "General Slocum." Washington, DC: Government Printing Office for the Department of Commerce and Labor, 1904.

Wreck of the Steamer Valencia. Report to the President of the Federal Commission of Investigation, April 14, 1906. Washington, DC: Government Printing Office, 1906.

Legal Cases

American Maritime Cases. Baltimore, MD: The Maritime Law Association of the United States, 1936: 1340.

American Maritime Cases. Baltimore, MD: The Maritime Law Association of the United States, 1938: 614

American Maritime Cases. Baltimore, MD: The Maritime Law Association of the United States, 1941: 111.

Index

A

Aberdeen, WA, 105-6, 120
Acapulco, Mexico, 108
Adamson (British steamer), 30
Adeline Smith (steam schooner), 126, 129
Admiral Benson (passenger ship), 22
Admiral Dewey (passenger ship), 42-43
Admiral Farragut (passenger ship), 43, 106
Admiral Line, 25, 42, 44, 106, 138
Admiral Schley (passenger ship), 148
Admiral Watson (passenger ship), 43, 106
aircraft, use in searches, 162-63, 178
Alaska, 19, 29, 30, 42, 47, 51, 73, 123, 160
Alaska Pacific Navigation Co., 106, 123
Alberni Inlet, BC, 52
Alcatraz tanker terminal, CA, 73
Alexander, Emma. See Emma Alexander
Alexander, H. F. (shipowner), 25
Allison, Charles (*Valencia* passenger), 65
American Bureau of Shipping, 47
American Maritime Cases, 181-85
American President Lines, 28
Anderson, Helen (*Leggett* passenger), 119
Anderson, Mrs. Nelson (*Leggett*, passenger), 119
Anderson, Walter (*Queen* officer), 39
Andrea Doria (Italian passenger ship), 4
Antofagasta, Chile, 86
Armstrong, F. (*Rosecrans* crew), 76
Arthur, President Chester A., 45
Asama (Japanese cruiser), 112
Ascunsion (tanker), 87
Associated Oil Company, 73, 78, 112, 139-40, 141, 145-46, 151, 159, 174-77
Astoria, OR, 86, 88-89, 106, 131, 141, 163, 173-77
Atlantic and Caribbean Navigation Co., 46

B

Bahada (tug), 61
Baird, W. J. (*South Coast* officer), 168
Ballard, Mrs. D. T. (*Santa Clara* passenger), 128
Ballard, Lucille (*Santa Clara* passenger), 128
Bamfield, BC, 57
Bandon, OR, 17, 23-24, 146-48, 149, 150-51, 155, 158, 163
bar ports, 17-18, 105
Barclay, Curle & Company, 72
Barkley Sound, BC, 57, 61
Bastendorf Beach, OR, 129
Bay City, OR, 17, 89
Bayside (tug), 198 (note 18)
Bear (passenger ship), 81
Beaver (passenger ship), 113-14, 115-16
"*Bedella*," (song), 32
Benson, Admiral. See Admiral Benson
Bessie K. (steam schooner), 158
Best, Don (photographer), 101
Biddle (dredge), 17
Big Sur coast, CA, 15
"Big Three." *See* San Francisco & Portland Steamship Co.
Binns, Jack (*Republic* radioman), 64
Black Ball Line, 65
Blacklock Point, OR, 143
Blackman, Russell (*Mimi* salvor), 96
Blue Magpie (Japanese freighter), 18
Blunts Reef, CA, 16, 81
Boulton, Bliss, and Dallett (ship owners), 47
Bowditch (navigation manual), 8
Breakwater (passenger ship), 196 (note 8)
breeches buoy, 14, 22, 61 74, 129-30
Brighton Beach, OR, 91, 92
Brookings, OR, 17, 161, 163
Brown, Giles T. (author), 25
Buck, Frank H. See Frank H. Buck
Buckman (passenger ship), 106
Bunker, Frank F. (*Valencia* passenger), 57-58, 63, 65
Burwell, William T. (*Valencia* commissioner), 67-70

C

C. T. Hill (schooner), 199 (note 32)

Cagna, "Dago Joe" (Rosecrans crew), 79-80, 81-82

Cahokia (Coast Guard tug), 162-63, 165-66

California Pacific Steamship Co., 172

Californian (British steamer), 12

Call-Post (San Francisco), 102

Callao, Peru, 86

Calmar Line, 15

Canadian Pacific Steamship Co., 28

Canberra (British passenger ship), 28

Cann, Thomas H. (captain, City of Topeka), 62

Cape Arago, OR, 20, 126

Cape Beale, BC, 52, 56-57

Cape Blanco, OR, 16, 20, 21, 88, 114, 141-44, 146, 153-54, 161, 163

Cape Disappointment Lighthouse, WA, 16, 21-22, 64, 77, 80, 82, 84, 174-75, 186

Cape Fermin, CA, 16

Cape Flattery, WA, 5, 16, 21, 36, 49, 53, 58, 68, 88, 105, 123, 142, 157-58

Cape Foulweather, OR, 15

Cape Lookout, OR, 21

Cape Meares, OR, 20-21

Cape Mendocino, CA, 16, 48, 68, 123, 142

Cape Perpetua, OR, 15

Carilel (Belgian steamer), 62

Carlson, C. (Santa Clara crew), 130

Carmanah Lighthouse, BC, 50, 52, 56-57, 58

Carrier Dove (schooner), 119

Cashen, Frank (Chanslor crew), 144

Castle Mail Service, 71

Castle Rock, OR, 143

casualties, marine, in past, 2-3

Cavendish, Lord Charles (British statesman), 71

Channel Islands, CA, 16

Chanslor, J. A. See J. A. Chanslor

Chanslor, J. A. (oilman), 139-40

Chehalis (steam schooner), 47

Chehalis River, WA, 105

Chelan (Coast Guard cutter), 175

Chevron Corporation, 159

Chilcott, Capt. Richard (critic), 64, 66

China Mail Line, 44

Chronicle (San Francisco), 48, 71, 91, 95, 144, 150, 162

Church, Alice (Santa Clara passenger), 127

City of Puebla (passenger ship), 47-48

City of Sydney (passenger ship), 108

City of Topeka (passenger ship), 59, 60-61, 66, 69, 148

Civilian Conservation Corps, 177

Clallam (passenger ship), 65

Clatsop Spit, OR, 29

Cleveland, USS (cruiser), 108

Clipperton Island, Mexico, 108

Clo-oose, BC, 57-58

Coast Pilot, 21, 107

Coast Seamen's Journal, 121

coastline, northwestern, features of, 14-16, 19-20

"cockbilling" of lifeboat, 130

Columbia (passenger ship), 103

Columbia (British/American steamer, aka Rosecrans), 72, 83

Columbia Pacific Shipping Co., 172

Columbia River, 16-17, 20, 22, 24, 29, 36, 75, 77-78, 83, 86, 88, 91, 105, 107, 110, 112, 114-15, 137-38, 141, 174-75, 178, 180, 183, 186

Columbia River Lightship, 21, 76-77, 80, 81, 88, 114, 180

Columbus Day Storm, 169

Comyn, MacKall & Co. (ship operators), 86

Condor (British naval sloop), 5, 157

Congress (passenger ship), 43-44

Connors (Valencia crew), 61

Conrad, Joseph (novelist), 6, 108

Coos Bay, OR, 17-18, 23, 27, 43, 116, 124-26, 131-32, 135, 142, 160, 163, 166

Coos Bay Times, 132

Coos Head, OR, 125, 126, 132

Copalis Beach, WA, 14

Coquille River, OR, 14, 20-21, 147-48, 150-51

Cortes Bank, CA, 16

Cousins, N. E. (captain of *Queen*), 30-32, 33, 35-38, 43-44, 52, 59, 61, 63, 68
Cramp Shipyard, 28, 45
Crescent City, CA, 16-17, 43, 160, 162
crews, nature of ships', 11, 48, 82, 161, 172
"Crossing the Bar" (poem by Tennyson), 186-87
Crowe, Capt. Albert (*Mimi* salvor), 89, 92-93, 96
Crowley, Mr. and Mrs. B. J. (*Santa Clara* passengers), 128
Curtis, Capt. Lebeus (marine surveyor), 154-55
Cyclops, USS (collier), 4
Czar (Canadian tug), 60, 63, 69

D

Daily Astorian, 194 (note 24)
Daisy Putnam (steam schooner), 114
Darling Creek, BC, 57
Daykin, Phil (*Valencia* rescue party), 57-58
Daykin, Roby, 58, 191 (note 34)
Daykin, Tom (lighthouse keeper), 57-58
Deshar, A. (*Santa Clara* officer), 130
Destruction Island, WA, 16, 21
Dewey, Admiral. See *Admiral Dewey*
diving on wrecks, recreational, 2, 152
Dodge, C. P. (shipowner), 123
"doghole" landings, CA, 17
Dollar, James. See *James Dollar*
Dollar Line, 25, 28, 87, 122-23
Dooley, Earl W. (*Chanslor* crew), 148-49, 150, 152, 153
Downing, E. W. (*Valencia* officer), 52
Dunn, Bridget (*Santa Clara* passenger), 127
Dunn, Marguerite (*Santa Clara* passenger), 127
Dunn, Roy (*Santa Clara* passenger), 127
Dunstan (lighthouse keeper), 126.

E

Edith (collier), 51
Edthofer, Frank (inspector), 178-80

Edwards, E. S. (inspector), 84
Elder, George W. See *George W. Elder*
Elizabeth (steam schooner), 162
El Segundo (tanker), 114
Emma Alexander (passenger ship), 44
Empire Woodlark (British steamer), 44
Empress of Australia (British passenger ship), 28
"Erin Kildare" (dog), 134
Eskildson, Lars (*Frank Buck* crew), 113
Eureka, CA, 17, 24, 123-24, 128, 135, 163
Everett, WA, 122

F

F. A. Kilburn (passenger ship), 135
Farallon Islands, CA, 16, 30
Farley, Capt. Robert (Lifesaving Service), 88, 92, 94, 96-98, 100
Farragut, Admiral. See *Admiral Farragut*
Farrell, Alexander (*Leggett* passenger), 107, 109, 113, 115-16, 117, 118
Fearless (tug), 79, 80, 88
Fee, Judge James A., 182, 185
Fischer, Frederick (aka William Fischer and Frederick Flagg, mate of *Mimi*), 92
Fischer, Mimi (daughter of captain of *Mimi*), 100-101
Fisher, Charles S. (salvor), 91-92, 94, 95, 100
Fisher Engineering and Construction Co. (salvors), 91, 96
Fisher, Capt. Walter (inspector), 179
fishing boat disaster of 1880, 169
Fleming, C. J. (*Leggett* radioman), 107, 115, 119
Florence, OR, 17, 23
Flying Dutchman (ghost ship), 5
Flying Enterprise (freighter), 4
fog, role of in accidents, 21-22, 48-49, 51, 58, 86, 142-43
Ford, J. C. See *J. C. Ford*
Ford Motor Company, 161
Fort Bragg, CA, 160
Fort Canby, WA, 23, 80
Fort Stevens, OR, 23, 80, 82
Forty, George (owners' representative), 154

Francis H. Leggett (passenger ship), 102-21, 141, 166-68, 170

Frank H. Buck (tanker), 112-13, 114-15, 116, 141, 152

Frye, Jesse (U. S. attorney), 66

Fuller, George F. (inspector), 84

G

Garibaldi, OR, 90

Garibaldi Lifesaving Station, 88, 92, 94-95

Gaviota, CA, 73, 74

General Petroleum Company, 161

General Slocum (steamer), 5, 67

Genereaux, Capt. E. C. (insurance adjustor), 89-90

George Loomis (tanker), 141, 158

George W. Elder (passenger ship), 124

Getty Oil Co., 73

Gibbs (*Frank Buck* officer), 113

Gibbs, James A. (author), 21, 132, 157

Glasgow, Scotland, 71, 85

Glenclova (British barque, aka German barque *Mimi*), 85

Gold Beach, OR, 17, 161, 164

Goleta, CA, 141

Goliath (tug), 79

Gomez, Rose (*Leggett* passenger), 119

Goodwin, O. E. (*Santa Clara* radioman), 126

Grant (Revenue Marine cutter), 61

Graves, Jack L. (author), 90-92, 100

Grays Harbor, WA, 15-17, 21, 23-24, 86, 103, 104, 105-7, 117, 120

Great Northern (passenger ship), 105-6

Great Northern Pacific Steamship Co., 25

Great Northern Railway, 25

Green, Ole (*Leggett* officer), 119

Greer, James (*Queen* crew), 40

Guide, The, 24, 87

Gulf Oil Co., 140

Gull Rock, OR, 143

H

Haida (British steamer), 158

Hammond, C. A. (lumberman), 104

Hammond Lumber Co., 103, 160

Hancock, Sam (*Valencia* crew), 61

Hanify, J. R., Co. (shipowners), 160

Hanlon, Dan (shipbuilder), 155

Harriman, E. H. (railway/ship owner), 25

Hawaii, 29, 73

Heceta Head Lighthouse, OR, 20

Hercules (tug), 42

Hibbard, Capt. Isaac N. (*Queen* passenger), 32, 38

Hicks-Hauptman Lumber Co., 104

Higgins, James S. (owner/master, *South Coast*), 160

Hill, C. T. See *C. T. Hill*

Hill, James J. (railway/ship owner), 25, 106

Hobbs Wall and Co. (lumber firm), 160, 162, 164, 170

Hohne, Adolph (*Chanslor* crew), 150-51

Holmes, Sherlock, 170

Holyfield, J. E. (salvor), 92-94

Homer (steam schooner/salvage ship), 155

Honolulu, HI, 5, 30, 73-74, 169

Hooper, John A. (shipowner), 100

Hoquiam, WA, 27, 105-6, 120

Hughes Brothers ranch, OR, 143-44, 146-47

Humphrey, William E. (congressman), 67

Hunter, G. O. (labor leader), 178

Huycke, Capt. Harold D. (author), 117-18

I

Idzumo (Japanese cruiser), 102, 109, 110-12, 113, 115, 121

Ilwaco, WA, 177, 186

Independent Steamship Company, 25

Industrial Workers of the World (IWW), 42

Ingals, Tillie (*Leggett* passenger), 119

Iowa (freighter), 171-87

J

J. A. Chanslor (tanker), 139-55

J. C. Ford (schooner), 199 (note 33)

Jackson, C. S. (newspaperman), 151

Jackson, Francis (*Chanslor* officer), 151-52

James Dollar (steamer, aka *Santa Clara*), 122

Japan, 28, 43, 172

Jensen, Capt. Jens (*Leggett* passenger), 108-9, 115, 119

Jesse, George H. (*Valencia* passenger), 64-65

Jetter (or Jeter), Howard W. (Oregon deputy sheriff), 147

Johanna Smith (steam schooner), 43, 148

John S. Kimball (steamer, aka *Santa Clara*), 122

Johnson, John (*Leggett* passenger), 120

Johnson, John (*Valencia* crew), 51, 190 (note 19)

Johnson, Lucien F. (captain of *Rosecrans*), 73-74, 75-76, 79, 82-84

Johnson, Oscar M. (captain of *Valencia*), 47, 48-52, 54-55, 60, 62, 67-68, 133

Johnson, Robert (Coast Guardsman), 147-48

Jones, Hugh B. (oil company executive), 154

Jones, M. J. (*Chanslor* officer), 151-52

Jordfeldt, T. (*Leggett* officer), 119

K

Kilburn, F. A. See *F. A. Kilburn*

Kimball, John S. See *John S. Kimball*

Kimball Steamship Company, 122-23

Klamath Mountains, OR, 15

Klanaway (also Klanawa and Clanawah) Point, BC, 52, 57

Klein, William (Oregon resident), 101

Klipsan Beach, WA, 23, 82

Kosei Maru (Japanese steamer), 173

Kreiger, Alfred (*Iowa* officer), 179

Kreiger, Mrs. Alfred (widow), 179

Kusher, Johan (aka Johan Koschr and Hans Konchord, *Mimi* crew), 95

L

Lake Benbow (freighter), 161

Lakeview Cemetery, Seattle, 67

Leggett, Francis H. See *Francis H. Leggett*

Leggett, Francis H. (merchant), 104

Lehn, Frank (*Valencia* crew), 54

Leipzig (German cruiser), 112

lifeboats, launching of, 4, 13, 31, 33, 54, 80, 109, 127, 130, 153, 165-66

lighthouses, siting and use of, 20-22

Lightship hull #50, 80

Lightship hull #88, 80-81

Lindmark, Eric (*Rosecrans* crew), 79-81

Linnton, OR, 141, 149

Loehneyson, Baron Wolf von (German consul, Seattle), 99

Lofstedt, August (captain of *Santa Clara*), 124-26, 130, 133, 135-36, 138, 174

Logan, Joe (*Valencia* rescue party), 57

Long Beach/San Pedro, CA, 18, 105, 137, 160

Longview, WA, 141, 172, 179, 182

Loomis, George. See *George Loomis*

Lord, Harry C. (inspector), 135, 138

Lord Jim (novel by Joseph Conrad), 108

Lord, Capt. Stanley, 12

Lorne (Canadian tug), 61

Los Angeles, CA, 24-25, 28, 72, 105

Ludwig, Fritz (*Mimi* crew), 95-96

Lurline (passenger ship), 28

Lyle guns, 13, 55-58, 74, 130

M

Macdonald, G. B. (captain of *Frank H. Buck*), 113, 141

MacVeagh, Franklin (Secretary of the Treasury), 84

Maguire, Robert F. (*Iowa* commissioner), 182-86

Marconi Company, 111, 194 (note 24)

Mariposa (passenger ship), 28

Maro, Charles (captain of *Francis H. Leggett*), 105, 107-08, 118

Marshall, Don (author), 111

Marshfield, OR, 124, 129

Martin, Charles H. (governor of Oregon), 179

Martin, Joe (*Valencia* rescue party), 57

Mason, E. W. (captain of *Beaver*), 114

Masterson, Patrick (author), 146-47, 154

Matson Line, 28, 72-73
Matson, William (shipowner), 73
Mattawean (collier), 157
McCarthy, T. J. (*Valencia* crew), 53-54,
  55-56
McCormick Steamship Co., 25, 104-5
McCredy, W. J. (*Queen* officer), 38-39
*McCurdy Marine History of the Pacific
  Northwest,* 111, 114
Melville, Herman (author), 6
Merchant Marine Act of 1936, 13
Merchant Marine Officers' Handbook, 12
Merchant Vessels of the United States,
  103, 123
Merkel, William (*Chanslor* crew), 145,
  149-50
Metcalf, Victor H. (U. S. Secretary of
  Commerce and Labor), 66
*Methven Castle (*British steamer, aka
  Rosecrans), 71
Meyer (*Queen* officer), 31
Meyers, F. (*Leggett* officer), 119
Michie (dredge), 44, 129
Mimi (German barque), 85-101
Monarch (tug), 43
Monterey, CA, 24, 75, 112, 124
Moody, William H. (U. S. Attorney
  General), 66
Morro Castle (passenger ship), 5
Mt. Pleasant Cemetery, Seattle, 67
Mullins, Thomas (*Rosecrans* officer), 79
Murray, Lawrence O. (*Valencia*
  commissioner), 67
Mussel Beach, OR, 129
Myers, Ralph (shipping executive), 164

N
Nanking (Chinese steamer, aka
  Congress), 44
Nann Smith (steam schooner), 116
National Archives, 83, 121
National Transportation Safety Board,
  166
navigational equipment, early 20th
  century, 3, 7, 20, 49-50, 68, 75
Neah Bay, WA, 23, 53, 64, 68-69, 70,
  120
Neakahnie Mountain, OR, 15, 88

"Nearer My God to Thee" (hymn), 54,
  134
Nehalem Bay and Spit, 88-89, 90, 94,
  99, 101
Nelson Steamship Company, 25
New Carissa (Philippine freighter), 18
New Electra Line, 25
Newport, OR, 17, 23, 114
Newport News Shipbuilding Co., 103,
  139
Nokomis (schooner), 108
Nolan, Capt. John H. (inspector), 178-
  80
North Head Lighthouse, WA, 19, 21,
  76-77, 78, 82, 83
North Pacific Steamship Co., 25, 106,
  123-24, 138
Northern Pacific (passenger ship), 106
Northern Pacific Railway, 25
Northern Pacific Steamship Co., 72
Northwestern Steamship Company, 123
Norton, Oliver (*Chanslor* officer), 144
Norwood (steam schooner), 47, 111,
  114
Noyes, W. T. (*Santa Clara* passenger),
  128

O
Oliver J. Olson (freighter), 14
Olson, B. W. (captain of *Adeline
  Smith*), 129
Olson, Lawrence (*Queen* crew), 55
Olson, Oliver J. See Oliver J. Olson
Olympia, USS (cruiser), 73
Olympic Mountains, WA, 15
Oneonta (tug), 79, 82, 88
Onondaga (Coast Guard cutter), 175,
  177, 180
Opposition Line, 25
Oregon Improvement Co., 47
Oregon Journal (Portland), 116, 151
Oregon Shipwrecks, 111
Oregonian (Portland), 92, 95, 99, 111,
  144, 178-79
Oriental Navigation Co, 174
Orion (Canadian whaler), 60-61, 63-64
Otter Crest, OR, 20
Otto, Henry E. (*Leggett* radioman),
  119-20

P

P. &. O. Line, 28

Pachena Bay, BC, 56

Pachena Point, BC, 52, 70

Pacific (dredge), 17

Pacific Coast Co., 28, 47, 60, 64

Pacific Coast Steamship Co., 22, 24-25, 28, 37, 42-44, 47, 57, 63, 66-67, 106

Pacific Lumber Ships, 166

Pacific Mail Line, 108

Pacific Packing and Navigation Co., 47

Pacific Rim National Park, BC, 56

Pacific Steam Whaling Co., 46

Palmer, C. R. (*Rosecrans* officer), 76

Parks, Mr. and Mrs. C. A. (*Leggett* passengers), 119

Patch, Lt. Cdr. R. Stanley (captain of *Onondaga*), 177

Peacock, USS (naval sloop), 77-78

Peacock Spit, WA, 22, 77-78, 81, 82, 84, 174, 177

Peckinbaugh, Miss L. (*Queen* passenger), 32

Pennsylvania (freighter), 158

Perry (Revenue Marine cutter), 61

Peterel (British gunboat), 112

Peters, Fred (*Rosecrans* crew), 76-77, 81

Pederson, L. (*Leggett* officer), 119

Peterson, P. E. (*Valencia* officer), 60

Pfantzsch, C. (*Chanslor* crew), 150

Philadelphia, PA, 28, 45, 123

Philippines, 37

Phillips, C. (*Santa Clara* crew), 127

Pigeon Point, CA, 16

Pillsbury & Curtis (shipowners), 154

pilotage, 18-19, 180-81

Pioneer (Canadian tug), 61

Plummer, Susie M. See Susie M. Plummer

Poelman, George (*Leggett* passenger), 107, 109, 112, 113, 115

Point Adams, OR, 22, 80, 84

Point Arena, CA, 16, 42, 107, 162

Point Arguello, CA, 13, 16

Point Bonita, CA, 124

Point Conception, CA, 16

Point Dume, CA, 16

Point Reyes, CA, 16, 42, 114

Point Sur, CA, 16, 43

Point Wilson, WA, 65

Port Angeles, WA, 178

Port Harford, CA 29

Port Logan (ship, aka *Mimi*), 85

Port Orford, OR, 17, 146-47, 154-55, 158

Port San Luis, CA, 24, 29, 124

Port Townsend, WA, 30, 36, 37

Portland, OR, 22, 23, 25, 27, 75-76, 84, 85, 86, 96, 99, 106, 112, 124, 131, 134, 141, 149, 151, 154, 162, 172-73, 177, 181

Portland Central Labor Council, 178

Poulsen, John (*Queen* crew), 39-40

Propeller Club of San Francisco, 162

Prudhout, L. (*Rosecrans* radioman), 78

Puebla, City of. See City of Puebla

Puget Sound, WA, 16, 22-24, 30, 36, 47, 68, 105, 141, 157

Punta Gorda, CA, 16

Putnam, Daisy. See Daisy Putnam

Q

Queen (passenger ship), 28-44, 58, 60, 65, 66, 68-69, 123

Queen City (Canadian coaster), 58

Queen of the Pacific (passenger ship, aka *Queen*), 28, 29, 45

Quinan, J. H. or Gay H. (Lifesaving Service Inspector), 84, 99-100

R

Red Star Line, 47

Red Wing (Coast Guard cutter), 163

Reedsport, OR, 17

Reece, Mark (*Queen* officer), 31

Reese, W. H. (*Chanslor* officer), 150

Reimers, E. L. (*Santa Clara* radioman), 126

Republic (freighter), 100

Republic (passenger ship), 64

Richfield Oil Co., 140

Riesenberg, Felix (author), 118

Rio de Janeiro (passenger ship), 62, 103

Roanoke (passenger ship), 106, 138, 168

Rogue River, OR, 163

Rohrbacker, C. A. (*Leggett* passenger), 119

Roosevelt, President Theodore, 65- 66, 67

Rosander, Otto (*Valencia* rescue party), 57

Rose, Edward A. (*Chanslor* officer), 144, 150

Rose City (passenger ship), 106, 148

Rosecrans (tanker), 71-84, 90, 99, 139, 140-41, 153

Rosecrans, General William S., 72

Ross, Donald (*Valencia* passenger), 65

Rossell, William T. See *William T. Rossell*

Rules of the Road, 22

Russell & Co. (shipbuilder), 85

Russell, Sir Charles (former *Queen* passenger), 29

S

St. George Reef, CA, 16, 21

Sakowis, BC, 58

Salvage Chief (salvage ship), 16

salvage techniques, 15-16, 91, 92-93, 100, 155

Salvor (Canadian salvage ship), 60, 61, 63, 69

San Diego, CA, 16, 25

San Francisco, CA, 17, 23, 24, 25, 27-28, 30, 41-43, 47, 49, 73, 84, 100, 105, 108, 116, 124, 135, 141, 154, 157, 159, 160, 167-68, 172, 173, 176, 179, 181

San Francisco Board of Underwriters, 89, 96, 180

San Francisco & Portland Steamship Co. ("Big Three"), 25, 113, 123

San Juan (passenger ship), 9, 103, 164

Santa Barbara, CA, 24, 124, 141

Santa Clara (passenger ship), 106, 122-138, 174

*Santa Monica (*steam schooner), 35

Santa Rosa (passenger ship), 13

Savage, Ernest (*Queen* crew), 39

Sawyer, A. A. (captain of *Chanslor*), 141-42, 146, 148, 149-50, 152-54

Schley, Admiral. See *Admiral Schley*

Schmidt, Hans H. (shipowner), 85

Scott, Alex (salvor), 154

Seattle, WA, 25, 26, 27, 29, 31, 32, 36-37, 40, 42-44, 47, 57, 64, 99, 105, 106, 120, 123

Seattle Chamber of Commerce, 65

Seattle Commercial Club, 65

Seattle Elks Club, 65

Sedro Wooley, WA, 128

Segalos, Joe (*Valencia* crew), 55, 62

Segundo, El. See *El Segundo*

Selja (Norwegian steamer), 114

Shamrock (Canadian steamer), 61

Shaw, Capt. Stephen B. (*Queen* passenger), 38

Shearer, Robert (*Santa Clara* crew), 128-29

Shelter Bight, BC, 52

shipping, tonnage of northwestern, 23-24

Shipwrecks of the Pacific Coast, 157

Shore Acres (coastal residence), OR, 129

Sinaloa (steamer), 146

Siskiyou Mountains, OR, 15

Siuslaw Inlet, OR, 20

Sixes River, OR, 147

Skelly Oil Co., 73

Slenning, Joseph (*Rosecrans* crew), 79-80, 82

Slocum, General. See *General Slocum*

Smith, Adeline. See *Adeline Smith*

Smith, Herbert Knox (*Valencia* commissioner), 67

Smith, Johana. See *Johanna Smith*

Smith, Nann. See *Nann Smith*

Snediger, Mr. and Mrs. Homer D. (*Leggett* passengers), 119

Snediger, Raymond (*Leggett* passenger), 119

Socony-Vacuum Oil Co., 140

Sorenson, Stanley (captain of *South Coast*), 160

South Coast (steam schooner), 156-70

South Coast Steamship Co., 159-60

South Portland (passenger ship), 144

Southern Pacific Railroad, 25, 124, 197 (note 1)

Spanish American War, 37, 47, 72-73

Spee, Admiral Graf, 100
Staffordshire (British barque, aka *Mimi*), 85
Stambourg, Pontus (*South Coast* officer), 167-68
Standard Oil Co. of California, 87, 114, 140, 141, 158
States Steamship Co., 158, 172, 174, 178, 180-82, 184, 185-86
steam schooners, characteristics of, 156, 159
steering gear, problems of, 125, 135-37, 183
Steiner, Anna (*Queen* passenger), 35
Stockholm (Norwegian passenger ship), 4
Strait of Juan de Fuca, 12, 16, 21-22, 49, 50, 53, 64, 65, 68-69, 105, 120, 157
Strathdon (British steamer), 30
Susie M. Plummer (schooner), 158
swastika, as company emblem, 172
Swatow, China, 158
Swiftsure Bank Lightship, WA/BC, 21-22, 49, 70
Sydney, City of. See *City of Sydney*

T
Tacoma, WA, 72
Tahiti, 100
Takahashi, S. (Japanese consul), 111
Tallaksen, A. J. (*South Coast* officer), 168
Tambaugh, Fred (*Chanslor* radioman), 146
Tanner Bank, CA, 16
Tatoosh (tug), 79
Tatoosh Island, 16, 56, 64
Taylor, W. O., & Co. (shipowners), 85
Tejon (tanker), 161, 163, 165
Tennyson, Alfred Lord, 186
Tenpaisan Maru (Japanese freighter), 14
Tessell (*Santa Clara* officer), 130
Texaco, Inc., 140
Tidewater Oil Co., 73, 140
Tillamook, OR, 17, 88-89
Tillamook Bay, OR, 23, 89-90
Tillamook Rock Lighthouse, OR, 16, 20, 31

Time Magazine, 12
Times (Seattle), 48, 51, 53, 66
Tioga, WA, 81
Titanic (passenger ship), 1, 5, 9, 12, 27
Topeka, City of. See *City of Topeka*
Tornstrom, Sven (captain of *Tejon*),161
Torrisdale (British barque), 86
Trout, Capt. Vance (shipping executive), 178
tule life jackets, 12-13, 54, 62, 65
Turner, Frank (inspector), 167
Turner, Robert. A. (inspector), 38-39, 65
Turret Island, BC, 61

U
U. S. Army Corps of Engineers, 17, 44, 129
U. S. Army Transport Service, 72
U. S. Bureau of Marine Inspection (and Navigation), 10, 167, 168, 178-79, 181
U. S. Coast Guard, 2, 10, 13, 18, 98-99, 129-30, 146-48, 162, 166-67, 170, 175-76, 177-78
U. S. Department of Commerce (and Labor), 65, 166, 180
U. S. Customs, 44
U. S. Lifesaving Service, 10, 13, 23, 84, 98-99, 117, 147-48, 150
U. S. Lighthouse Service, 10, 20, 23
U. S. Revenue Marine Service, 10, 61, 63, 99
U. S. Shipping Board, 43, 139, 171-72
U. S. Steamboat Inspection Service, 10, 38, 65, 84, 99, 132, 137-38, 164, 167, 170
U. S. Commission on *Valencia*, 48, 62, 67-70
Uhler, Inspector-General (Steamboat Inspection Service), 66
Umatilla Reef, WA, 16, 21, 49-50
Umpqua River, OR, 20
Union Iron Works, 41, 168
Union Oil Co., 140
Union Pacific Railroad, 25
Upton, Monroe (author), 145

V

Valencia (passenger ship), 12, 45-70, 103, 123, 135, 148

Vallenga, Louis (*Santa Clara* officer), 197 (note 33)

Vancouver, BC, 87, 110

Vancouver Island, BC, 52, 56, 63, 64, 67

Van Wyck, Laura (*Valencia* passenger), 65

Victoria, BC, 47, 53, 56, 58, 60, 69

Volant (schooner), 199 (note 32)

W

Wake, USS (gunboat), 112

Walküre (German steamer), 100

Walla Walla Reef, BC, 52

Watson, Admiral. See *Admiral Watson*

Watt and Holyfield (salvors), 91

Wasson, Tom (Oregon resident), 132

weather, marine in Northwest, 19-20

Weaver, J. B. (Director, Bureau of Marine Inspection), 179

Weeks, W. H. (*Chanslor* officer), 144, 150

West Cadron (freighter, aka *Iowa*), 172

"West Coast"-type ship, 171-72

Western Pipe & Steel (shipyard), 172

Western World (Bandon), 150

Westphal, Ludwig (captain of *Mimi*), 86-87, 88, 93-94, 95-96, 97-98, 99, 100

Weyerhaeuser Lumber Co., 135, 172

Whiskey Run Beach, OR, 149, 151

Whitney, Capt. Bion B. (inspector), 38, 65, 135, 138

White, Charles G. (shipyard), 122, 159

Whitelaw Salvage Co., 74

Wicklund, Capt. Oscar S. (Lifesaving Service), 84

Wilkes, Charles (explorer), 78

Willapa Bay, WA, 15, 17, 21, 23-24, 82

William T. Rossell (dredge), 17

Wilmington, DE, 47

Winchester Bay, OR, 23

Winslow, Stewart V. (river pilot), 172

Woodlark, Empire. See *Empire Woodlark*

World War I, 7, 42, 87, 100-101, 110, 112, 114, 141, 171

Y

Yaquina (dredge), 17

Yaquina Bay, OR, 18

Yaquina Head Lighthouse, OR, 20, 114

Yates, Edgar L. (captain of *Iowa*), 172, 174, 183, 185-86

Yokohama, Japan, 43

Yorkmar (freighter), 16

Z

Zeh, George (officer/captain of *Queen*), 39, 42